Ages in Chaos

Volume II:
Ramses II and His Time

Immanuel Velikovsky

Paradigma

New, unchanged edition (2010).
Notes by the publisher are marked by { }.

Original edition (1978) by Doubleday & Company, Inc., Garden City, New York

Cover design based on a drawing by Dino Idrizbegovic

Published by   Paradigma Ltd.
                Internet: www.paradigma-publishing.com
                e-mail: info@paradigma-publishing.com

ISBN 978-1-906833-14-5 (Softcover edition)
     978-1-906833-54-1 (Hardcover edition)

Contents

4

Introduction

The More Proper Title for this volume would have been *Ramses II and Nebuchadnezzar,* since both of them play dominant roles in this volume, or in this part of history. But revealing in this way the subject of the book—and the contemporaneity of two well-known figures of antiquity, separated in conventionally written history by seven hundred years—would have added sensation to what is perforce a revolutionary reconstruction of the past. Although the entire work of reconstruction covers over twelve hundred years, each volume is organized in such a way that it presents, as far as feasible, a separate fraction of ancient history.

On the pages to follow an effort is made to reconstruct the period of Chaldean domination in the Middle East. This period is also known in history books as the time of the Neo-Babylonian Empire; in the Scriptures, Nebuchadnezzar is known as king of Babylon and king of the Chaldeans; Chaldeans, however, were not indigenous to Babylon.

The thesis presented and evidenced in this volume is that the so-called Hittite Empire, dubbed the Forgotten Empire because it was supposedly discovered less than one hundred years ago, is nothing but the kingdom of the Chaldeans; further, that the pictographic script found on monuments from the western shores of Asia Minor to Babylon, but mainly in central and eastern Anatolia and northern Syria, is most probably the Chaldean script. The "Hittite" emperors are alter egos of the great kings of the Chaldean Dynasty of Babylon. Thus the "Hittite Empire" in its most exalted period, the placement of which in the fourteenth and thirteenth centuries before the present era has caused innumerable difficulties and led to much consternation among archaeologists, vanishes after having "lived" in books and articles for more than a century.

No lesser upheaval takes place in Egyptian historiography. The so-called Nineteenth Dynasty, whose main representatives are Seti the Great, Ramses II, and Merneptah, reveals itself as identical with the so-called Twenty-sixth Dynasty of Psammetich, Necho, and Apries, whose true activities are known to us partly from Greek historians and partly from the scriptural texts (Books of Kings, Chronicles, and Jeremiah) but not from the extant Egyptian texts. This identification entails the removal of Seti the Great, Ramses II, and Merneptah from the time in the fourteenth and thirteenth centuries usually ascribed to them to the seventh and sixth centuries. Actually, the process of identifying the early pharaohs of the Nineteenth Dynasty, Seti I (Sethos), Haremhab, Ramses I, and Seti the Great, occupies the volume dealing with the Assyrian domination which covers the time from about -840 to -612. There it is shown in some detail that Seti I (Sethos of Herodotus) was a contemporary and adversary of King Sennacherib; that Haremhab, his brother, was appointed a viceroy of Egypt by the decree of the Assyrian king and later crowned as a pharaoh, while still in vassalage to Nineveh; that Ramses I is known to us from the Greek historians as the Necho I who reigned for only a short period before he was killed by the Ethiopians, who for more than fifty years contested with the Assyrians for supremacy in Egypt; and that Seti the Great,[1] as just said, is Psammetich of the Greek historians. Thus the beginning of the task of identifying the Nineteenth Dynasty with the Twenty-sixth in the list of Manetho's succession – a most confused and deliberately extended and misleading list of the Egyptian dynasties and kings – has been delegated to the volume covering the time of the Assyrian domination up to the fall of Nineveh in about -612.

I weighed in my mind whether I should draw the demarcation line between these two volumes at -663, the year of the fall of Thebes before Assurbanipal, and I was motivated by the desire to have in one volume the story of the great Egyptian dynasty from the time Seti the Great began his career, which marked the growth of Egypt from vassalage to independence; but after some deliberation it appeared more desirable to draw the line at the fall of Nineveh about fifty-five years later. Nevertheless in subsequent chapters of the present volume, though not from the start, the reader will be led back to the times when Seti, no more a vassal of Assyria but an ally, took part in the protracted struggle in which the Chaldeans and the Medes faced the Assyrians and the Egyptians, with the Scythians finally deciding the outcome.

---

[1] Seti I of the conventional chronology but Seti II of this reconstruction.

Thus this volume starts with the first confrontation of two ambitious and famous kings supposedly separated by seven hundred years, Ramses II and Nebuchadnezzar – a confrontation renewed again and again for nineteen years until it was terminated in a peace treaty the text of which is still extant. Judea was caught between the two contesting great powers and suffered until it lost its statehood; the population was exiled to Babylon, while a minor part escaped to Egypt only to be removed to Babylon, too, on the strength of a provision stipulated in the same treaty.

Merneptah-Hophrama'e, sometimes thought to be the Pharaoh of the Exodus, is shown to be the Pharaoh of the Exile, and an enormous stretch of time separates these two events in the history of the Jewish people–the Wandering in the Desert, the Conquest of Canaan, and the period of the judges and the Kings down to the last king of the Davidian Dynasty.

Having exposed here the main theme of this volume, let me express the hope that every thoughtful reader will postpone judgment until he has considered the evidence in all its details, which range from ancient texts in cuneiform, hieroglyphics, and Hebrew, to autobiographies and portraits, to ancient topographical maps and plans of battle, to archaeological stratigraphy. The centuries both preceding and following[1] the decades described in this volume constitute together, in the reconstruction of ancient history, a monolithic oneness.

---

[1] The centuries preceding are the subject of my *Ages in Chaos*, Vol. I, *From the Exodus to King Akhnaton* (1952); *Oedipus and Akhnaton* (1960); and the forthcoming volumes in which I deal with the Assyrian conquest and the dark age of Greece. The centuries following the present volume are the subject of my *Peoples of the Sea* (1977).

Chapter 1

The Battle of Kadesh-Carchemish

Who Was Pharaoh Necho, the Adversary of Nebuchadnezzar?

The Assyrian Empire tottered and fell. Despite the aid of Egypt, the Babylonians and the Medes captured Nineveh and burned it. In the ensuing years they were busy dividing Assyria.

In -608 the king of Egypt moved toward the Euphrates (II Kings 23:29), marching with his troops on the military road that ran along the coast. When he came to Megiddo Pass he found his way obstructed by Josiah, the king of Jerusalem. The king of Egypt sent emissaries to him, saying: "I come not against thee this day. ... Nevertheless Josiah would not turn his face from him." In the battle King Josiah was mortally wounded by Egyptian dart throwers (II Chronicles 35:21–24).

The pharaoh proceeded northward toward Carchemish on the Euphrates. In Jerusalem the people chose Jehoahaz, the second son of Josiah, to be king. But after three months the pharaoh put him in chains in Riblah in the land of Hamath and sent him to Egypt. The pharaoh then appointed Eliakim, the elder brother of Jehoahaz, to be king in Jerusalem and changed his name to Jehoiakim. From the land of Judea he exacted a tribute of one hundred talents of silver and one talent of gold (II Kings 23:33–34).

During the following years Riblah in northern Syria was the military headquarters of the pharaoh, who apparently visited there yearly.

Three years after the first campaign the pharaoh brought from Egypt a great army and fought at Carchemish on the Euphrates against Nebuchadnezzar and the Chaldean army. The Egyptian host was defeated and dispersed, and the pharaoh hurriedly retreated toward Egypt. Nebuchadnezzar pursued the beaten army but stopped at the border of Egypt and because of some dynastic troubles returned to Babylon. For the next few years Syria and Palestine were under the undisputed domination of Babylon. Riblah was made the military headquarters of Nebuchadnezzar, and Jehoiakim became his vassal.

Some time later the pharaoh renewed his military and political activities in southern Palestine. After capturing Askelon, he proceeded northward. Jehoiakim rebelled against Babylon and Nebuchadnezzar sent an army of Chaldeans and Syrians against Jerusalem. Jehoiakim was captured and executed,[1] and Nebuchadnezzar placed the young Jeconiah (Jehoiachin), son of Jehoiakim, on the throne of his father in Jerusalem. The Egyptian army retreated to the borders of Egypt, behind the river (Wadi) el-Arish. Jeconiah reigned only three months. Nebuchadnezzar, suspicious and uncertain whether the new king of Jerusalem would keep faith with Babylon, once more marched against Jerusalem and besieged it. The boy king, in his desire to save the city and its people, went out to Nebuchadnezzar to establish his loyalty. He was sent to Babylon together with "all the princes, and all the mighty men of valour, ten thousand captives, and all the craftsmen and smiths." Only the poor were left. Jeconiah remained in prison in Babylon for thirty-seven years, until the death of Nebuchadnezzar (II Kings 25:27).

When Jeconiah was taken to Babylon, Zedekiah, the third son of Josiah, was appointed to be king. The removal of the wealthy, the influential, and the skilled from Jerusalem did not insure against a new rebellion. Despite all that had happened before, the freedom-loving people of Jerusalem desired a war of independence, in which they expected help from the pharaoh. Eight years after Zedekiah was appointed king he revolted. Nebuchadnezzar came with all his forces against Jerusalem and besieged it. The pharaoh moved along the coast with his troops into southern Palestine. The Chaldean army withdrew from Jerusalem "for fear of Pharaoh's army" (Jeremiah 37:11) and, in order not to be outflanked, marched against the Egyptians. However, no battle took place, and apparently some agreement was reached, as a result of which the Egyptian host returned to Egypt and the Chaldean army renewed the siege of Jerusalem. After eighteen months the Chaldeans captured and burned the city and carried the people of Jerusalem away into Babylonian captivity.

Detailed material on this war is found in the last chapters of the Books of Kings and of Chronicles, and especially in the Book of Jeremiah. Nebuchadnezzar, whose name is mentioned in the Scrip-

---

[1] *Midrash Breshith Raba,* 94; *Midrash Va'yikra Raba; Seder Olam,* 25; Josephus Flavius: *Antiquities,* X, 6:3. Cf. L. Ginzberg: *Legends of the Jews,* (Philadelphia, 1925-38), VI, 379. Compare also II Kings 24:6 and II Chronicles 36:6.

tures more than ninety times, was the mighty king of a great empire. Several Greek authors also wrote about him. He erected grandiose buildings, some of which have been unearthed. His prayers and building inscriptions are read by archaeologists, and "If in the field of Irak [Iraq] you find a brick with cuneiform signs, most probably it contains the name of Nebuchadnezzar."[1]

The pharaoh, his adversary for two decades, is called in the Scriptures Pharaoh Necho. He must have been a very formidable monarch indeed if, despite his reverse at Carchemish, the fate of Syria and Palestine remained unsettled for almost two decades; the Egyptian party in Jerusalem was stronger than the Babylonian, and the army of Nebuchadnezzar interrupted its siege of Jerusalem through fear of the pharaoh.

Who was Pharaoh Necho?

Books on Egyptian history tell an extensive story of Necho (II)'s wars against Nebuchadnezzar, but this story is based on the rich material of the Scriptures; his other activities are described with the help of information gleaned from Herodotus.[2] Egyptian inscriptions have been searched for mention of a pharaoh named Necho and of his campaigns. Egyptian archaeology could not supply the story of the long war. The only extant inscription of any historical value that is related to Pharaoh Necho is supposed to be the Serapeum stele, which records the burial of an Apis by His Majesty Nekau-Wehemibre. "This god (the bull Apis) was conducted in peace to the necropolis, to let him assume his place in his temple," where Nekau-Wehemibre prepared "all the coffins and everything excellent and profitable for this august god."[3] Then follows the biography of the bull with the exact day and month of his birth.

Historiography is content with this single monumental relic of the rich past of Pharaoh Necho.

It is strange indeed that in the annals of Egypt no account has been found of the long war between Nekau-Wehemibre and Nebuchadnezzar; no record of the civic activities of Nekau-Wehemibre is extant; no law published in his day has been found; no temple built by him has been

---

[1] C. J. Gadd: *The Fall of Nineveh* (London, 1923).

[2] See especially F. K. Kienitz: *Die politische Geschichte Aegyptens vom 7. bis zum 4. Jahrhundert vor der Zeitwende* (Berlin, 1953), Ch. 2.

[3] J. H. Breasted: *Ancient Records of Egypt* (Chicago, 1906), Vol. IV, Secs. 977, 979.

unearthed; no written scroll discovered; no mummy or coffin.[1] Judged by the Egyptian material, he must have been a ruler of few achievements. But then how could he have been a match for Nebuchadnezzar for almost a generation? How could he have succeeded in making the Palestinian kings, Jehoahaz, Jehoiakim, and Zedekiah, believe that he would be able to free Palestine from the yoke of the mightiest monarch Babylon had ever known?

My effort at reconstructing the history of the Nineteenth Dynasty has led me to identify the father of Necho II, Psammetichus, with Seti the Great (Ptah Maat), and the grandfather of Necho II, Necho I, with Ramses I. I show that Ramses I was appointed to rule Egypt by Assurbanipal after the sack of Thebes in -663. These earlier identifications, which are the subject of *The Assyrian Conquest,* bring me to the proposition which I will attempt to substantiate in this volume, that in the monuments of Ramses II are described the same events that Jeremiah and Herodotus record with reference to Pharaoh Necho (II).

Herodotus (II, 159) tells of the biblical Pharaoh Necho, calling him by the similar name of Necos. Of the Asian wars of Necos he wrote: "With his land army he met and defeated the Syrians at Magdalos, taking into possession the great Syrian city of Cadytis after the battle."[2]

Besides recording Necos' battle with the Syrians, Herodotus also wrote that he "was the first to attempt the construction of the canal to the Red Sea, a work completed afterward by Darius the Persian."[3] It was a great undertaking and Herodotus narrates that, before Necos despaired of completing the canal that would open a waterway from the Mediterranean to the Red Sea, one hundred and twenty thousand workers perished in digging it.

---

[1] The objects attributable to Nekau-Wehemibre were enumerated by F. Petrie in *A History of Egypt,* Vol. III (London, 1905), pp. 335-36. A few additional small objects were discovered since.

[2] The identity of these two places is uncertain. Cadytis may be Gaza or, possibly, Jerusalem. F. Hitzig: *De Cadyti urbe Herodotea* (Göttingen, 1829), identified Cadytis with Gaza. P. H. Larcher: *Historical and Critical Comments on the History of Herodotus* (London, 1844), favored Jerusalem (Vol. I, p. 391). J. T. Wheeler: *The Geography of Herodotus* (London, 1854), concurred with the opinion of Rawlinson that Cadytis is Gaza. For recent discussion of the problem, see H. de Meulenaere: *Herodotos over de 26ste Dynastie* (Leyden, 1951), pp. 57-59; Kienitz, op. cit., p. 22, note 1.

[3] *Herodotus,* II, 158, transl. G. Rawlinson. See also Diodorus Siculus, I, 33, 9.

Historical testimony was found to the effect that Ramses II had built a canal connecting the Mediterranean with the Red Sea.[1] This led to a discussion: who started building the canal, Ramses II or Nekau-Wehemibre, seven hundred years later? Herodotus related that it was Necos who was *first* to build it, while modern historians, on the basis of ancient evidence, concluded that Ramses II had already built the canal connecting the Mediterranean with the Red Sea. It was resolved that Herodotus was wrong and that Necho simply continued the work which Ramses II, seven hundred years earlier, had begun.[2]

And even if Ramses II was the first to undertake the project and Necos of Herodotus, or Necho of the Scriptures, was not the first, the question still stands – why did Nekau-Wehemibre of Egyptian monuments leave no inscription in stone or on papyrus to memorialize this stupendous effort of continuing the work of Ramses II? Of Ramses' work hieroglyphic testimony survived; Darius, too, put on record his effort: he erected steles along the route of the canal, to glorify his achievement.

Herodotus (IV, 42) also narrates that Pharaoh Necos dispatched Phoenician sailors to circumnavigate the continent of Africa and to explore its shores; they remained away for almost three years on their voyage of exploration, sowing and reaping while on the way. They started along the Red Sea and returned in glory through the Strait of Gibraltar (the Pillars of Heracles).[3]

Nekau-Wehemibre, who was too modest to leave a memorial to any of his military undertakings, was equally reticent about leaving word of his civil activities – really great enterprises on any scale. How to explain this?

---

[1] E. A. W. Budge: *A History of Egypt* (London, 1902-4), VI, 219; K. Sethe: *Untersuchungen zur Geschichte und Altertumskunde Aegyptens*, Vol. II (1902), 23; cf. Posener in *Chronique d'Egypte*, XIII (1938), 259-73.

[2] Budge, op. cit., VI, 219: "He (Necho) gave orders for fleets of triremes to be built for him, both in the Mediterranean Sea and the Red Sea. In order to give these vessels the opportunity of being employed upon both seas, he conceived the idea of connecting them by means of a canal, which he intended to join the old canal that was already in existence in the days *of* Rameses II."

[3] Ramses II gave a son of his for a husband to a daughter of a Phoenician sea captain, Ben-Anath. The thought may occur, was not Ben-Anath in pharaoh's favors for some unusual achievement? See J. H. Breasted: *A History of Egypt* (New York, 1905), p. 449.

Ramses II built large palaces and temples and left to posterity numerous inscriptions on steles, obelisks, and walls. Many of these inscriptions contain accounts of his battles, some are illustrated with maps of
the battlefields and with pictures showing his armies and those of his
enemies. A peace treaty that put an end to hostilities is preserved in its
entirety. In accordance with Egyptian custom, the personal name of
the opposing king is not given in the description of the battle, but in
the text of the treaty the personal name of the adversary of Ramses II
is inserted. Seals of Ramses II are found in great number in Egypt and
in Palestine. A papyrus written by an Egyptian scribe under Ramses II
depicts the Palestine of his day.

On the other hand, the Books of Kings, Chronicles, and Jeremiah
furnish precise data concerning times and places; they can and must
be compared with the description of the wars, the calendar of events,
the pictures, and the battle charts of Ramses II.

Figure 1: Ramses II:
A statue of the king now
in the Turin Museum

The Early Campaign of Ramses II

When Ramses II was on his first march across Palestine from south to north, the king of this land came out to do battle with him.

A fragment of a mural from a Theban temple of Ramses II, preserved in the Metropolitan Museum of Art in New York, shows a Palestinian prince, mortally wounded by a dart or a lance thrown by one of the Egyptian warriors, and the army of this prince in great dismay.[1]

On a stele at Aswan erected in "year 2," Ramses, proud of his momentous victory, carved the record of this campaign:

> He has overthrown myriads in the space of a moment . . . he has extended its boundaries for ever, plundering the Asiatics (St-tyw) and capturing their cities.[2]

The Scriptures relate the encounter, fatal to the king of Judah:

> II CHRONICLES 35:20 ... Necho king of Egypt came up to fight against Carchemish by Euphrates: and Josiah went out against him.

> 21 But he sent ambassadors to him, saying, What have I to do with thee, thou king of Judah? I come not against thee this day, but against the house wherewith I have war... .

> 22 Nevertheless Josiah would not turn his face from him ... and came to fight in the valley of Megiddo.

Josiah had no more than drawn up his army in formation when the missile of an Egyptian dart thrower decided the outcome of the battle.

> II CHRONICLES 35:23 And the archers[3] shot at king Josiah: and the king said to his servants, Have me away; for I am sore wounded.

> 24 His servants therefore took him out of that chariot and put him in the second chariot that he had; and they brought him to Jerusalem, and he died... .

According to a parallel narrative in II Kings (23:30), Josiah died before reaching Jerusalem.

---

[1] H. E. Winlock: *Excavations at Deir el Bahari, 1911-1931* (New York, 1942), p. 12 and Plate 6g.

[2] Breasted: *Records,* Vol. III, Sec. 479.

[3] The Hebrew text has "yoru ha-yorim" and a correct translation is "the hurlers *(ha-yorim)* hurled *(yoru),*" or the "shooters shot." The same verb is used but with the addition of "ba-keshet", "with a bow" if a bow and arrow are the weapons. See I Samuel 31:3 and I Chronicles 10:3; cf. also Genesis 21:10 and Isaiah 21:17; 22:3.

Figure 2: Part of a granite doorjamb of Ramses II: probably Josiah, father of Jehoiakin, falling at Megiddo. From *Excavations at Deir el Bahari, 1911 - 1931* by H. E. Winlock, New York, 1942, plate 69

After Josiah died the people of Jerusalem put his son Jehoahaz on the throne of Judah. But in a short while "the king of Egypt put him down" and "carried him to Egypt" (II Chronicles 36:3-4).

An obelisk of Ramses II at Tanis mentions "carrying off the princes of Retenu (Palestine) as living prisoners." The word "princes" is written on the obelisk with a hieroglyph of a size disproportionate to the rest of the inscription, emphasizing their royal status.[1]

According to the biblical record, the pharaoh, at that time in northern Syria, put Jehoahaz in shackles.

II KINGS 23:33 And Pharaoh-Necho put him in bands at Riblah in the land of Hamath... .

34 ...and [he] took Jehoahaz away: and he [Jehoahaz] came to Egypt, and died there.

Having "condemned the land in an hundred talents of silver and a talent of gold" (II Chronicles 36:3), the pharaoh placed Jehoiakim on the throne vacated by his brother.

---

[1] See *Kêmi, Revue de philologie et d'archéologie égyptiennes et coptes,* V (1935), Plate 26, and p. 113.

II Kɪɴɢs 23:35 And Jehoiakim gave the silver and the gold to Pharaoh; but he taxed the land to give the money according to the commandment of Pharaoh... .

The inscription on the obelisk of Tanis says of Ramses II that he was "plundering the chiefs of the Asiatics in their land."

In return for the tribute the pharaoh gave protection to Judah. "They sit in the shadow of his sword, and they fear not any country," wrote Ramses on the Aswan stele.

On his frequent visits to his headquarters at Riblah, Ramses II used to have carved commemorative tablets at Nahr el-Kelb (Dog River), near Beirut on the Syrian coast. He had them cut in the rock next to the tablet of Esarhaddon, king of Assyria, son of Sennacherib. The accepted viewpoint is that Esarhaddon's tablet was carved close to those of Ramses II, erected six hundred years earlier. As may be gathered from this reconstruction of ancient history, Esarhaddon's tablet had already been in existence three quarters of a century when Ramses had his inscriptions cut.

Figure 3: Nahr el-Kelb: Stelae of Esarhaddon (left) and of Ramses II. From *Records of the Past* II (1904).

It has been presumed that Esarhaddon, carving his inscriptions next to those of Ramses II, was perpetrating an act of irony.[1] But there was no irony on the part of either the Assyrian king or the pharaoh. Esarhaddon, who put down the Ethiopian rule in Egypt and whose son Assurbanipal established there the dynasty of Ramses I, was regarded by the Ramessides as a liberator of Egypt, and for this reason Ramses II did not destroy the inscriptions of Esarhaddon.

Ramses wrote his texts on the rock by the Dog River in the second, third (?), and fourth years of his reign; the year "2" on one plate and year "4" on another are still legible, but the text is almost completely destroyed mainly by weathering. We may suppose that the text of the second year was to some extent like that of the Aswan stele, also of Ramses' second year.

In the fifth year of his reign Ramses II again moved toward the Euphrates. A great battle was joined, the famous battle of Kadesh. It was a fateful campaign.

Tell Nebi-Mend

The battle which, in historiography, earned the name of "the battle of Kadesh" is pictured in a series of bas-reliefs engraved on the walls of the Ramesseum near Thebes and of the temples at Luxor, Karnak, Abydos, and Abu-Simbel. An official record of the battle accompanies the pictures in the Ramesseum, at Luxor, and at Abu-Simbel; the pictures contain plans of the battle-ground.

These bas-reliefs are famous; they have been well known to tourists in Egypt since days of old, as the quotation from Hecataeus (of the fifth century before the present era) by Diodorus of Sicily proves. After a brief description of the army of the pharaoh, consisting of infantry and cavalry, the whole divided into four divisions, Diodorus cites Hecataeus: "the king, he says, is represented in the act of besieging a walled city which is surrounded by a river, and of leading the attack against opposing troops."[2]

---

[1] D. D. Luckenbill: *Records of Assyria* (1927), Vol. II, Sec. 479.
[2] Diodorus, transl. Oldfather (1933), I, 48.

Besides the official record, a poetic description of this battle is written on the walls of the Karnak, Luxor, and Abydos temples; it is also preserved on rolls of papyrus[1] and has been given the name of the *Poem of Pentaur*. Pentaur might have been only a copyist of one of the papyri.[2]

The city, on the approaches to which Ramses II fought his battle, was a northern Syrian city north of Mount Lebanon. The city of Kadesh of this battle is different from the Kadesh captured by Thutmose III in Palestine, or Jerusalem.[3] It is also different from Kadesh in Coele-Syria, a city stormed by Seti, father of Ramses II. As Seti's drawings show, the Kadesh attacked by him was on a forested hill; there was no river front;[4] Syrians and not the "Kheta people" defended the city.

In this all agree, that neither Kadesh in Palestine nor Kadesh in Coele-Syria, between the ridges of Lebanon and Hermon, is identical with Kadesh of Ramses' fame. "Kadesh," or "holy city," was an eponym of great temple cities; so in our day the designation "Holy City" is often substituted for Jerusalem, the Vatican, Mecca, and Lhasa.

Champollion, the decipherer of the hieroglyphics, was misled by Diodorus of Sicily into placing the site in Bactria, close to the north-western parts of India.[5] Other Egyptologists of the first half of the nineteenth century placed the city in Mesopotamia, or close to the Taurus, not far from Aleppo, or again in Edessa beyond the Euphrates.[6] But in the second half of that century scholars, looking for a site whose topography would correspond with the charts of the battleground as they were drawn by the artists of Ramses II, located this Kadesh on the river Orontes in Syria. Restricting the search for Kadesh to the flow of the Orontes was caused by a reading of the name of the river in hieroglyphic texts that we will have reason to dispute.

The charts, differing among themselves as they do, nevertheless show that the place of the battle was on the banks of a wide river and that

---

[1] The Papyri *Raifet* (the beginning) and *Sallier* III (the rest). The first page is lost; *Papyrus Raifet* is the second page and *Papyrus Sallier* III, pp. 3-12.

[2] A. Erman regards Pentaur as merely a copyist and is followed by other scholars.

[3] *Ages in Chaos*, Vol. I, »Kadesh in Judah«.

[4] See W. Wreszinski: *Atlas zur altägyptischen Kulturgeschichte*, Vol. II, Part 2 (Leipzig, 1935), Plate 53.

[5] J. F. Champollion: *Lettres écrites d'Egypte* (Paris, 1833). He identified the foes of Ramses II as Scythians.

[6] Literature in G. C. Maspero: *The Struggle of the Nations* (New York, 1897), pp. 140-41, note 4.

Kadesh was surrounded by the water of a lesser stream, a confluent of the river. Any attempt to locate the battleground of Kadesh must hinge on this topographical peculiarity which "is mandatory for every site that might be identified as Kadesh."[1]

The river Orontes, starting in central Syria and flowing north, passes through several lakes in the first of which there is a small island. The basin is called Bahret el-Qattine, and the scholar[2] who placed Kadesh on the island in the middle of the lake could show that in the Middle Ages the lake had been called Bahr el-Kedes.[3] This identification was abandoned, however, as the lake is an artificial one, created by a dam, and did not exist in ancient times. Both Talmuds attribute the dam to Diocletian,[4] the Roman emperor (284-305).

Then a place only a few miles to the south of the lake, up the Orontes, was found to meet all requirements. It is Tell Nebi-Mend, or Laodicea of Lebanon, an artificial hill thirty meters high and one kilometer long, bounded by the Orontes and by a small confluent stream as by the two sides of an angle.[5] A mill in the vicinity was called "Qudas," and this was pointed to as proof of the correctness of the identification. The mill probably is a Turkish building.[6]

Since the 1880's a number of ardent supporters of the last-mentioned theory have tried to show that in Tell Nebi-Mend, and there only, all the conditions of the Egyptian texts and charts are satisfied.[7] Until now Tell Nebi-Mend as the site of Kadesh remained an undisputed thesis in archaeology.

Excavation was undertaken there in 1921-22. No buildings or city walls were unearthed which would suggest the existence of a city in the period under investigation. True, only a very small portion of the mound

---

[1] "Elle était encerclée par les eaux: or, cette condition est nécessaire pour tout site qui voudra s'identifier avec Qadesh." M. Pézard: *Qadesh. Mission Archéologique à Tell Nebi-Mend, 1921–1922* (Paris, 1931), p. 26.

[2] H. K. Brugsch: *Geographische Inschriften altägyptischer Denkmäler* (Leipzig, 1857-60), II, 22.

[3] Abulfeda (1273-1331): *Tabulae Syriae* (Leipzig, 1786), p. 157: "The lake at Qades. Now it is the same as the lake of Homs."

[4] *The Jerusalem Talmud*, Kilaim 60. 5; *The Babylonian Talmud, Baba Batra* 74b. Abulfeda (1273–1331), also referred to the fact that the lake is artificially constructed.

[5] Claude R. Conder: »Kadesh«, *Quarterly Statement of the Palestine Exploration Fund*, 1881, pp. 163-73.

[6] Pézard: *Qadesh*, p. 2.

[7] J. H. Breasted: *The Battle of Kadesh* (Chicago, 1903), uses the map of Tell Nebi-Mend for the reconstruction of the famous battle.

was explored; the ruins of Kadesh, we are assured, are concealed by the mound, awaiting future excavators.

Neither the geographical position nor the topography of Tell Nebi-Mend warrants its identification as Kadesh of the battle. What suggested this identification? First, it is the name of the river on the shore of which the city was situated; second, it is its position in an angle between two streams. We shall consider both the geographical and the topographical grounds for the identification.

From several centuries earlier, a reference to the position of the northern Kadesh is found in the tomb inscription of one Amenemheb, an officer in the military service of Thutmose III: it strongly suggests that the city must have been situated farther north than Tell Nebi-Mend. The officer, in a short record, mentioned the battles in southern Palestine (Negeb), the arrival in Mesopotamia (Naharin) and later in the mountains in the region of Aleppo, then the expedition to the land of Carchemish, the crossing of the river, and the capture of Kadesh. Scholars concluded that the officer was very inaccurate in his enumeration of the places through which he marched on the victorious campaign of Thutmose III,[1] for he placed the northern Kadesh in the land of Carchemish, west of the Euphrates, which he and his troops, coming from the east, crossed.

The victorious army of Thutmose could not take Aleppo and some regions in Mesopotamia without first taking Tell Nebi-Mend, on the military road, when marching from Egypt to the north.

But was Kadesh of Ramses' fame on the Orontes? In the *Poem of Pentaur* the name of the river is spelled "r-n-t" and it may seem hardly justifiable to raise the question not raised for ninety years, from the day Conder identified Tell Nebi-Mend as Kadesh of the battle. The phonetic similarity is too good to doubt. However, in the *Papyrus Sallier* dealing with the same campaign the river's name is given as "n-r-t"; the designations "r-n-t", "n-r-t", and "p-n-r-t" are found in quite a few documents in hieroglyphics; the confusing geographical whereabouts of these designations long ago caused two scholars, Bürnouf and Lagarde, to theorize that "r-n-t" was the name of many rivers and mountains.

---

[1] "It appears that the tomb inscription of Amenemheb records the campaign events in a very loose order: Negeb, Naharina, Aleppo, (land of) Karchemish, Qades (Kadesh) and so forth. Naturally Qades must have been conquered first before northern Syria and Naharina (Mesopotamia) and before the Euphrates could have been crossed." R. Kittel: *Geschichte des Volkes Israel* (5th ed.; Stuttgart, 1923-25), I, 79, note 1.

If, however, the oft-mentioned "p-n-r-t" or "r-n-t" is the Orontes, then, strangely enough, the great river Euphrates has no name in Egyptian. Its Babylonian name was Puratu and similarly its Hebrew name is Prat. In the Egyptian the initial p could be omitted if it was understood as the definite article, a procedure for which other examples are known. It would not be surprising if the Orontes were not mentioned in Egyptian sources, but how could it be that the great and famous Euphrates – next to the Nile, the largest river in the world the Egyptians knew – was nameless?

According to Strabo, the river in Syria did not receive its name Orontes until the fourth century before the present era. Strabo provides the following information: "Though formerly called Typhon, its [the river's] name was changed to that of Orontes, the man who built a bridge across it."[1]

This Orontes was a Bactrian[2] by origin, son of Artasyras; he married a daughter of Artaxerxes II Mnemon, the Persian king,[3] and was active in Syria and Asia Minor.[4] In -349 or -348, by decision of the Athenians, Athenian citizenship was bestowed upon him.

Thus a river that obtained its name from the name of a well-known Bactrian general who built a bridge across it in the fourth century could not possibly have had the name of this general presumably a thousand years earlier. However, this specific argument, sounding so conclusive, does not necessarily settle the issue. In the inscriptions of Shalmaneser III with the record of his war with Hazael of Damascus, he refers to throwing the remnants of Hazael's army into the river Arantu, which could be either the Orontes or the Euphrates. As we just read of the opinion of the early orientalists, it appears that similar or even identical designations "r-n-t", "n-r-t", and "p-n-r-t" were applied to more than one stream in the region. Therefore we are compelled to turn to the topography of the battle of Kadesh but later to consider also the localities

---

[1] Strabo: *The Geography,* transl. M. L. Jones, XVI, 750.
[2] Bactria was a Persian satrapy between the mountain range of Hindu Kush and the Oxus (Amu Darya).
[3] Xenophon: *Anabasis,* II, iv, 8; Plutarch: *Lives,* »Artaxerxes«, 27.
[4] He was second in command, under Tiribazos, in the war against Euagoras of Cyprus, and without the knowledge of Tiribazos concluded a peace treaty with Euagoras (Diodorus of Sicily, XV, ii, 2). He served as a satrap of Armenia (Xenophon: *Anabasis,* III, v, 17). In Asia Minor he became an open enemy of the Persian king; in Syria he was besieged by Artaxerxes III (Ochus). The Athenians presented him with a golden wreath together with citizenship.

named in the hieroglyphic texts of Ramses II as situated on the way to Kadesh, in order to settle the problem of the river of the famous battle.

The topography of Kadesh as pictured by Ramses II contradicts, too, the topography of Tell Nebi-Mend. On the bas-reliefs of Ramses II, as already mentioned, the city of Kadesh is surrounded by water: a large river flows north of the city and a small stream encircles the city from the south. But Tell Nebi-Mend is not surrounded by water on all sides, since the base of the triangle, two sides of which are formed by the Orontes and the confluent stream, is not closed by a water barrier. Moreover, the position of the river with respect to the mound is different at Tell Nebi-Mend from the plans of Ramses II.

The *Poem of Pentaur* indicates that the pharaoh halted north of the city of Kadesh, on the western bank of the river; also the official record of the battle narrates that Ramses II was to the northwest of Kadesh when the battle began. "But if the side of the Egyptian drawing where the Pharaoh is, is north, then it represents him as on the east side of the river. Or again, if, as the texts state, he should be on the west side of the river in the Egyptian drawing, then the drawing represents him as south of the city and charging northward. In no way can any of the four ancient drawings of this battlefield be made to coincide with the data of the inscriptions."[1]

Kadesh, as shown on the pictures of Ramses II, was fortified by one embankment in the form of a horseshoe and by another, a shorter one, touching the large river. The two embankments were connected by two bastions, and the fortified area was oval in shape. Outside the embankment a trench surrounded the city, and a double wall completed the fortifications. High tower bastions stood out from the wall; a crown of triangular battlements running along the edge served to protect the soldiers on the wall and on the bastions.

Neither the double wall with its bastions and towers nor the trenches have been unearthed at Tell Nebi-Mend. If the walls are still covered by the earth of the mound, at least vestiges of trench work around the mound should have been preserved. But this has not yet been uncovered.[2]

The lack of conformity between the plans and the actual topography and position of Tell Nebi-Mend and its fortifications did not serve as a

---

[1] »Poem of Pentaur« in Breasted: *Records,* Vol. III, Sec. 335.
[2] Wreszinski: *Atlas,* Vol. II, Part 4, Plate 173.

warning that this might be the wrong place; the scholars who stressed the divergencies between the Egyptian plans and the site itself still did not doubt that Tell Nebi-Mend was the Kadesh of Ramses II's battle.

In a section soon to follow, the topography of the battle maps of Ramses II will be compared with the topography of Carchemish. But what, then, does Tell Nebi-Mend-a great mount–represent? Which historical place does the mound conceal?

Only a few miles from Tell Nebi-Mend is an Arab village named Riblah, actually the populated place closest to the mound. The village of Riblah has no tell or mound; yet it is generally assumed that the village occupies the place of the ancient fortress by this name. Riblah, the fortress in the "land of Hamath," played an important role as the military headquarters first of Pharaoh Necho and thereafter of Nebuchadnezzar. There the pharaoh put Jehoahaz, king of Jerusalem, in bands (II Kings 23:33); there Nebuchadnezzar blinded King Zedekiah (II Kings 25:7, Jeremiah 39:7).

Pézard, in his abortive exploration of Tell Nebi-Mend, found a fragment of a stele of Seti the Great, father of Ramses II. It appears that Seti built the fortress of Riblah.[1]

Pézard died soon after he started the work; had it been continued, most unexpected finds would have come to light. Hidden under a kilometer-long mound is not Kadesh but Riblah, the military headquarters of Seti; and of Pharaoh Necho; and shortly thereafter of Nebuchadnezzar. But between Seti and Necho supposedly seven hundred years have elapsed. The tell conceals a rich reward for those who would resume the work of Pézard, whose shovels have lain rusted now for over fifty years.

The Army of Ramses II

The Egyptian *Poem of Pentaur* was meant to glorify the personal heroism of the pharaoh and to tell about "the victory ... he achieved in the land of Khatti, Nahrin ... Carchemish, Kedy, [the] land of Kadesh. "[2]
...

---

[1] Pézard: *Qadesh,* pp. 19-21, Plate XXVIII.
[2] A. Gardiner: *The Kadesh Inscriptions of Ramesses II* (Oxford, 1960), p. 7.

Another poem, written by Jeremiah, is entitled: "Against the army of Pharaoh-Necho king of Egypt, which was by the river Euphrates in Carchemish."[1]

In the tenth month of the fifth year of his reign Usermare Setepnere (Ramses II) passed the fortress of Tharu on the Egyptian frontier,

> ... all foreign countries trembling before him and their chiefs bringing their gifts ... bowing down through fear of His Majesty's might.[2]

Jeremiah described the start of this campaign in the following words:

> JEREMIAH 46:8 Egypt riseth up like a flood ... he saith, I will go up, and will cover the earth. ...

All lands on pharaoh's way, Judea included, were overawed by the show of force. Uneventfully and unopposed, the pharaoh proceeded northward.

Ramses II passed the region of cedars and the fortress of Riblah. "His Majesty proceeded northward [and] reached the hill-country of Kadesh."

His enemy was the "wretched chief of Khatti." The foe was not alone: Syrian allies were with the troops of "the king of Khatti."

> Now the wretched Fallen one of Kadesh was come and had collected together all the foreign countries as far as the end of the sea; the entire land of Khatti was come ... [here the north Syrian cities are called by name].[3]

Similarly we read in Jeremiah that the cities of northern Syria were allies of Nebuchadnezzar, and "the army of the Syrians" was acting in support of "the army of the Chaldeans" (Jeremiah 35:11).

The army of Ramses is described in the Egyptian texts as composed of four divisions:

> The division of Amon... the division of Re... the division of Ptah . . . the division of Sutekh.

According to the Hebrew poem of Jeremiah, this army was composed of Egyptians, Ethiopians, Libyans "that handle the shield," and Lydians "that handle and bend the bow" (Jeremiah 46:9). To these divisions are applied the words of the prophet:

---

[1] Jeremiah 46.
[2] Gardiner: *The Kadesh Inscriptions of Ramesses II,* p. 8.
[3] *Ibid.,* p. 8.

JEREMIAH 46:3 Order ye the buckler and shield, and draw near to battle.

4 Harness the horses; and get up, ye horsemen, and stand forth with your helmets; furbish the spears, and put on the brigandines.

The Egyptian poem prominently mentions the mercenaries of the pharaoh, called "the Sardan." Mercenaries of the pharaoh also appear in the poem of Jeremiah (46:21):

Also her [Egypt's] hired men are in the midst of her like fatted bullocks...

Since days of old the Egyptian army had recruited warriors from the neighboring countries, Ethiopia and Libya. In the days of Seti Ptah-Maat, the father of Ramses II, the Sardan, a division of mercenaries, became a permanent contingent in the Egyptian army. It can be shown that of the two theories of the land of origin of the Sardan mercenaries, whether from Sardinia or from Sardis (in Lydia), the latter identifi-

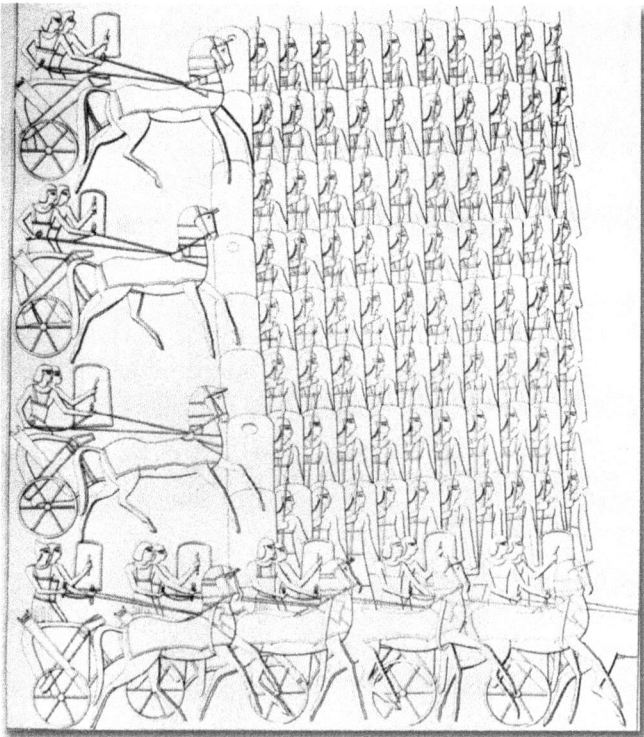

Figure 4: The infantry and chariotry of Ramses II.
From *Monuments de l'Egypte et de la Nubie*, Vol. 1, plate 33, Jean-François Champollion, Paris (1835-45)

cation is correct and the former wrong: to Seti, the Psammetich of Greek authors, Gyges, king of Sardis, dispatched mercenaries who arrived by sea and for whom the pharaoh built camps in Defenneh (Daphnae) in the eastern part of the Delta.

In establishing the identity of Ramses II and Pharaoh Necho, we look also for an explanation from Jeremiah: Who were the Sardan soldiers of fortune in the Egyptian army?

Jeremiah (46:9) named, next to the Egyptians, the Ethiopians, Libyans, and Lydians as contingents of the Egyptian army, "which was by the river Euphrates in Carchemish" and battled with Nebuchadnezzar. The Libyans and Ethiopians were neighbors of Egypt proper. At different times in Egyptian history Libyans and Ethiopians ruled over the entire domain, and Greater Egypt comprised at least parts of Libya on the west and Ethiopia on the south. The Lydians (in Hebrew "Ludim", plural of "Lud", Lydia) were people in western Asia Minor. There can be no mistake: the Lydians of Jeremiah were the Sardan of Ramses II. Sardis was the capital of Lydia. Sardan means "the men of Sardis."

The Battle of Kadesh-Carchemish

The famous battle of Kadesh took the following course. Ramses II, not suspecting that the army of the enemy was close by, marched with the division of Amon and reached a point northwest of Kadesh. He voiced his complaint:

> This is a great crime that the governors of foreign countries and the chiefs of Pharaoh have committed in not causing to be tracked down for them the Fallen one of Khatti wherever he was, that they might make report of it to Pharaoh every day.[1]

Ramses did not lay siege to Kadesh, planning to capture the city by assault. The troops of the enemy, expected from the north, were hidden behind the city. At the appropriate moment they marched from behind the city and, coming from the south, attacked the army of Re that followed the army of Amon.

---

[1] Gardiner: *The Kadesh Inscriptions of Ramesses II*, p. 30.

Figure 5: Relief sculptures from Charchemish showing two soldiers in battle dress.

Figure 6: Lydian soldiers from Sardis at the battle of Kadesh-Charchemish.

Figure 7: Soldiers of the army of Nebuchadnezzar at Carchemish. From Egyptian bas-reliefs. From *Die Welt der Hethiter*, M. Riemenschneider, Gustav Kilpper Verlag, Stuttgart.

Figure 8: Egyptian soldiers lined up for battle at Carchemish. From *La Bataille de Kadesh*, Kuenz (1928)

They had been made to stand concealed behind the town of Kadesh, and now they came forth from the south side of Kadesh and broke into the army of Pré in its midst as they were marching and did not know nor were they prepared to fight. There-upon the infantry and the chariotry of His Majesty were discomfited before them. ...[1]

The Egyptian host, taken unawares, retreated to the north. The "Annals of the War" repeat the story of the poem and give the direction of the retreat.

... The wretched Fallen one of Khatti was come with his infantry and his chariotry, as well as the many foreign countries who were with him, and they had crossed over the ford which is to the south of Kadesh. Then they entered into the midst of His Majesty's army as they were marching and did not know. Then the infantry and chariotry of His Majesty were discomfited before them whilst going northward to where His Majesty was.[2]

This harassed retreat of the loudly acclaimed and much-feared army is described by Jeremiah (46:5-6):

JEREMIAH 46:5 Wherefore have I seen them dismayed and turned away back? ...

6 Let not the swift flee away, nor the mighty man escape; they shall stumble, and fall toward the north by the river Euphrates.

Jeremiah and Ramses both stated that the retreat of the Egyptian army was northward. Why was it important to mention in what direction the Egyptians retreated? Usually a retreating army flees toward the land from which it came. Pursued from the south, the Egyptians retreated to the north, away from their land and their supply bases.

Meanwhile, the troops of "the wretched Chief of Khatti" surrounded the bodyguard of His Majesty. This is Ramses' own statement:

All foreign countries were combined against me, I being alone by myself, none other with me, my numerous infantry having abandoned me, not one looking at me of my chariotry.[3]

---

[1] *Ibid.*, pp. 8-9.
[2] *Ibid.*, p. 30.
[3] *Ibid.*, p. 10. Breasted: *Records,* Vol. III, Sec. 327, translates the last phrase: "Not one among them stood to turn about."

A similar picture of this panicky flight of the Egyptian army is given by Jeremiah:

> JEREMIAH 46:5 ... their mighty ones are beaten down, and are fled apace, and look not back: for fear was round about.

The pursuers "covered the mountains as grasshoppers in their multitude," wrote Pentaur. "They are more than the grasshoppers, and are innumerable," said Jeremiah (46:23) of them.

In this perilous situation the Egyptian king saved himself from capture by a desperate effort: he charged into the army of "the wretched Chief of Khatti." "Like a fierce-eyed lion," the pharaoh battled for a way out.

> So then His Majesty went to look about him and he found 2,500 chariots hemming him in on his outer side ... they being three men on a chariot acting as a unit.

How much truth there is in the poetical description of the courage of the king, forsaken by his troops, is difficult to establish. The Egyptian author ascribed the valor of a lion to his king. (The poem is written as if King Ramses II were the author, using the pronoun "I" for himself.) It was certainly a difficult and hazardous feat to find one's way out of the battle. The Hebrew prophet, too, made it clear that the pharaoh escaped with his life. As we shall learn later, he was helped by a contingent of "naarim," or "youths" in Hebrew.

The descriptions of the battle and its outcome, in the Hebrew and the Egyptian sources, are much alike: it was disaster, defeat, and flight. The prestige of Egypt was shattered.

The Egyptian author heaped shame on the army but not on the king, who was presented as a hero reproaching his forces for their cowardice.

> How cowardly are your hearts, my chariotry, nor is there any worthy of trust among you any longer... .
> But behold, you have done a cowardly deed, combined in one place. Not a man has stood among you to give me his hand when I was fighting. [1]

Of himself the pharaoh said, while admonishing his army:

> The nations have seen me: they will repeat my name even in far away regions.

---

[1] Gardiner: *The Kadesh Inscriptions of Ramesses II,* p. 11.

But Jeremiah disagreed:

JEREMIAH 46:12 The nations have heard of thy shame, and thy cry hath filled the land... .

According to the poem, Ramses succeeded in reaching, by a side road, the two divisions that did not participate in the battle; he consulted with his officers and heard their advice to return to Egypt. It was a hurried return.

In Jeremiah's words,

JEREMIAH 46:15 ... the Lord did drive them.

16 He made many to fall, yea, one fell upon another: and they said, Arise, and let us go again to our own people, and to the land of our nativity, from the oppressing sword.

The immediate result of the battle was that the rest of the Egyptian army escaped to Egypt, and Syria and Palestine were lost to the pharaoh and came under the sway of Nebuchadnezzar.

"Strategically the result was a defeat for the Egyptians, and they had to retire homeward with nothing to show for their efforts ..." wrote a historian of the reign of Ramses II; "the revolt [of Syria-Palestine] must have spread far south..."[1]

Table of the Battle of Kadesh-Carchemish

Hebrew sources about Pharaoh Necho:	*Egyptian sources about Ramses-Setepnere (Ramses II):*
TIME	
Four years after the first invasion of Palestine by Pharaoh Necho. Cf. II Chronicles 35:20; 36:2,4; Jeremiah 42:2	Four years after the first invasion of Palestine by Pharaoh Ramses II. Cf. stele of the 2nd year at Nahr el-Kelb; Assuan stele; *Annals*; *Poem of Pentaur*
PLACE	
"By the river Euphrates in Carchemish." Jeremiah 46:2	"In the land of Khatti, Nahrin (Naharaim), Carchemish, Kedy, the land of Kadesh." *Poem of Pentaur*

---

[1] R. O. Faulkner: in *The Cambridge Ancient History,* II, 2 (1975), p. 228.

TOPOGRAPHY

Near a fortress, surrounded on all all sides by water; the fortress has a double wall and moats; it projects into a large stream; nearby is a sacred lake. Cf. the description and plans of the Carchemish excavation	Near a fortress, surrounded on sides by water; the fortress has a double wall and moats; it projects into a large stream; nearby is a sacred lake. Cf. the four plans drawn on the walls of Karnak

POSITION

Carchemish is north of Bab	The field of battle was north of Baw

ALLIES

"The army of the Syrians" warring on the side of the Chaldean (Babylonian) army. Jeremiah 35:11	"Armies of the Syrian cities" on the side of the army of Hatti

PHARAOH'S ARMY

Four divisions: Egyptians, Ethiopians, Libyans, Lydians. Cf. Jeremiah 46:9. Of these, Lydians were mercenaries, "hired men." Jeremiah 46:9 Chariotry participated in the battle. Jeremiah 46:9	Four divisions – of Amon, Re, Ptah, and Sutekh. Cf. *Poem of Pentaur.* Mercenaries in the army were the Sardana, or the warriors from Sardis, in Lydia. Chariotry participated in the battle. *Annals* of Ramses II, *Poem of Pentaur*

THE COURSE OF THE BATTLE

The Egyptian army was "dismayed and turned back." Jeremiah 46:5	Suddenly attacked, "the infantry and chariotry of His Majesty were discomfited." Poem of the battle of Kadesh; *Annals*

THE RETREAT DEVELOPS INTO A FLIGHT OF THE EGYPTIAN ARMY

"Their mighty men are beaten down, fled apace, and look not back." Jeremiah 46:5	"My numerous infantry having abandoned me, not one looking at me of my chariotry." *Annals* of Ramses II

THE FLIGHT TOOK THE DIRECTION TO THE NORTH, AWAY FROM EGYPT

"... stumble and fall toward the north."	"Then the infantry and chariotry of His Majesty were discomfited before them whilst going northward."

The Fortress of Carchemish

Jeremiah reveals the site of the battle: it was at Carchemish. If Jeremiah and Pentaur described the same battle, it follows that Tell Nebi-Mend on the Orontes was not the scene of the great contest. We must now investigate whether Carchemish conforms to the drawings of Ramses II.

Carchemish is identified with the mound of Jerablus on the western bank of the Euphrates. [1]

The road from Aleppo runs northeast, passes Bab, Arima, and Hierapolis of Greek and Roman times, then crosses the valley of the Sadjur, a tributary flowing into the Euphrates, and reaches Jerablus on the Euphrates.

A large ancient mound dominates the western (here, because of winding, southern) bank of the Euphrates where now the Baghdad Railway crosses the river close to the Syrian-Turkish frontier. Great slabs with "Hittite" inscriptions and figures were discovered there even before the mound was excavated. They attracted attention and suggested the identification of the mound with Carchemish.

The site, as described by its excavators, "is marked by a horse-shoe embankment" and by "a high citadel mound which rises on the river bank to a height of some hundred and twenty feet above the mean water level of the Euphrates, and almost fills the riverain space between the two points of the horseshoe." [2] The two embankments – that in the shape of a horseshoe and that of the citadel – together form an oval. [3] The horseshoe embankment is surrounded by a deep trench. "The embankment rises very steeply to heights varying from 30 to even 50 feet from this depression." [4] "The mound rose twenty metres above the original surface; outside it was a fosse, some five metres deep." [5]

Another trench was on the inner side of the embankment. Thus two trenches, filled with water, ran along the embankment.

---

[1] First identified by W. H. Skene and G. Smith. See D. G. Hogarth: *Carchemish; report on the excavations at Djerabis on behalf of the British Museum conducted by C. Leonard Woolley and T. E. Lawrence*, Pt. 1, Introductory (London, 1914).

[2] *Ibid.*, p. 1.

[3] R. Koldewey: *Die Architektur von Sendschirli* (Berlin, 1898), p. 179, describes it as a circle.

[4] Hogarth: *Carchemish*, Pt. 1, *Introductory*, p. 1.

[5] C. L. Woolley: *Carchemish*, Vol. 2: *The Town Defences* (London, 1921), p. 44.

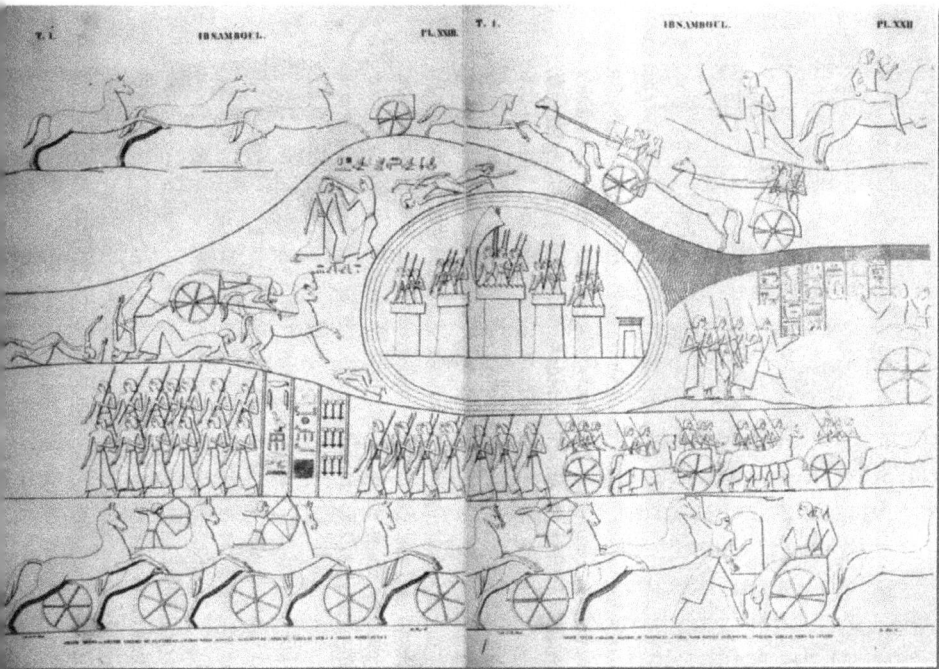

Figure 9: The fortress wall of Carchemish from the reliefs of Ramses II and from the Balawat Gate of Shalmaneser III.

The pictures of Ramses II fit this plan of the fortifications. The horse-shoe fortress is surrounded by trenches. "Kadesh is in a low valley surrounded by moats."[1] "The city is shown with a double moat."[2]

Tell Nebi-Mend, we recall, is not surrounded by moats; nor have any vestiges of an embankment been found there.

The horseshoe embankment of Carchemish was topped by a double wall, and also "the river wall was a double one."[3] In addition to the inner defenses the city also had outer defenses which "consisted of two parallel walls about nine metres from each other."[4]

The drawings of Ramses II of the city of Kadesh also show four parallel lines representing two walls running around the fortress.

On the map of the excavators of Carchemish two forts can be seen between the citadel mound and the horseshoe embankment, to the northwest and southeast of the citadel. "The transition from mound to walling was marked by a great fort" at "the north-west corner, close to what was then the bank of the little stream," and a similar fort-bastion was at the southeast.[5]

On the drawing by Ramses' artist two squares break the line of the walls, indicating two forts or bastions.

Besides the two forts the walls of Carchemish were interrupted by towers. "Brick towers were built on the wall face."[6]

The drawings of Ramses also show these towers. They can be compared with the picture of them made by Shalmaneser III. This king had occupied Carchemish two hundred and fifty years before Nebuchad-nezzar, and let his artist depict the front view of Carchemish on the bronze gate of Balawat.[7]

There is another detail: on the pictures of Ramses II and on those of Shalmaneser III alike the towers and the wall carry a crown of triangles. Some of these triangles or merlons were found in Carchemish in the course of excavation.[8]

---

[1] Breasted: *Records*, Vol. III, Sec. 340, note.
[2] Conder: *Quarterly Statement of the Palestine Exploration Fund*, 1881, p. 164
[3] Woolley: *Carchemish*, Pt. 2, pp. 46 and 47.
[4] *Ibid.*, p. 50.
[5] *Ibid.*, p. 47.
[6] *Ibid.*, p. 46.
[7] L. W. King: *Bronze Reliefs from the Gates of Shalmaneser* (London, 1915). During two centuries and a half since Shalmaneser III, Carchemish had been repeatedly stormed and occupied by Assyrian kings.
[8] Woolley: *Carchemish*, Pt. 2.

The city of the battle, pictured at the Ramesseum in western Thebes, is described as follows: "A fortress surrounded by a river and situated not far from the border of a lake" which is on the left of the fortress.[1]

"Just south of the western gate-gap" of Carchemish is found a depression. "This depression, which is bare of any trace of building, probably marks an open space, or even, may be, a sacred lake."[2]

The citadel-mound of Carchemish is poised on a rock, its northern face 'bowed out into the Euphrates'[3]

This situation suggested to the artists of Ramses his drawing of the fortifications on the waterfront itself. "We here see the city of Kadesh, by which the battle was fought, so thoroughly moated that it seems to lie in the very Orontes itself, rather than on it."[4] But this description does not fit Tell Nebi-Mend.[5]

It does fit the site of Carchemish. "The river Euphrates, coming from the north, here turns east of south after receiving the water of a small stream which descends a valley from the west. After passing the hamlet of Yunus, one mile up this rivulet throws off a millstream on the right, and finally reaches the main river about a hundred yards above the citadel."[6]

The Euphrates, the tributary Yunus, and the millstream surround Jerablus (Carchemish) on all sides with a water barrier. A sketch map of the "city of Jerablus" in a book published in 1754 illustrates this.[7]

This topography of a city surrounded by water satisfies the condition which "is mandatory for every site that might be identified as Kadesh."[8] No other suggested site, Tell Nebi-Mend included, meets this requirement.

The topography of the site of the fortress, the plan of its fortifications and their architectural design identify Kadesh of Ramses II as Carchemish.

---

[1] Conder: *Quarterly Statement of the Palestine Exploration Fund,* 1881, p. 164.
[2] Hogarth: *Carchemish,* Pt. 1, p. 2.
[3] *Ibid.*
[4] Breasted: *Records,* Vol. III, Sec. 335.
[5] "In the reliefs the town is wrongly depicted as an island in the river." Gardiner: *The Kadesh Inscriptions of Ramesses II,* p. 16.
[6] Hogarth: *Carchemish,* Pt. 1, p. 2.
[7] Alexander Drummond: *Travels ... as Far as the Banks of the Euphrates* (London, 1754); the map is reproduced in Hogarth: *Carchemish,* Pt. 1, p. 4; see overleaf.
[8] Pézard: *Qadesh,* p. 26.

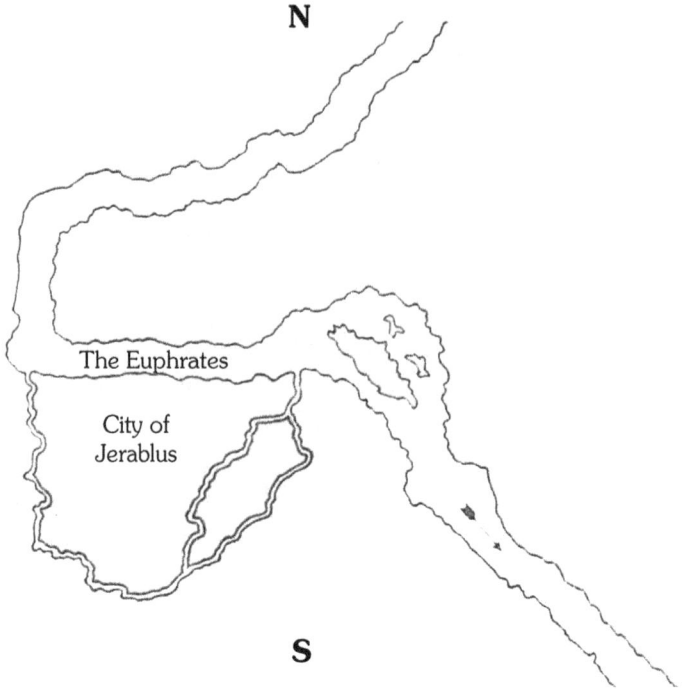

N

The Euphrates

City of
Jerablus

S

The Plan of the Battle

Now we can reconstruct the position of the armies of the pharaoh
Ramses II. When he, with the division of Amon, was northwest of
Carchemish, the division of Re crossed the ford of the river Nrt (or Rnt
or P-rnt) and approached Carchemish.[1] The divisions of Ptah and Sutekh
were "to the south of the town of Aronama (Arinama)."[2] This is Arima
of today.[3] Their officers were a few miles farther to the south in a place
called Baw or Bav.

---

[1] The Semitic "parat" changed to "ranat" in Egyptian, the letter "n", as often in this language,
being only slightly pronounced, and the letter "p" being dropped, as the Egyptians might
have mistaken it for "the" ("pi") before the name of the river.

[2] *Poem of Pentaur*, Gardiner, op. cit., p. 8.

[3] The original name of the place was "Arne, the city of Arame," the name of the king whose
capital it was in the days of Shalmaneser III. Shalmaneser wrote of the campaign of his tenth
year: "Against the cities of Aarame (personal name) I drew near. Arne, his royal city, I captured." Luckenbill: *Records of Assyria*, Vol. I, Sec. 567. A. Erman: *Life in Ancient Egypt*
(London, 1894), p. 335, and A. Gardiner: *Egyptian Grammar* (London, 1927), pp. 52–53
59, 63, discuss instances of words containing an internal m or n that is often not written
"with apparently no reason for the omission" (Erman), or "probably due to calligraphic reasons" (Gardiner, p. 52, § 59).

"Now the division of Re and the division of Ptah were on the march; they had not yet arrived and their officers were in the forest of Baw."[1] Thus wrote Ramses in the annals of the battle.

Baw is Bab of today. Bab and Arima are successive points on the road from Aleppo to Jerablus (Carchemish). The archaeologists who looked for Kadesh of the battle should have taken this reference to Baw and Arinama as clues.

Ramses mentioned the "forest of Baw." It is therefore of interest to read, in the report of the excavations at Carchemish, the following about the road from Aleppo to the site of the excavations: "The feature of the country which most strikes the newcomer is its treelessness. To the north and east the mountain regions still preserve something of their ancient forests. ... But the land as a whole is bare and shadeless. ... This was not always the case: An English traveller of the seventeenth century could lose himself in the interminable forests between Aleppo and Bab, where not a tree grows now. ...There is no doubt that a vast amount of deforestation has taken place, and it is probable that in Hittite times the Carchemish country was a well-wooded one."[2]

With Kadesh placed at Tell Nebi-Mend, Arinama and Baw to the south of Kadesh could not be identified, and "just where [were their locations] it is impossible to determine."[3]

The army of the enemy was so well concealed behind the city of Kadesh that the pharaoh and the division of Amon, which had already passed to a point northwest of the city, did not notice their presence.

See, they stand equipped and ready to fight behind Kadesh the Old.[4]

That the topography made it possible to set this trap may be seen from the following description of the position of Carchemish: "Carchemish is right down on the river's edge, so low that from a kilometre inland its citadel mound is hidden from sight by the intervening con-

---

[1] Breasted: *Records*, Vol. III, Sec. 340. Breasted vocalized "Bewey" in *Records* and "Baui" in *The Battle of Kadesh*.

[2] Woolley: *Carchemish*, Pt. 2, pp. 33-34.

[3] Breasted: *The Battle of Kadesh*, p. 23.

[4] Annals of Ramses II. Breasted translated "Kadesh the Deceitful," but it is assumed by Erman-Grapow: *Wörterbuch der ägyptischen Sprache*, I, 128, that the meaning is "Kadesh the Old," the adjective being a part of the name. See also A. Jirku: *Zeitschrift der Deutschen Morgenländischen Gesellschaft*, 86 (1933), 179; A. Gardiner: *The Kadesh Inscriptions of Ramesses II*, p. 32.

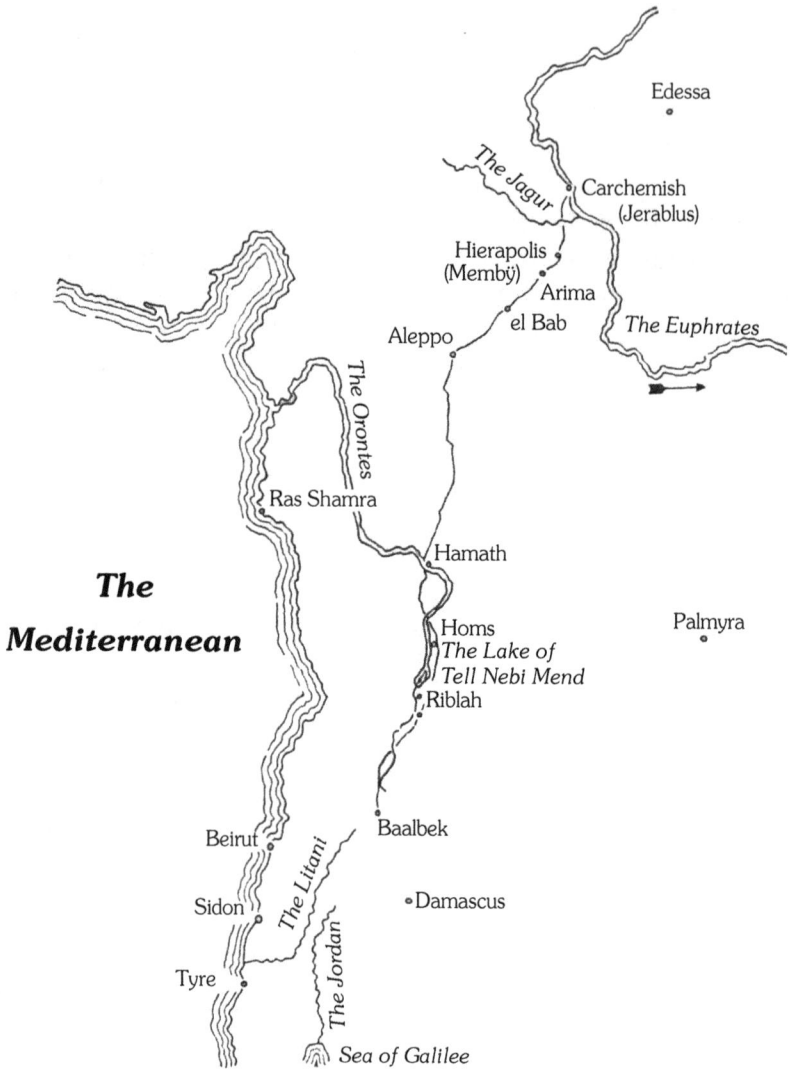

Edessa

The Jagur

Carchemish
(Jerablus)

Hierapolis
(Membÿ)

Arima

Aleppo

el Bab

The Euphrates

The Orontes

Ras Shamra

Hamath

The
Mediterranean

Homs

Palmyra

The Lake of
Tell Nebi Mend

Riblah

Baalbek

Beirut

The Litani

Sidon

Damascus

The Jordan

Tyre

Sea of Galilee

Northern Syria

tours. But low as it lies in relation to the main plateau, it none the less commands the head of the rich hollow land."[1]

As soon as the pharaoh and the division of Amon started to set up camp northwest of the city the enemy appeared in the field. A part of them, who were on the other side of the Euphrates, crossed the river, probably upon a darn to the south of the fortress, and attacked the division of Re marching unprepared for battle after having crossed the valley of the Sadjur. Cut off from retreat, they fled to the north. The pharaoh and the division of Amon, meanwhile, were attacked by another force emerging from south of the city. The battle was fought on the Syrian bank of the Euphrates. There the river forms a bend, and the drawing of the Egyptian artist, showing the pharaoh charging toward the river in the direction of the fortress from the starting point northwest of the fortress, accords with the topography of the place.

Already alarmed at the flight of the division of Re, which was attacked first, the pharaoh sent a messenger by a side route farther to the west to speed the arrival of two other divisions from Arinama (Arima) and Baw (Bab). Meanwhile, however, the division of Amon, which was with the pharaoh, was, like the division of Re, faced with disaster and, if we are to believe the *Poem of Pentaur*, deserted him and his charioteer. It was then that he put up his heroic fight in the style of a Roland and escaped captivity when *naarim* came to his help.

"Naarim" in the *Poem of Pentaur* is a Hebrew word meaning "boys" or "young men." Ramses, deserted by his troops, ascribed his survival to his own bravery but also to the "naarim" who came to his assistance, cutting through the ranks of the surrounding enemy and saving him in the nick of time.

> The arrival of the Nearin-troops of Pharaoh – life, prosperity, health! – from the land of Amurru [Syria].[2]

Naarim (Nearin) helped Ramses II to find his way to his troops cowering on the road and not daring to approach the battlefield where two other divisions had already been smashed and thrown to the north.

We learn that warriors, most probably from Judah, a unit separate from the four army divisions, participated in the campaign, acting as

---

[1] Woolley: *Carchemish*, Pt. 2, p. 38.
[2] Transl. J. A. Wilson in J. B. Pritchard, ed.: *Ancient Near Eastern Texts* (Princeton, 1950), p. 256.

an auxiliary force, and to some extent also decided the ultimate outcome of the campaign by saving Ramses II from death or captivity.

Naarim as choice warriors are referred to in the Scriptures in the
time of Ahab;[1] the existence of *naarim* as choice troops is twice mentioned in a writing by an Egyptian scribe discussing Palestine in the
days of Ramses II, a document we will consider on a later page.

Carchemish, the Sacred City

In the inscriptions of Ramses II, Carchemish is usually called Kadesh,
but he knew the other name too. As often as the names of the allies of
the "chief of Kheta" are mentioned in the *Poem of Pentaur*, either
Kadesh or Carchemish is referred to, but not both. The only exception
is the sentence, already quoted, which enumerates the allied lands and
cities under the "chief of Kheta" and includes "Carchemish, Kode, the
land of Kadesh," Kadesh in this instance having the sign not of a city
but of a country.

Carchemish means the city (Car) of Chemosh. Being a city named
after or dedicated to a god, it was a holy city (Kadesh).[2] The worship of
Chemosh was widespread – more than two centuries earlier, King Mesha
of Moab described on his stele how under protection of Chemosh he
was victorious over Ahab, king of Samaria.[3]

Carchemish was the site of a large temple; its foundations were discovered when the place was surveyed and partly excavated by an expedition of the British Museum. On a later page we shall discuss the
divergence of opinion among archaeologists concerning the age of
various structures and bas-reliefs and of finds in the tombs of Carchemish: significantly for our thesis, the age evaluations are consistently
divided between the thirteenth century and the end of the seventh. We
will have the chance to learn about this divergence of opinion but we
can already guess the cause of it.

---

[1] I Kings 20:14-19. See also J. Macdonald: »The Na'ar in Israelite Society«, *Journal of Near Eastern Studies*, 35 (1976), p. 169.

[2] Joachim Ménant: »Kar-Kemish«, *Mémoires, Académie des Inscriptions et Belles Lettres*, XXXII (1891), 210.

[3] *Ages in Chaos*, Vol. I, »Mesha's Rebellion«.

Not only the temple and the city but the entire area was consecrated to the protecting deity. About twenty miles southeast from Carchemish, on the road to Aleppo, is located Hierapolis, or "Holy City" in Greek, a name equivalent to the Semitic Kadesh. In the days we describe it was most probably called Shabtuna, a site referred to by Ramses II on the road to Carchemish, north of Baw (Bab) . In Hellenistic times Hierapolis became an important temple city; but despite its name it was not the Kadesh of the battle. The battle maps of Ramses II show Kadesh on the waterfront but Hierapolis is ten miles away from the Euphrates and there is no river at Hierapolis.

The center of the battle was ten to twenty miles north of Hierapolis. Only the two divisions, or half of the army, which did not participate in the battle stood still farther to the south, at Arinama (Arima) and Baw (Bab). Although a part of the battle took place on the plain between Hierapolis and Carchemish, where the division of Re was attacked after crossing the valley of the Sadjur, almost halfway from Hierapolis to Carchemish, the pictures do not leave room for doubt: the fortress Kadesh of the battlefield was on a river and was surrounded by water. The city of the battle was Carchemish but in the inscriptions of Ramses II it bears the name of a city twenty miles away. What is the reason for this?

Lucian, the Roman writer, himself a native of the area, in his book *De Dea Syria (The Syrian Goddess),* gave a detailed description of the cult of Hierapolis. He began the book with these words: "There is in Syria a city not far from the river Euphrates: it is called the Sacred City, and is sacred to the Assyrian Hera."[1]

Lucian supplies the answer to the question just posed. Stratonice, the queen of King Antiochus (-280 to -261), ordered that the city of Carchemish, which lost its military and religious significance during Persian times (-539 to -332), should be transplanted, as a sacerdotal center, twenty miles to the south, to the place called Mabog by the Assyrians, Shabtuna by the Egyptians, and later Hierapolis by the Greeks and the Romans. "As far as I can judge," writes Lucian, "this name [Hierapolis] was not conferred upon the city when it was first settled, but originally it bore another name."

---

[1] Lucian: *The Syrian Goddess,* transl. H. A. Strong (London, 1913). The authorship of this book is sometimes questioned.

Impoverished under the Persians, the sacred cult of Chemosh was soon replaced by the Hellenized Syrians with the cult of the "Syrian Goddess," compared by Lucian with Hera.[1]

Already in antiquity the transfer of the cult to a new locality resulted in a certain confusion among writers. The Syriac translation of the Scriptures (Peshitta) renders Carchemish as Mabog, whereas Hierapolis is Mabog.[2] Strabo (XVI, i, 27) identified Carchemish with Hierapolis, and were it not for the explicit statement of Lucian, one would be lured into locating Hierapolis at Jerablus-Carchemish. Procopius was better informed when he wrote that Hierapolis lies within easy distance from Europos on the Euphrates[3] – Europos was the name the Romans gave to Carchemish-Jerablus.[4]

Ammianus Marcellinus, the Roman historian of the fourth century of the present era, himself born in Syrian Antioch, in his enumeration of the cities of the Commagene district on the Euphrates, mentions a city, "the Ancient Hierapolis" or "Hierapolis the Old."[5] This designation seems to have originated after Stratonice transferred the holy precinct from the site of Carchemish to the south. But, strangely, already the war annals of Ramses II call the city of the battle "Kadesh the Old," which proves not only that Carchemish was a sacred city (Hierapolis) but also that in Ramses' time, long before Stratonice, the city was called by the name by which Marcellinus knew it.

Carchemish (Car Chemosh) was the Carian name of the city; Kadesh was its Semitic eponym; Hierapolis was the Greek translation of the Semitic Kadesh.

---

[1] Sacred prostitution became the predominant feature of the cult, and every married woman was required, at least once in her lifetime, to offer herself to a stranger in the precincts of the temple.

[2] In II Chronicles 35:20 the Syriac version substitutes Mabog for Carchemish; in II Kings 23:29, where the Hebrew text reads "to the river Euphrates," the Syriac version is "to Mabog which is on the river Euphrates." The Arabic version follows the Syriac and has "to Menbaj" (Membidj or Mabog). Also Ephrem, the Syrian saint (*Commentaire sur l'Ecriture Sainte, Opera Omnia*, IV), renders Carchemish as Mabog.

[3] Procopius: *Histories, Persian Wars*, II, 20.

[4] The name "Jerablus" is considered a corruption of the names "Europos" (the Roman city on the site of Carchemish) and "Hierapolis" (Hogarth: *Carchemish*, Pt. 1, pp. 23-25). Travelers of the eighteenth and nineteenth centuries placed Hierapolis in Jerablus or Carchemish. J. S. Buckingham in *Travels in Mesopotamia* (London, 1827), wrote about "ruins of Hierapolis, now called Yerabolus."

[5] Ammianus Marcellinus, IV, 8, 7. See Hogarth: *Carchemish*, Pt. 1, p. 23.

Ramses II and Nebuchadnezzar in War and Peace

Palestine's Three-Year Revolt and the Capture of Ashkelon

Between the fifth and eighth years of Ramses II all Palestine revolted against Egypt.[1] The battle of Kadesh took place in the fifth year of Ramses, and the "revolt of Palestine" followed the unfortunate outcome of this contest. This three years' revolt is described also in the Second Book of Kings. The battle by the river Euphrates took place in the fourth year of Jehoiakim (Jeremiah 46:2); as a consequence of it Syria and Palestine were exposed to Babylonian conquest. The tribute which had been paid to the pharaoh (II Kings 23:35) was discontinued.

II Kings 24:1 In his (Jehoiakim's) days Nebuchadnezzar king of Babylon came up, and Jehoiakim became his servant three years.[2]

It took the Egyptians these three years to recover sufficiently to send an army of reconquest to Palestine. An inscription of the eighth year of Ramses II records such an attempt by him.[3] He invaded the Philistine shore and besieged Ashkelon. A relief at Karnak shows the city of Ashkelon being stormed by the Egyptians under Ramses II. A laconic inscription reads:

The wretched town which his majesty took when it was wicked, Ashkelon. It says: "Happy is he who acts in fidelity to thee. ..."[4]

---

[1] Faulkner in *The Cambridge Ancient History*, II, 2 (1975), p. 228.
[2] Jehoiakim revolted against Nebuchadnezzar in his (Jehoiakim's) eighth year, after three years of submission; therefore his defection from the pharaoh occurred in his fifth year.
[3] Wilson in Pritchard: *Ancient Near Eastern Texts*, p. 256.
[4] Wilson: loc. cit.

This third period of the war is described by Jeremiah in the chapter, "against the Philistines, before that Pharaoh smote Gaza" (Jeremiah 47:1).

> JEREMIAH 47:5 Baldness is come upon Gaza; Ashkelon is cut off with the remnant of their valley.

The impending invasion of the pharaoh was a signal to Jehoiakim. In his eighth year he rebelled against the Chaldeans. For a few years Judea was again in the domain of the pharaoh Ramses II. His campaign brought him as far as Beth-Shan, where a stele of his ninth year was found. But a few years later, in the eleventh year of Jehoiakim, Nebuchadnezzar moved into Palestine, encircled Jerusalem, captured its king, and forced the pharaoh out of the country.

> II KINGS 24:7 And the king of Egypt came not again any more out of his land: for the king of Babylon had taken from the river of Egypt unto the river Euphrates all that pertained to the king of Egypt.

Figure 10: The storming of Ashkelon by Ramses II

Nebuchadnezzar placed Jehoiachin (Jeconiah) on the throne of his father Jehoiakim. After three months, however, he returned to Jerusalem and removed Jehoiachin to Babylonia, together with "all the princes, and all the mighty men of valour," and also "all the craftsmen and smiths." He installed Mattaniah, the third son of Josiah, as a vassal king in Jerusalem, and changed his name to Zedekiah. For eight years Zedekiah bore the burden of vassalage to the king of the Babylonians. Then he renounced his allegiance to Nebuchadnezzar and, like his brother Jehoiakim, relied on the help promised by the pharaoh. Nebuchadnezzar brought his army into Judea and besieged Jerusalem.

The End of the Kingdom of Judah

Twenty years had passed since Josiah, true to his treaty with the Babylonians, defended with his life the Megiddo Pass against the overwhelming odds of the Egyptian army under Ramses II. Jehoahaz, Josiah's son, spent his life in an Egyptian prison; Jehoiakim, another son, was killed by the Babylonians; Jeconiah (Jehoiachin), a son of Jehoiakim, was held in a prison in Babylon; Zedekiah, the third son of Josiah and the last king onthe throne of David, was besieged in Jerusalem by the army of Nebuchadnezzar. Secretly, without the knowledge of the princes and elders of Jerusalem, he had Jeremiah brought from prison to the palace to hear from him a prophetic word.

Since his youth, for more than thirty years, Jeremiah had admonished the people of Jerusalem: "Do no wrong, do no violence to the stranger, the fatherless, nor the widow, neither shed innocent blood" (22:3). Daily he went through the streets of Jerusalem and its broad places, warning the population of the city: "I cannot hold my peace, because thou hast heard, O my soul, the sound of the trumpet, the alarm of war. Destruction upon destruction is cried" (4:19-20).

Jeremiah stood behind Josiah and his pledge to defend Babylonia against attack by Egypt, and though Josiah lost the battle at Megiddo, the prophet remained all his life true to his Babylonian orientation. He saw that the people were not aware of the growing might of the Chaldeans and were relying on the erroneous assumption of the equality or even superiority of Egypt under Ramses II.

The seer did not console the people with promises of God's help, as Isaiah had done one hundred years before when Sennacherib threatened Jerusalem. Jeremiah cried in the streets of Jerusalem: "Woe unto us! for the day goeth away, for the shadows of the evening are stretched out" (6:4).

Jerusalem witnessed the titanic struggle of Nebuchadnezzar and Ramses II for domination of the ancient world, and the city became the prize between them. The Egyptian party in Jerusalem was stronger than the Babylonian because the pompousness of Egypt under Ramses II misled them; and the cruel treatment by the Babylonians made enemies of many. Therefore Jerusalem repeatedly rebelled against Nebuchadnezzar.

Jeremiah was persecuted. In the days before the final siege and before Jerusalem fell exhausted by famine, Jeremiah was repeatedly taken into custody that he might not cause to falter the hearts of the soldiers who had taken upon themselves the herculean task of resisting Nebuchadnezzar. It is remarkable that he was not put to death for treason. He antagonized the entire population by proclaiming Nebuchadnezzar to be a servant of the Lord, whom nations and even beasts of the field were obliged to revere. Jerusalem could not believe that this was the word of the Lord. Zedekiah was among the very few who believed that Jeremiah was a true prophet. In the secret audience with the prophet brought from his prison the king inquired: "Is there any word from the Lord? And Jeremiah said, There is: for, said he, thou shalt be delivered into the hand of the king of Babylon" (37:17).

Jeremiah was not returned to his prison but was sent to the detention yard close to the palace and received there daily upon the command of the king a piece of bread out of the bakers' street until all the bread in the city was spent.

When the leaders among the defenders heard that Jeremiah had said in the detention yard, "He that remaineth in this city shall die by the sword, by the famine, and by the pestilence: but he that goeth forth to the Chaldeans shall live; for he shall have his life for a prey" (38:2), they cast him into a dungeon so that nobody should hear his words, and he remained there.

Zedekiah had him drawn out of the mire with ropes and brought again into the palace through a secret entrance that was in the House of the Lord. The king said to Jeremiah: "I will ask thee a thing; hide nothing from me." Then Jeremiah said to Zedekiah: "If I declare it unto thee, wilt thou not surely put me to death?" Zedekiah, the king, swore secretly to Jeremiah, saying: "As the Lord liveth, that made us this soul, I will not put thee to death, neither will I give thee into the hand of these men that seek thy life." Jeremiah then said: "If thou wilt not go forth to the king of Babylon's princes, then shall this city be given into the hand of the Chaldeans, and they shall burn it with fire, and thou shalt not escape out of their hand" (38:14-18).

It was too late. "For death is come up into our windows and is entered into our palaces" (Jeremiah 9:21). There occurred no miracle as in the days of the Pharaoh of the Exodus or King Sennacherib. Jerusalem endured the renewed siege for eighteen months. The famine grew dreadful, but the people would not submit. The storming machines at last breached the walls. When the city wall was broken in, the last of the defenders fled and went out of the city by night "by the way of the king's garden, by the gate betwixt the two walls: and he (Zedekiah) went out the way of the plain." The army of the Chaldeans pursued the starved warriors and overtook Zedekiah on the plains of Jericho; all his army was scattered from him.

Zedekiah was brought before Nebuchadnezzar in Riblah. Nebuchadnezzar slew the little children of Zedekiah before his eyes and then put out his eyes. The sight of his children in their agony was the last thing he saw in his life. The blind king was bound in chains, dragged to Babylon, and thrown into prison. He was thirty-two years old.

The people in Jerusalem, also in chains, followed their king into exile. They were dragged entirely unclothed. They were not permitted to rest on the way.[1] But they bore with them vessels containing the earth of Jerusalem, narrates the Arabian historian Yaqut.[2]

> This people hath a revolting and a rebellious heart; they are revolted and gone (Jeremiah 5:23).

When they reached the Euphrates, Nebuchadnezzar arranged a feast on his royal ship. The captives of Jerusalem were ordered to sing their

---

[1] *Pesikta Rabba* 28.
[2] "This is told in the ancient chronicles: When the Jews went from Jerusalem ... and became exiles in Iraq, they carried with them earth and water of Jerusalem." Yaqout (Yakut): *Dictionnaire geographique, historique et litteraire* (transl. from Arabic by Barbier de Meynard, Paris, 1861), p. 613.

sacred songs: "… they that carried us away captive required of us a song; and they that wasted us required of us mirth, saying, Sing us one of the songs of Zion. How shall we sing the Lord's song in a strange land? If I forget thee, O Jerusalem, let my right hand forget her cunning. If I do not remember thee, let my tongue cleave to the roof of my mouth; if I prefer not Jerusalem above my chief joy" (Psalm 137:3-6).

The pious writer of the Book of Chronicles says that Zedekiah "did that which was evil in the sight of the Lord his God, and humbled not himself before Jeremiah the prophet." For trying to restore the freedom of his people he was branded by the scriptural annalist as a sinner. The *Talmud* did not share this verdict of the Scriptures and pronounced him to be righteous and his tormentor vicious.[1]

Haunted by the vision of the siege and famine of Jerusalem and still hearing the cries of his own children, Zedekiah, with dry holes in his face, unable to weep, lived and died in prison, which was dark for him day and night alike. He left the throne of David and started the procession of serfs and priests of sorrow which moved through the days of the Roman Caesars, the Christian Inquisition, and down to the present day.

Palestine was a desolate waste; the fruitful place was a wilderness. The fields remained unfilled. Stork, turtledove, crane, swallow, and every cheerful and singing bird of the sky flew away from the gruesome land, and vultures came in their place. The sound of the millstones was heard no more in Judea, nor was the light of a candle seen.[2]

The prophet was left to bewail the end of his city and his nation. After his prophecy had been fulfilled he asked himself: "Wherefore hath the Lord done thus unto this great city?"

Jerusalem was a heap of ruins, the Temple destroyed. Everyone who passed wagged his head. An obstinate nation was deported in chains along the road trodden by the tribes of Israel after the fall of Samaria about one hundred and thirty years earlier.

It is nowhere said that Judah found the Ten Tribes in Assyria or Babylonia. They had been moved northward and eastward into the depths of Asia. Some splinters of Israel and Judah presumably reached the mountains of the Himalaya and the forests of India.

---

[1] *Tractate Shabbat* 149a, *Sanhedrin* 103a.
[2] Jeremiah 25:10.

In the year -586 Jerusalem was destroyed. A decade or two later Buddha was born; a few years later still Confucius was born; Lao-tse was their contemporary.[2] Just as after the second destruction of Jerusalem, when the Temple and the city were burned by Titus, a hot blast of Hebrew prophecy shattered the Occident and "conquered the conquerors," so after the first destruction of Jerusalem a wind out of the tempest that swept the prophets of Judea reached the Far East and kindled the tongues of seers and preachers.

The Lachish Conflagration

Before World War II the spades of the archaeologists raised from the ground the ashes of -586.

Together with Jerusalem, Lachish and Azekah were the last strongholds to oppose the Chaldean army.

> JEREMIAH 34:7 ... the king of Babylon's army fought against Jerusalem, and against all the cities of Judah that were left, against Lachish, and against Azekah: for these defenced cities remained of the cities of Judah.

Between 1932 and 1938 excavation work at Tell ed Duweir in southern Palestine brought ancient Lachish to light.[1] It was one of the ranking strongholds in Judea. In -702 Sennacherib assaulted the city and had his artist depict this assault in low relief in his palace at Nineveh – it is one of the most famous reliefs of the Assyrian warfare. Now, one hundred and fifteen years later, the city suffered another siege – by the troops of Nebuchadnezzar.

Under the crumbled walls of a city destroyed by fire, potsherds inscribed with Hebrew letters were found. Reading of the messages dis-

---

[1] The time of Lao-tse is disputed. *Journal of the American Oriental Society,* LXI (1941), 215-21; LXII (1942), 8-13, 300-4.

[2] Earlier in the century Lachish was erroneously identified in the mound of Tell el Hasi. Following a suggestion by W. F. Albright, J. L. Starkey dug at Tell ed Duweir. He suffered death at the hands of Arab terrorists who mistook him for a Jew; the mound was left only partially excavated. The publication of the results absorbed the next twenty years and was executed by Olga Tufnell, a member of Starkey's staff. *Lachish (Tell ed Duweir),* Vol. I, *The Lachish Letters* (1938) (Torczyner of the Hebrew University at Jerusalem read and edited the letters); Vol. II, *The Fosse Temple,* by O. Tufnell, C. H. Inge, and L. Harding (1940); Vol. III, *The Iron Age,* by O. Tufnell (1953); Vol. IV, *The Bronze Age,* ed. O. Tufnell (1958).

closed that these potsherds date from the time of the siege of Jerusalem by Nebuchadnezzar.

The commander of a small outpost to the north of Lachish, Hoshayahu, wrote to Yaush, the military governor of Lachish, his superior:

> For the signal stations of Lachish we are watching, according to all the signs which my lord gives, because we do not see the signals of Azekah.

It is conjectured that this message from the commander of the outpost to the governor of Lachish was written when Azekah was crumbling under the siege, and only Lachish was sending fire signals and also written orders to the outpost, probably Kiryath-Yearim.

The ostraca were discovered under a layer of ashes and the burnt debris of a shattered bastion in the city defenses. The stones of the walls appear to have been "split by thermal fractures, or are partly calcined" and the mortar was reduced to a pink grey powder.

> It is quite certain that the conflagration inside the room near the gates was directly connected with the firing of the bastion from without, and is contemporary with the final assault, as evidenced at so many points along the line of the city's outer defense wall. Huge bonfires had been maintained to breach it, though the northwest corner of the mound and the bastion bore the brunt of the attack. Our first season's work on the defenses indicated that the firing should be equated with the destruction of the city at the end of the Judaean kingdom, at the time of Nebuchadnezzar's campaign before he destroyed Jerusalem in 586 B.C. The burnt olive stones found in the embers of the fire suggest the autumn as a season date. [1]

The local temple of Lachish, described in the second volume of the published reports, "was founded after the crushing of Hyksos power in Palestine." It was rebuilt in the el-Amarna period: a plaque of Amenhotep III was found under the foundation of the rebuilt temple. [2]

Various small objects were discovered amid the ruins. "The ivories, the beads, and the vases of glass, faience and stone belong fairly consistently to the XVIIIth and XIXth Dynasties. Scarabs and plaques with royal names range from Thothmes (Thutmose III) (1501-1447) to Ramses II (1292-1225). This indicates only that the Temple cannot have come to an end be-fore 1292 B.C." [3] All these dates are derived from the conventional chronology.

---

[1] *Lachish,* Vol. I, p. 12.
[2] *Ibid.,* Vol. II, p. 20.
[3] *Ibid.*

Together with Egyptian objects of the Eighteenth and Nineteenth Dynasties, local objects of the ninth and eighth centuries were found in the temple. The following explanation of their presence together with Egyptian objects was offered.

> The objects from graves which were later dug down into the filling of the rooms and the surrounding soil are all ca. 900-800 B.C. They can only prove that the temple was well buried and forgotten by that time. [1]

Scarabs and seal impressions of the Egyptian pharaohs of the Eighteenth and Nineteenth Dynasties are often found in Palestine in the strata of the Israelite period, but these seals are regarded as antedating the strata in which they are discovered and are explained either as antiquarian amulets used by the Israelites five or six centuries after they were cut or impressed, or as contemporary but counterfeit seals of ancient pharaohs.

On the basis of these often repeated explanations one should assume that the Egyptian objects in the temple of Lachish were pieces of antiquity or counterfeits. But in this case the principle was disregarded because "the scarabs are notoriously dangerous objects to use for dating purposes except when they are in bulk,"[2] and here they were found in bulk; it was disregarded also because of the plaque of Amenhotep III placed under the foundation of the temple when it was rebuilt. This placing of a plaque was a formal act, and only a genuine and contemporary plaque would have been used.

Ultimately the temple of Lachish burned down in a conflagration. "The temple was destroyed by fire," and soon thereafter, before any salvage work was done, rain washed in sand and filled the debris with it. "This suggests that the destruction occurred just before or during the rainy season."[3] In Palestine the rainy season lasts from late fall until spring.

"Signs of fire and destruction" were found to be widespread and indicate that the burning of the temple had been "only a part of a far wider catastrophe."[4]

Concerning the date of the destruction of the temple by fire, the archaeologists wrote: "On the evidence of the large collection of vessels found within the rooms of the building in the ashes covering the

---

[1] *Ibid.*
[2] *Ibid.*, p. 68.
[3] *Ibid.*, p. 44.
[4] *Ibid.*, p. 23.

floor, it seems impossible that this should be dated later than the middle point of Ramses II's reign, about 1262 B.C."[1]

Some time after the destruction of the temple of Lachish, a few stones were rolled together "by a remnant of the faithful, lacking the resources necessary to rebuild the ruins," on which to place their offering. These stones reminded the excavators of a similar occurrence after the destruction of the Temple in Jerusalem supposedly seven hundred years later. The excavators wrote: "A notable parallel could be found in Jeremiah 41:5"[2]

In the ruins of a rectangular structure which served as an extension of the bastion in which the Hebrew ostraca of the time of Nebuchadnezzar were found, objects dating from the reign of Ramses II were discovered in the ashes. "Although the building is destroyed, the rubbish filling its foundation is of greatest interest to us." The potsherds were found to be "unmistakably" of the time of the Eighteenth and Nineteenth Dynasties; "it became evident that the horizon level from which they came had been dug into by these later builders. Quantities of sherds were from vessels of the local decorated type of the late XVIIIth – XIXth Dynasty, similar to those found in the graves producing the scarabs. ... From this same deposit comes a finely engraved carnelian scarab bearing the name User-Maat-Ra, Setep-en-Ra, Ramesses II. This scarab has certainly been subjected to fire, its surface has a greyish patination, and discoloring and fusing is a feature of so many of the decorated sherds in this deposit. It was here also that we collected twenty-five fragments of a small open pottery bowl, inscribed spirally both inside and out." The script was recognized as "Egyptian hieratic of the thirteenth – twelfth centuries." The inscription referred to the year "four," evidently of the pharaoh Ramses II."[3]

In a layer of pure black ash covering a trench, at the bottom of the foundation, the excavators tried at the end of the 1937 season to find the origin of "all this ballast for the iron age builders." "In the ash bed, we collected gold foil, fragments of a green glaze faience bowl and pieces of a small buff pottery bowl, of a type found in the upper levels of our XVIIIth – XIXth Dynasty temple, with the ivory toilet objects and scarabs, buried in the ashes which produced the fragments of the Tell

---

[1] *Ibid.*, p. 47.
[2] *Ibid.*, p. 45.
[3] J. Cerny maintains that the fourth year refers to the fourth year of Merneptah, the successor to Ramses II. See Albright: *Bulletin, American School of Oriental Research,* LXXIV (1939), 21.

ed Duweir ewer.[1] Here, once again we find that the burning of the temple was not an isolated event in the city's history, but was part of a general calamity which marked the end of Egypt's control, in the twelfth century, towards the close of the XIXth Dynasty."

Thus we have the following situation: in the ashes and ruins of the temple of Lachish destroyed by fire in the days of Ramses II (so dated because of the seals of this pharaoh), objects of the period of the Jewish kingdom were found in great number, andit was decided that these objects of the later period were *dug into* the level of Ramses II, presumably an earlier period. In the ashes and ruins of the citadel of Lachish, destroyed by fire in the days of Nebuchadnezzar (so dated because of the Hebrew letters to the defenders of the city), a vase with hieratic writing of the Nineteenth Dynasty and seals of Ramses II were found, and it was decided that these objects, presumably of an earlier period, were *dug up* in the days of the Jewish kings and thus became mingled with objects of a later age (that of Nebuchadnezzar).

Were these two destructions by fire separated by seven hundred years? Our reconstruction of history, according to which Ramses II and Nebuchadnezzar II were contemporaries, brings us to a different conclusion.

The temple of Lachish was built in the days of Solomon and Thutmose III. It was rebuilt in the days of Amenhotep III and Jehoshaphat. The third structure was erected on the site – the archaeologists discovered three consecutive constructions of the temple – after the siege of the city by Sennacherib.

The city and the temple were destroyed by Nebuchadnezzar in the days of Ramses II, in the twenty-first year of Ramses II's reign.

Treaty Between Ramses II and Nebuchadnezzar

Two giants, Egypt under Ramses II and Babylon under Nebuchadnezzar, fought nineteen years for domination over the Middle East. Judea was the victim in this deadly struggle. She was devastated by the troops first of one despot and then of the other, but the lands of the contestants were spared the horrors of the prolonged war.

---

[1] A ewer is a kind of a wide-mouthed jug.

To secure victory over rebellious Judea, Nebuchadnezzar finally proposed a peace treaty to the pharaoh. Historians take it for granted that
during the last siege of Jerusalem a treaty was negotiated between
Babylonia and Egypt. [1] The pharaoh was glad to insure the integrity of
his own country and sacrificed Judea, his ally.

Jerusalem suffered an eighteen months' siege, followed by destruction.
The war between Babylonia and Egypt had terminated, and Egypt did
not come to the aid of the besieged. More than this, Egypt and Babylonia
pledged loyalty to each other and obligated themselves to extradite
political refugees.

The peace treaty is preserved in the Egyptian language, carved on
the wall of the Karnak temple of Amon. A text in the Babylonian
(Akkadian) language, written on clay in cuneiform and found at the
beginning of this century at Boghazkoi, a village of eastern Anatolia, is
a draft of the same document. The original of the treaty was written on
a silver tablet not extant today. The original language of the treaty was
Babylonian, and the Egyptian text is a translation, as some expressions reveal.

The treaty was signed by Usermare Setepnere, son of Menmare,
grandson of Menpehtire (the royal name of Ramses II, son of Seti,
grandson of Ramses I), and by Khetasar, son of Merosar, grandson of
Seplel. The treaty in the Akkadian language was signed by Hattusilis,
son of Mursilis, grandson of Subbiluliumas. [2]

The man whose name was read Khetasar in the Egyptian and Hattusilis
in the Boghazkoi text must have been the king whom we know as
Nebuchadnezzar, son of Nabopolassar. More than fifty times in the
Scriptures his name is spelled Nebuchadrezzar; more than thirty times
he is called Nebuchadnezzar. [3]

---

[1] F. K. Kienitz: *Die politische Geschichte Aegyptens vom 7. bis zum 4. Jahrhundert vor der Zeitwende* (Berlin, 1953), p. 24: "Thus Necho and Nebukadnezar came to an understand-
ing, and probably even concluded a formal treaty." R. P. Dougherty: *Nabonidus and Belshazzar*
(London, 1929), p. 55: "It is natural to suppose that a treaty [with Egypt] was negotiated. ...
Breasted takes it for granted."

[2] This reading of the foreign royal names by Egyptologists follows other usages, the sounds "r"
and "l" being represented by the same sign in hieroglyphics.

[3] The name of one of the two legates who brought the treaty in the name of Hattusilis to
Ramses II is preserved in the text of the treaty itself. He is called T-r-t-s-bw. In the Book of
Jeremiah (39:3), among the chiefs of Nebuchadnezzar, Nergal-Sharezer, Sarsechim, and Rab-
saris are named. These names are sometimes regarded as names of offices. It is possible but
far from certain that the first or second of these was the above-mentioned ambassador.

The adversary of Ramses II is called in the treaty the king of Hatti. Hatti, as can be learned from many cuneiform texts, was a broad ethnographical or territorial designation. In a Babylonian building inscription Nebuchadnezzar wrote: "The princes of the land of Hatti beyond the Euphrates to the westward, over whom I exercised lordship."[1] The treaty has an "oath and curse" clause. Gods of many places were invoked to keep vigilance over the treaty and to punish the one who should violate it. In the list of the gods and goddesses, the goddess of Tyre is followed by the "goddess of Dan." But in the days before the conquest of Dan by the Danites, in the time of the Judges, that place was called Laish (Judges 18:29), and it was Jeroboam who built there a temple. The name of a place called Dan in a treaty of Ramses II, presumably of the first half of the thirteenth century, sounds like an anachronism.

The purpose of the treaty was to bring about the cessation of hostilities between the two lands. It is obvious from its text that Syria and Palestine no longer belonged to the domain of Egypt.

This is in agreement with the biblical data. The major part of the treaty is given over to the problem of political refugees. The paragraphs are written in a reciprocal manner; it is apparent that it was the great king of Hatti who was interested in the provisions for extradition of the political enemies of the Chaldeans. A special paragraph in the treaty deals with Syrian (Palestinian) fugitives:

> Now if subjects of the great chief of Kheta transgress against him ... I will come after their punishment to Ramses-Meriamon, the great ruler of Egypt ... to cause that Usermare-Setepnere, the great ruler of Egypt, shall be silent ... and he shall turn [them] back again to the great chief of Kheta.[2]

It was only shortly before this that a similar accord had existed between the pharaoh and the king of Jerusalem. The prophet Uriah had fled from the sight of Jehoiakim to Egypt. "And Jehoiakim the king sent men into Egypt. ... And they fetched forth Uriah out of Egypt, and brought him unto Jehoiakim the king" (Jeremiah 26:22-23). Now, ten or fifteen years later, the population of Palestine and Edom were also fleeing into Egypt from the sight of the Chaldeans. Egypt was the place of refuge for those who feared the Chaldeans.

---

[1] S. Langdon: Building Inscriptions of the Neo-Babylonian Empire (Paris,1905), p. 151.
[2] Breasted: Records, Vol. III, Sec. 381.

Jeremiah foretold that these Jewish refugees would be removed from Egypt.

JEREMIAH 44:14 ... none of the remnant of Judah, which are gone into the land of Egypt to sojourn there, shall escape or remain. ...

The following provision of the treaty was a fulfillment of what Jeremiah had foretold a few years before.

[If] one or two people flee ... and they come to the land of Egypt in order to change allegiance, then User-Ma'at Re, Chosen-of-Re, the great ruler of Egypt, shall not tolerate them, but he shall cause that they be brought back to the great chieftain of Hatti.[1]

It was the fate of Jeremiah that against his will he became a fugitive in Egypt when the last remnants of Judah decided to migrate there.

JEREMIAH 41:17 And they departed ... to go to enter into Egypt,

18 Because of the Chaldeans: for they were afraid of them. ...

The *Talmud* has preserved the story of the end of Jeremiah and those who forced him to go to Egypt. Nebuchadnezzar took the fugitives out of Egypt to Chaldea.[2] This he did by virtue of the treaty he had concluded with Ramses.

The treaty contained a paragraph calling for humane treatment of the fugitives who were handed over.

If people flee from the land of Hatti ... and they come to User-Ma'at-Re, Chosen-of-Re, the great ruler of Egypt ... [and] they be brought back to the great chieftain of Hatti, [then] the great chieftain of Hatti shall not [arraign their] crime against them and one shall not destroy his [house], his women or his children, and one shall not slay him nor shall one trespass against his ears, against his eyes, his mouth, or his legs. ...[3]

Ramses found it necessary to include this humanitarian provision in the treaty for the protection of the unfortunates whom he was now obliged to hand over. For it was Nebuchadnezzar who had killed the children of Zedekiah and put out his eyes.

Ezekiel in his parable about the population of Jerusalem foretold:

---

[1] John D. Schmidt: *Ramesses II: A Chronological Structure for His Reign* (Baltimore, 1973), p. 116.

[2] *The Jerusalem Talmud, Tractate Sanhedrin*, I, 19a; *Seder Olam* 26. See also Ginzberg: *Legends,* Vol. VI, p. 399, n. 42.

[3] Schmidt: *Ramesses II,* p. 118.

23:23 The Babylonians, and all the Chaldeans... and all the Assyrians with them ...

25 ... they shall take away thy nose and thine ears... .

The treaty provision dealt with an actual situation. It casts additional light on the story of martyrdom as told by the Scriptures: the story of mutilated prisoners, slaughtered children, and deportations; and the story of these few who escaped from the horrors of torture, of their flight to Egypt, and of the long arm that reached out for the refugees in the land of their asylum.

Events of the War in the Scriptures and in the Inscriptions of Ramses II Compared

Comparison of the military chronicle of Ramses II with the biblical records reveals no point of contradiction but numerous points of correspondence.

According to both sources, the war started with a campaign of the pharaoh across Palestine into northern Syria (II Kings 23:29; stele at Nahr el-Kelb; obelisk of Tanis).

On his march through Palestine the Egyptian king met opposition and had to fight his way through (II Chronicles 35:22ff; II Kings 23:29; Aswan stele). His archers shot the opposing king (II Chronicles 35:23; Egyptian mural in the Metropolitan Museum of Art from the temple of Ramses II). The pharaoh reached the north of Syria and established a camp and an outpost at Riblah in the land of Hamath (II Kings 23:33; inscription of the second year of Ramses II at Nahr el-Kelb).

From this campaign he brought back captives of the royal house in Palestine (II Chronicles 36:4; II Kings 23:34; obelisk of Tanis). He imposed a tribute on the land (II Chronicles 36:3; II Kings 23:35; obelisk of Tanis).

In the following years the pharaoh returned to northern Syria. He then undertook a second campaign (II Kings 23:33ff; Aswan stele; the official records of the battle) and came to the region of Kadesh-Carchemish (Jeremiah 46:2ff; the official records of the battle; the *Poem of Pentaur*).

He brought four divisions (Jeremiah 46:9; *Poem of Pentaur*; the official records of the battle). Mercenaries from Sardis were in his army (Jeremiah 46:21; *Poem of Pentaur*). Cities of northern Syria were allied with his adversary (Jeremiah 35:11; *Poem of Pentaur*; the official records of the battle).

The Egyptian troops were taken by surprise and were driven northward toward the river (Jeremiah 46:10; *Poem of Pentaur*; the official records of the battle), that is, not back in the direction of Egypt but away from their home base. It was the defeat and dispersal of a much-feared host (Jeremiah 46:8; *Poem of Pentaur*; the official records of the battle). The pharaoh hurriedly retreated by a roundabout way with the remnants of his troops to Egypt.

As a direct result of this campaign Palestine was conquered by the Chaldean-Akkadian forces (Hatti) and for a period of a few years was under their control (Jeremiah 24:1; compare Faulkner in *The Cambridge Ancient History*, II, 2 (1975), p. 228).

The Egyptian king subsequently opened a new offensive in an attempt to reconquer Palestine (Jeremiah 47:2; compare Faulkner, op. cit., p. 228). In the land of the Philistines was the immediate objective. It was besieged, stormed, and captured (Jeremiah 47:5; bas-relief on the outer south wall of the great hypostyle hall at Karnak).

For a while Palestine came once more under the control of Egypt (stele at Beth-Shan; bas-relief and inscription in the Ramesseum; Faulkner, op. cit., p. 228). But then the Egyptians retreated under the pressure of the Akkadians-Chaldeans, and Palestine for the second time was lost by Egypt (II Kings 24:7; Breasted: *Records,* Vol. III, Sec. 366).

Hostilities continued for many years without another pitched battle being fought. The war was brought to an end after almost two decades, and as the ultimate result the Egyptian Empire acquiesced in the loss of its Asiatic provinces; but its own endangered sovereignty was safeguarded. Egypt was accused of having been "a staff of reed to the house of Israel" (Ezekiel 29:6).

The problem of political refugees from Syria and Palestine was one of the main issues of the peace negotiations, and Egypt agreed to extradite them (*Jerusalem Talmud, Sanhedrin* I, 19a; treaty of Ramses and Hattusilis).

The events, their sequence, and the places where they occurred are the same in the Egyptian records of Pharaoh Ramses II and in the scriptural narrative of Pharaoh Necho.

We can also investigate the exact intervals between all the phases of this long war and see whether the Egyptian (of Ramses II) and the Hebrew sources are again in harmony.

There is nothing more trying than detailed chronology. But if this mathematics of history is scrutinized not for its own sake but for establishing identities, and if it serves as proof of these identifications, then it may become an exciting study.

The correspondence of the figures in the Egyptian and the scriptural chronologies of the period under investigation in this chapter is complete. It goes without saying that synchronism of the whole means correspondence in details too; but if the contemporaneity of the epochs is disputed, how shall the synchronism of details be explained?

The first campaign of Ramses II into northern Syria took place in the second year of his reign. This is the date of his earlier stele at Nahr el-Kelb; the obelisk at Tanis seems to refer to the same events.

In the beginning of the first campaign of the king of Egypt directed toward the Euphrates, Josiah, king of Jerusalem, was killed at Megiddo. Three months later (II Chronicles 36:2-4) Jehoiakim was made king of Jerusalem. The beginning of the reign of Jehoiakim corresponds to the second year of the reign of Ramses II.

In the fourth year of King Jehoiakim the pharaoh undertook his second military campaign and reached Carchemish (Jeremiah 46:2). The fourth year of Jehoiakim started in the fifth year of Ramses II; accordingly, this second campaign must have taken place in Ramses' fifth year. This conforms with the Egyptian sources: Ramses II started his second campaign leaving Egypt on the ninth day of the tenth month of the fifth year (*Poem of Pentaur*).

The fourth year of Jehoiakim was also the first year of Nebuchadnezzar, king of Babylon (Jeremiah 25:1). It follows that Nebuchadnezzar counted the years of his reign from the year that he fought the second battle at the Euphrates.

At the time he was commander-in-chief of the Babylonian army Nebuchadnezzar was king of Assyria, a part of the Babylonian Empire. At first he was called king of Assyria (II Kings 23:29), later king of Babylon or king of the Chaldeans.[1]

---

[1] There is a discrepancy between Jeremiah 25:1 and Daniel 1:1 – in the latter Nebuchadnezzar is called king of Babylon in the third year of Jehoiakim. For Nebuchadnezzar's later claims to have been the legitimate king of Babylon immediately following the death of *(cont'd)*

Figure 11: Victory stela set up by
Ramses II at Beth Shan.

Nebuchadnezzar's first year fell in the latter part of the fifth year of Ramses and the earlier part of the sixth.

According to the Egyptian sources, Palestine was in revolt against Egypt from the end of the fifth to the eighth or ninth year of Ramses' reign. Those years following the defeat of the Egyptians at Kadesh-Carchemish correspond to the period from the fifth to the eighth year of Jehoiakim; these years are mentioned in II Kings 24:1: "In his days Nebuchadnezzar, king of Babylon, came up, and Jehoiakim became his servant three years: then he turned and rebelled against him."

At the end of this time Jehoiakim revolted against the Babylonians, as the same verse in Kings states; thus he revolted in his eighth year. The time when Ashkelon was stormed is recorded as the ninth year of Ramses II.[1] Since the ninth year of Ramses II was the eighth year of Jehoiakim, the siege of Ashkelon by Ramses II was coincident with Jehoiakim's revolt against Nebuchadnezzar. The Karnak bas-relief of the storming of Ashkelon and Chapter 47 of Jeremiah give prominence to this event. The presence of Egyptian soldiers in Beth-Shan in the ninth year of Ramses is testified to by a stele of his erected there in his ninth year.

Three years after that, early in the eighth year of Nebuchadnezzar (II Kings 24:12), which was the twelfth year of Ramses and the eleventh year of Jehoiakim, Jerusalem was again subdued by Nebuchadnezzar, and three months later Jehoiachin, the son of Jehoiakim, was deported to Babylon. During the three months of Jehoiachin's reign (II Kings 24:8) and from the first year of Zedekiah until his eighth, Jerusalem was a tributary of Babylon.

In his eighth year Zedekiah revolted, and Nebuchadnezzar laid siege to Jerusalem. At that time the pharaoh's army, which since the deposal of Jehoiakim (the twelfth year of Ramses) had not left Egypt (II Kings 24:7), strengthened itself and crossed the border of Palestine (Jeremiah 37:5). The army of the Chaldeans withdrew from Jerusalem to meet the Egyptian army, but Jeremiah predicted that the pharaoh's army "shall return to Egypt into their own land" (37:7) and that the Chaldeans would come again and fight against Jerusalem. The interval was long enough for the inhabitants of the city, who had freed their

---

(cont'd) Nabopolassar see the section »Changing History« in Chapter V. See also, on the methods of calculating the reigning years in Babylonia and Judea, E. R. Thiele: »The Chronology of the Kings of Judah and Israel«, *Journal of Near Eastern Studies,* III (1944), 137-86; *The Mysterious Numbers of the Hebrew Kings* (Grand Rapids, Mich., 1965).
[1] According to Petrie and Maspero.

slaves, to believe that the danger was over and try to void the release (Jeremiah 34:11). In the tenth month of the ninth year of Zedekiah, after the Egyptians had returned to their country without offering battle, Nebuchadnezzar went back to Jerusalem and renewed the siege (II Kings 25:1).

As the result of the agreement between the two empires Egypt yielded Syria and Palestine to Nebuchadnezzar, leaving Jerusalem without support. This treaty between the king of Egypt and the king of the Chaldeans was concluded sometime before the tenth day of the tenth month[1] of the ninth year of Zedekiah, on which day the Chaldeans renewed the siege of Jerusalem (II Kings 25:1; Jeremiah 39:1; Ezekiel 24:1).

The ninth year of Zedekiah was the seventeenth year of Nebuchadnezzar (since the tenth year of Zedekiah was the eighteenth year of Nebuchadnezzar – Jeremiah 32:1); thus it must have been the twenty-first year of Ramses II. Actually the treaty between Ramses II and the king of Hatti was signed on the twenty-first day of the fourth month of the twenty-first year of Ramses II.

The entire conflict between Egypt and the Hatti (Akkadians-Chaldeans) lasted nineteen years, from the second year of Ramses II (his first march to the north) until his twenty-first year (when the treaty of peace was signed).

A check with the Hebrew data gives the following figures: the time from the death of Josiah at Megiddo (the first march of the pharaoh to the north) to the beginning of the last siege of Jerusalem by the Chaldeans comprises three months of Jehoahaz (II Kings 23:31), ten years and a number of months of Jehoiakim, three months of Jehoiachin, and eight years and nine months of Zedekiah (the renewal of the siege). Since II Chronicles 36:11 speaks of the eleven years of Zedekiah, whereas in Jeremiah (39:2) it is the eleventh year, the eleven years of Jehoiakim referred to in II Chronicles 36:5 likewise may be taken to signify the eleventh year. Thus nineteen years passed from the first march of the pharaoh through Palestine and the death of King Josiah to the withdrawal of the Egyptian army and the beginning of the final siege of Jerusalem. According to the data of the Scriptures and of the records of Ramses alike, for nineteen years Egypt participated in the war.

---

[1] The months of the reigns of the kings of this period are described in the Scriptures as first, second, and so on, as calendar months of the year. So the date of destruction of the Temple – the fifth month (II Kings 25:8) – was the fifth month from the vernal equinox. This destruction is still mourned by the Jews in the fifth month or the month of Ab, late in the summer.

The Egyptian and Hebrew sources agree on the order and the length of all stages of the Egyptian-Chaldean war. The exact data in the Egyptian and Hebrew sources made possible this cross checking, and that with a precision unattained by the historiography of many periods a thousand or even two thousand years closer to us.

The conventional history of Egypt assumes that Ramses II was the Pharaoh of Oppression at the time of Moses (if the Israelites left Egypt in the days of Merneptah), or that he was the ruler of Egypt and Palestine at the time of the Judges (if the Israelites left Egypt before the beginning of the Nineteenth Dynasty). Consequently the campaigns of Ramses II in northern Syria and in Palestine are supposed to have taken place either in the days of the Israelite bondage in Egypt or in the days when the Judges ruled the tribes in Palestine. However, no mention is made in the Book of Judges of an Egyptian ruler or of any campaign of a pharaoh against Syria and Palestine.

By the same token, with Ramses II removed to the remote past, it could be presumed in advance that the records of the Books of Kings, Chronicles, Jeremiah, and Ezekiel on the war of Nebuchadnezzar with Pharaoh Necho will find no counterpart in Egyptian history.

Reference to a pharaoh by the name of Necho and to his campaigns was sought among the Egyptian inscriptions, but Egyptian archaeology could not supply the story of the war. The only monumental inscription that mentions the name of one Nekau-Wehemibre is an epitaph on the tomb of a bull.

If we follow conventional history there is no account of Ramses' wars in the Scriptures and the wars of Nebuchadnezzar against Egypt are likewise not accounted for in extant records of the country on the Nile. But the wars of Ramses II correspond precisely with the biblical account of Pharaoh Necho.

Or did the same occurrences, battles, and sieges of the same cities occur some seven hundred years apart at exactly the same intervals? It would be miraculous if records of two such identical series of events had come down to us. But there are no Egyptian records of the wars of Nekau-Wehemibre.[1]

---

[1] Four clay impressions of a seal of Nekau were found in the ruins of a house at Carchemish, together with seals of Psamthek. As I show in *Peoples of the Sea* (Part I, Ch. 5, »A Comedy of Errors«), this person is to be identified with Psamshek: a Persian high official mentioned in the *Elephantine papyri*. The seals of Nekau found next to those of Psamshek would seem to place also Nekau Wehemibre in the fifth century when Egypt was under Persian occupation. See L. Woolley and T. E. Lawrence, eds.: *Carchemish*, II (1915-1952), pp. 126-128; Pl. 26c.

Chapter 3

The Tomb of King Ahiram

The Speedy Scribe

The *Poem of Pentaur* contains a few Hebrew words which had infiltrated into the Egyptian language and were used instead of their Egyptian equivalents. So the word "katzin" is used for "officer" and "sesem" ("sous") for "horse."[1] "Naarim", who saved Ramses at Kadesh, as already mentioned on an earlier page, is "boys" in Hebrew.

Among the texts composed in the time of Ramses II there is a letter written by a scribe named Hori to a scribe named Amenemope.[2] Hori was insulted by Amenemope and charged with being ignorant; Hori replied in a sarcastic letter, proved his own erudition, and exposed the ignorance of his opponent. The field of knowledge in which he thought himself an authority was Palestinology. It is possible that the letter was written in Palestine.

The letter mentions many geographical names; they are spelled in an easily legible and recognizable form: "Kiryath-n-b" is "Kiryath-anab".

Even more impressive than the list of Palestinian cities is the use of numerous Hebrew words by the scribe.[3] Thus "flour" is called "kemakh", "bramble" is "koz", "quiver," "ashep", and even an entire Hebrew sentence is inserted in the letter: "Avadta kmoari, mahir noam."[4] It is not so important to know what was in the mind of the scribe when he wrote the sentence; it may be that he wished only to boast of his knowledge of Hebrew.

The generally accepted conclusion is that Hebrew words were acquired by the Egyptians from the natives of Canaan and that the popu-

---

[1] De Rougé: *Œuvres diverses*, Vol. V (Paris, 1914), pp. 318-343.
[2] *Papyrus Anastasi I*, ed. and transl. by A. H. Gardiner: *Egyptian Hieratic Texts*, I (Leipzig, 1911).
[3] M. Burchardt: *Die Altkanaanäischen Fremdworte und Eigennamen im Aegyptischen* (Leipzig, 1909-10).
[4] "You have perished like a lion, said the speedy scribe."

lation of pre-Israelite Palestine, sometimes said to have been of Hamitic stock (see Genesis 9:18), spoke Semitic Hebrew. This conclusion, implied by the Hebrew words inserted in the Babylonian texts of the el-Amarna letters written from Palestine, has been regarded as indisputable since the discovery of the Ras Shamra texts.

The conclusion that the population of pre-Israelite Canaan not only spoke Hebrew but must also have had speedy scribes writing in this language has been avoided, though it follows from Hori's text: Hori used the Hebrew words "sofer yodea" for a learned scribe, and "mahir" for a speedy scribe. The latter word appears throughout the papyrus, as it was the intention of its author to explain the duties of a *mahir*, who must calculate quickly and instantly orient himself in any situation.

"A pen of *a mahir*" or "a pen of a speedy writer" is found in the opening passage of Psalm 45. Scribes were a professional class from the days of the first Jewish kings in Palestine,[1] and a "speedy scribe," or one who could write down words as they were spoken, is a late development of skill in the art of writing.

Did the art of writing flourish in the days of the Canaanites, and was it entirely forgotten in the early days of the Israelites in Palestine?

Correct chronology does not require of the population of pre-Israelite Canaan that they should have used the Hebrew language, or of the Egyptians that they should have learned it from them; however, if through some not yet discovered material the use of Hebrew in Canaan before the migration of the clan of Israel to Egypt could be proven, the art of writing Hebrew in the age of the patriarchs would not follow from the Hebrew texts of Ras Shamra (written in an alphabetic cuneiform) or from the el-Amarna letters with occasional Hebrew words in them: these two series of documents date from the ninth, not the fourteenth, century.[2] On the other hand, it is not surprising that during the actual intercourse between Hebrew Palestine and Egypt, from the days of Saul and Kamose to the time of Jeremiah and Ramses II, a number of Hebrew words became absorbed into the vocabulary of Egyptian scribes.[3]

The papyrus of Hori most probably was written between the second and fifth years of Ramses II, between his first, successful, and second, unsuccessful, campaigns, apparently shortly after the pharaoh passed through Megiddo, as described in II Kings 23:29-30. The papyrus con-

---

[1] I Chronicles 2:55; II Samuel 8:17; 20:25; I Kings 4:3.
[2] See *Ages in Chaos*, Vol. I, »Ras Shamra« and »The El-Amarna Letters«.
[3] Another example of the use of Hebrew words by an Egyptian scribe of that time is presented by the *Papyrus Koller*, ed. and transl. by Gardiner: *Egyptian Hieratic Texts*, I (Leipzig, 1911).

tains the following words of the scribe addressed to his opponent: "Cause me to know the way of crossing over to Megiddo." Under the circumstances we might well expect that an inscription in Hebrew letters would be found together with some signs documenting the age of Ramses' reign.

The Tomb of Ahiram

In a preceding section I had occasion to discuss the question: Did Ramses II build the canal connecting the Mediterranean with the Red Sea, as the Egyptian sources state, or was it Necho (Necos) who started this work, as Herodotus says? Again, was it Seti-Ptah-Maat, the predecessor of Ramses II, who first employed Greek Mercenaries, or was it Necho's predecessor, Psammetich of Herodotus?

The reader may be depended on to solve a similar question without the help of the author.

Byblos, the modern Jebeil, or Gebel, on the Syrian coast, north of Beirut, Gwal of the Old Testament and of Phoenician inscriptions, or K-b-ny in Egyptian, was an old and venerated royal city. It traded with cedars of Lebanon and with papyri imported from Egypt.[1]

In the nineteenth century Ernest Renan, the celebrated religious historian, dug at Byblos and also at Tyre, Sidon, and Arvad, all on the Phoenician coast.[2]

Sixty years later, in 1921, Pierre Montet renewed digging at Byblos. Several months passed and on February 16, 1922, a land-slide on the seaward slope of the excavations revealed a royal tomb with funerary gifts of Amenemhet III of the Middle Kingdom in Egypt. Eight more royal tombs, dating from various periods, were discovered in the same area. The most important find was King Ahiram's tomb. A shaft cut into the rock led to a burial chamber; after the burial a wall was built separating the chamber from the shaft. The chamber had three sarcophagi, two plain, containing only bones, and one ornate, of King Ahiram.[3] "Hiram" or "Ahiram" was a name of more than one Phoenician king.

---

[1] The word "Bible" is derived from "Byblos", which means "papyrus" in Greek.
[2] *Mission de Phenicie* (Paris, 1864).
[3] P. Montet: *Byblos et l'Egypte, Quatre Campagnes de Fouilles à Gebel (1921-1924)*, (Paris, 1928), Ch. IV.

A short Hebrew inscription was cut into the southern wall of the shaft:

Attention! Behold, thou shalt come to grief below here!

The warning against desecrating the sepulcher was repeated and extended, incised on the lid of the sarcophagus:

The coffin which Ithobaal, son of Ahiram, King of Gwal [Byblos], made for his father as his abode in eternity. And if any king or any governor or any army commander attacks (Gwal) and exposes this coffin, let his judicial scepter be broken, let his royal throne be overthrown, and let peace flee from Gwal; and as for him, let a vagabond efface his inscriptions![2]

On one side of the sarcophagus King Ahiram is represented in relief seated on a throne with winged sphinxes guarding him and courtiers facing him. The other side shows a procession of persons carrying offerings. Each of the two ends of the sarcophagus has figures of four lamenting women.

Near the entrance to the burial chamber several fragments of an alabaster vase were found, and one of them bore the name and royal nomen of Ramses II. Another fragment, also of alabaster, with Ramses II's cartouche was in the chamber; there was also an ivory plaque found and evaluated by R. Dussaud as of Mycenaean age; but pottery of Cyprian origin was also there and it looked like seventh-century ware.

The tomb was violated, probably in antiquity, argued the historians, despite the warnings in Hebrew (Phoenician) letters. The scholars had to decide on the time in which King Ahiram lived.

The Phoenician inscriptions on the sarcophagus did not reveal it. Montet, the discoverer, assigned the tomb to the time of Ramses II, thus to the thirteenth century. He subscribed to the view that all objects in the tomb, the Cyprian vases included, were of the time of Ramses II. But the age of the Cyprian pottery was claimed by other scholars to be that of the seventh century. Dussaud, a leading French orientalist, agreed that the tomb dated from the thirteenth century, the time of Ramses II, but he insisted that the Cyprian ware was of the seventh century. Dussaud also assumed that in the seventh century tomb robbers broke in and left there pottery of their own age. Signs of intrusion and violation were obvious: the lid of the sarcophagus had

---

[2] Transl. by W. F. Albright: *Journal of the American Oriental Society,* LXVII, 1947, pp. 155-56. The translation by R. Dussaud quoted by Montet reads in part: "... *le throne de la royauté se renversera et la paix regnera sur Gobel"* (... and peace will reign over Gwal).

Figure 12: The sarcophagus of Ahiram. Note the Phoenician inscription on the side of the lid. From *Byblos Through the Ages*, Dar el-Machreg, Beirut (1968)

been moved from its proper position, alabaster vases were broken, jewelry was missing.

Dussaud wrote: "Together with Mycenaean relics, Montet found fragments of Cypriote pottery, characteristic of the seventh century, which thus fixes the time of the tomb violation. No fragment of a more recent date was found." He continued: "There is no doubt that, [faced with a choice] between the age of Ramses II and the seventh century [as the time when the tomb was built and the inscriptions were made], the first must be accepted."[1] But intruders certainly would not have brought six- or seven-hundred-year-old vases into the sepulchral chamber. Why they would have brought any vessels into the mortuary chambers they had come to loot is not satisfactorily explained.

What is the correct conclusion?

---

[1] "Avec des vestiges myceniens, M. Montet ait trouve ... des fragments de poterie chypriote, caractéristiques du VIIe siècle, qui fixent ainsi l'époque de la violation. Aucun fragment plus récent n'a été découvert. Or, il est certain que les inscriptions de l'hypogée V ne peuvent descendre à une date aussi base. Entre l'époque de Ramses II et le VIIe siècle, il n'y reste aucun doute qu'il ne faille adopter la première." R. Dussaud: »Les Inscriptions phéniciennes du tombeau d'Ahiram, roi de Byblos«, *Syria, Revue d'art oriental et d'archéologie*, V (1924), 143-44.

Even if it were possible to explain the presence of the Cyprian vessels in the tomb of Ahiram as the work of thieves, there was something in the tomb that could not be attributed to looters: the inscriptions.

An inscription in Hebrew letters at the entrance warns against any sacrilegious act and invokes a curse on any king, soldier, or other person who should disturb the peace of the sepulcher. The other inscription, on the sarcophagus, says that a king, whose name is read Ithobaal[1] and who speaks in the first person, built the sarcophagus for his father, Ahiram, king of Gwal (Byblos).

The two inscriptions are carved in the same characters and are of one age. If the tomb was prepared in the days of Ramses II the inscriptions were written in his time. But inscriptions in Hebrew characters in the time of Ramses II, in the thirteenth century, were quite unexpected.

A hotly waged dispute took place and was not concluded in five decades. On one side were the archaeologists, who regarded the archaeological proofs of the origin of the tomb under the Nineteenth Dynasty, or in the thirteenth century B.C. as conclusive. On the other side were the epigraphists, who would not concede that the inscriptions of Ahiram's tomb were of a period as early as the thirteenth century; they found a close similarity between these characters and the characters inscribed by Abi-baal and Elibaal, Phoenician kings, on statues of their patrons, the pharaohs of the Libyan Dynasty, Sosenk and Osorkon respectively, presumably of the tenth to the ninth centuries. From the time the inscribed statues of Sosenk and Osorkon came to the notice of scientists until the discovery of Ahiram's tomb, the dedications on these statues in the names of Abibaal and Elibaal were supposed not to have been contemporaneous with the statues themselves: the letters of the dedications were intermediate between the Mesha stele letters of about -850 and the Hezekiah letters chiseled into the rock wall of a water conduit of the Shiloah spring near Jerusalem, of about -700, and must have been written between these two time points.

But the inscriptions of Ahiram compelled an epigraphic reconsideration of the inscriptions on the statues. Finally the difficulties arising from a comparison of the characters of Abibaal and Elibaal with those of the Mesha stele and the Hezekiah letters were ascribed to some anomalies in the development of the Hebrew script.

---

[1] Dussaud: *Syria,* VI (1925), 104.

Figure 13: Cartouche of Ramses II on an alabaster vase found in the tomb of Ahiram.

According to the conventional chronology, Ahiram, being a contemporary of Ramses II, must have lived and died almost four centuries before Sosenk and Osorkon. In four centuries a script must have undergone considerable change. But there were no marked changes in the characters from the time of Ahiram to that of Abibaal and Elibaal.

Let a few of the disputants make their own statements. The participants in the debate who are quoted below are all historians of great repute.

"From the discovery of two alabaster vases inscribed with the name of Ramses II in the tomb of Ahiram, we can deduce beyond any uncertainty (sans qu'il puisse subsister la moindre incertitude) that the tomb, the sarcophagus, and its inscription date from the thirteenth century before our era."[1]

"It is strange that there should be agreement on this dating of the thirteenth century because of two fragments with the name of Ramses II, though there is not the slightest reason for such dating ["obwohl dazu am allerwenigsten Veranlassung ist"]. After the tomb of Ahiram was

---

[1] R. Dussaud: *Syria*, V (1924), 142.

robbed in the eighth to the seventh century and stood open, grave robbers in a new visit deposited in it vases from some other tomb, a more ancient one. It follows that the tomb and the inscriptions were made before the seventh to the eighth century, but when can be determined only by the epigraphists, who must pay not the slightest attention ["nicht die geringste Rücksicht"] to the vases with the name of Ramses II."[1]

The first writer assumes that the Cyprian vases of the seventh century were brought into the tombs by the thieves. The second scholar accepts this explanation and has the thieves also bring the Ramses vases into the same tomb.

"The date of this tomb is furnished by an ensemble of testimonies concordant and conclusive: ceramics of Mycenae of a good style, Mycenaean ivory, with no specimen of a later time, and two vases of alabaster with the cartouches of Ramses II."[2] The sculpture of the sarcophagus is also stressed as indicating the time of Ramses.

> The sarcophagus and with it the use of the alphabet are pushed back into the thirteenth century, the time of Ramses II. But it is unthinkable and contradicts everything ["es ist undenkbar und widerspricht allem ..."] we know about the history of writing that here the script should have remained unchanged for four centuries. Ahiram could have lived only shortly before Abibaal, say about 1000.[3]

> The evidence of the ornament on this coffin seems decisive as to date. It cannot be later than the thirteenth century. The forms of the letters have induced the epigraphists to doubt the excavator's conclusions, and some play has been made with the sherds found in the tomb. The epigraphic argument is not sound.[4]

The archaeologists are unshakable and insist that Ahiram's burial dates from the time of Ramses II, the middle of his reign in the first half of the thirteenth century, and are prepared to deduct no more than fifty years if this will satisfy the epigraphists. The epigraphists, unable to refute the archaeological evidence, bargain for every half century so as to bring the date of Ahiram's inscription as close as possible to the time of the Mesha stele.

---

[1] W. Spiegelberg: »Zur Datierung der Ahiram-Inschrift von Byblos«, *Orientalistische Literaturzeitung,* XXIX (1926), cols. 735-37.
[2] Dussaud: *Archiv für Orientforschung,* V (1929), 237.
[3] Eduard Meyer: *Geschichte des Altertums,* II (1931), Pt. 2, p. 73.
[4] Sidney Smith: *Alalakh and Chronology* (London, 1940), p. 46.

It is true that an alabaster vase with the cartouches of Ramesses II [Ramses II] and the fragment of another naming the same king were found in the tomb, which may well, therefore, go back to the thirteenth century. But the differences between the forms of Ahiram and those of Abibaal and Elibaal are exceedingly small, and it seems just possible that the true date of Ahiram may be somewhat nearer to the Bubastite age (tenth century).[1]

Compromise was rejected from the very beginning, even before it was proposed.

It does not suffice to put forth such a hypothesis, it is necessary to demonstrate it. If the work executed in the thirteenth century as well as the violation in the eighth – seventh century left very clear testimony in ceramics, the burial of a hypothetical eleventh century must be proved by pottery that was placed with the dead. But no vestige of this epoch (eleventh century) was found.[2]

The epigraphists, embarrassed enough by the demand of the archaeologists that the inscriptions of Abibaal and Elibaal be placed a century before the stele of Mesha, have been unwilling to date the inscription of Ithobaal on the grave of his father Ahiram four centuries before the stele of Mesha.

The vases of the seventh century that covered the floor of the tomb were explained as having been brought in by thieves. The epigraphists would ascribe the vases of Ramses II to robbers also, but this would not do, as the sarcophagus and the Mycenaean ware are of the time of Ramses II. The last recourse would be to attribute the inscriptions to the thieves.

"Were the inscriptions made by robbers?" asked a scholar, and he answered himself: The inscription on the sarcophagus is contemporary with the sarcophagus, because Ithobaal declared that he had had it made. The shorter inscription at the entrance, written in the same characters, was a warning not to violate the grave, and curses on desecrators were invoked by Ithobaal in the inscription on the sarcophagus. Violators did not write it. "It cannot be attributed to violators."[3]

When an art historian, H. Frankfort, developed the view that the sarcophagus belonged to the thirteenth century but that the inscription on it could have been added later, early in the tenth century when the

---

[1] A. H. Gardiner: *Quarterly Statement of the Palestine Exploration Fund,* 1939, p. 112.
[2] Dussaud: *Syria,* V (1924), 144.
[3] *Ibid.* p. 142.

sarcophagus was re-used, a protagonist of the argument that the sarcophagus was of the early tenth century wrote:

> Absolutely indefensible is Frankfort's position that the Ahiram sarcopha-
> gus belongs to the 13th century and the inscription (whose early tenth-
> century date he is willing to concede) was inscribed on the occasion of a
> later re-use of the stone coffin. This assertion defies common sense,
> since the inscription begins: 'The coffin which Ittobal [Ithobaal] son of
> Ahiram, king of Byblos, made for his father as his abode in eternity ...'
> Another inscription in the same script is carved on the walls of the en-
> trance shaft of the tomb. No ancient oriental ruler is likely to have been
> guilty of such a crude falsehood, for which there was no object.[1]

The author of these lines, the late William F. Albright, added: "The
tenth century date ... becomes inevitable after the latest epigraphic
discoveries in Palestine."

In the same year as this was written, Pierre Montet, who thirty-three
years earlier had discovered the tomb of Ahiram, wrote, almost deri-
sively:

> The oldest alphabetic inscription then known was that of Mesha, king of
> Moab, dating from the ninth century. The new texts [of Ahiram's tomb]
> put back the use of the alphabet by four centuries. Some scholars main-
> tain that the presence of the vases of Ramses II – as a matter of conve-
> nience they speak of 'a vase' – does not mean anything, but as new
> alphabetic inscriptions, even more ancient, have been subsequently found
> at Byblos, all their laborious argumentation can no longer convince any-
> body ["leur laborieuse argumentation ne peut plus convaincre personne"].[2]

The debate embraced further problems. "The sarcophagus of Ahiram
opens a new chapter in the history of Phoenician art."[3] It was found
that Phoenician art had been very conservative, because after many
centuries it used the same forms: even a similar sarcophagus, also with
figures of lamenting women, is well known; it was discovered in Sidon
and is ascribed to the fourth century.[4]

---

[1] W. F. Albright in *The Aegean and the Near East*, studies presented to Hetty Goldman,
1956, p. 159. Albright's earlier treatment of the subject is found in *Journal of the American
Oriental Society*, LXVII, 1947, pp. 154ff.
[2] P. Montet: *Isis* (Paris, 1956), p. 194.
[3] Dussaud: *Syria*, XI (1930), 181.
[4] "Si l'on considère le traditionalisme, qui est un des traits caractéristiques de l'art et des cultes
phéniciens, le célèbre sarcophage de Sidon, dit des pleureuses et conservé à Stambul, est de
dernier état de la représentation qu'apparaît sur le sarcophage d'Ahiram." Dussaud: *Syria*, XI
(1930), 183.

Figure 14: The weeping women, from the sarcophagus of King Ahiram. From *Byblos Through
the Ages*, Dar el-Machreg, Beirut (1968)

An Israeli scholar[1] wrote a paper on the bas-reliefs on the sarcophagus of Ahiram and paid special attention to the mourning women,
four at each end of the sarcophagus: "two of them slap their hips[2]
while the other two hold their heads in their hands." The scholar cited
several examples of hand slapping in the Old Testament as a sign of
profound grief, notably in Jeremiah 31:19 and Ezekiel 21:12. "The
other two women place their hands on their heads – another regular
accompaniment of lamentation, of grief and pain" – Jeremiah and
Ezekiel were contemporaries of Nebuchadnezzar.

---

[1] M. Haran in *Israel Exploration Journal*, Vol. 8, No. 1 (1958).
[2] The photograph of one of the two scenes with the mourning women shows two beating their
breasts, not hips, two others lifting their arms over their heads: Plate 97 in N. Jidejian:
Byblos Through the Ages (Beirut,1968).

Would that only the question of the age of Ahiram's tomb and the problem of Phoenician art were involved! But here the entire research on the development of the Hebrew script and the very question of the origin of the alphabet are inseparably tied together.

"Dating of the Ahiram script is highly important in studying the history of the alphabet."[1] "The discovery of new Semitic inscriptions not only pushed back the invention of the alphabet but also made possible the assumption of its earlier adoption by the Greeks."[2]

The Inscriptions of Ahiram
and the Origin of the Alphabet

The invention of the alphabet is regarded as one of the greatest achievements of all times. Before its creation writing was either pictorial or syllabic, the latter form employing of necessity hundreds of different signs.

"The alphabet originated probably about -1300 on the shore of Syria, probably in Byblos."[3] The tomb of Ahiram is the basis for this statement. The inscriptions of the tomb of Ahiram are regarded as the earliest legible texts in Hebrew letters yet discovered.[4]

"No scholar doubts now that the alphabet was created at least in the first half of the second millennium."[5] The date is shifted back a few more centuries because the inscriptions of Ahiram show a developed stage of an alphabet and also because a few sherds with a small number of archaic characters of undefined age were found at Lachish and other places.[6] Finally, the cuneiform signs for the letters of the Hebrew alphabet also form an alphabetic writing, and it is in this script that the poems found at Ras Shamra, presumably of the early fourteenth century, are written. A few inscriptions found in Sinai, not yet satisfactorily

---

[1] B. Ullman: »How Old Is the Greek Alphabet?« *American Journal of Archaeology,* XXXVIII (1934), 362.
[2] *Ibid.,* p. 379.
[3] H. Bauer: *Der Ursprung des Alphabets* (Leipzig, 1937), p. 43.
[4] J. Leibovitch (*Bulletin de l'Institut Français d'Archéologie Orientale,* XXXII [1932], 84) rates the inscription of Yehimilk as older than the Ahiram inscription.
[5] D. Diringer: »The Palestinian Inscriptions and the Origin of the Alphabet«, *Journal of the American Oriental Society,* LXIII (March 1943).
[6] The finds are enumerated by Diringer.

deciphered, are regarded by some scholars as having originated when the Eighteenth Dynasty ruled in Egypt, and by others as dating back to the time of the Hyksos. The relation of these signs to Hebrew and to the origin of the alphabet is a dark problem because of the scarcity and obscurity of the material.

The Greek alphabet copied from the Hebrew the forms of many letters, their order in the alphabet, and their names – "alpha" meaning "aleph" ("ox"); "beta", "beth" ("house"); "gamma", "gimmel" ("camel"); "delta", "deleth" ("door"), and so on. The problem of when the Greek alphabet was derived from the Hebrew (Phoenician) can best be answered by comparing the earliest Greek letters with the various stages in the development of the Hebrew script. The earliest Greek inscriptions found date from the eighth century – until the middle of the sixth century they were written from right to left – and from the shape of their characters a scholar in the 1860's was able to reconstruct the early Hebrew letters in the form in which, a few years later, they were found on the stele of Mesha of the ninth century before the present era.[1] Because of the similarity of the archaic Greek letters to the letters of the Mesha stele, many scholars regard the ninth century as the time when the Greek alphabet was derived from the Hebrew.[2] But the fact that no Greek inscriptions from before the seventh century have been found suggested to a few scholars that the Greek alphabet was derived from the Hebrew alphabet as late as about -700.[3] Another extreme viewpoint would have the Greek alphabet originate from the Hebrew before -1200.[4] To prove their arguments the disputants turned to the Hebrew (Phoenician) inscriptions of various ages in order to show that the small variations in some letters of these respective epochs are reflected in the earliest Greek letters.

The result of these comparisons gave equal support to both sides.[5] The Hebrew characters of presumably the thirteenth century (Ahiram's inscription) and the Hebrew characters of the seventh century have

---

[1] Kirchhoff in 1863. See Meyer: *Geschichte des Altertums*, Vol. II, Pt. 2 (1931), p. 72.

[2] So Eduard Meyer and his school; F. G. Kenyon argues for the tenth century.

[3] R. Carpenter: »The Antiquity of the Greek Alphabet«, *American Journal of Archaeology*, XXXVII (1933), 8-29. More recently it has been claimed that the earliest Greek inscription, found on a vase from the Kerameikos cemetery (Athens), dates from c. -740.

[4] Ullman: *American Journal of Archaeology*, XXXVIII (1934); also among earlier epigraphists, M. Lidzbarski: *Handbuch der nordsemitischen Epigraphik* (Weimar, 1898).

[5] "I find the closest relation of early Greek writing in inscriptions ante-dating the Moabite stone, Carpenter finds them in later inscriptions." Ullman: op. cit., p. 366.

the same slight deviations from the characters of the Mesha stele of the ninth century. Whereas, for example, the letter "heth" in Ahiram's inscriptions is made with three horizontal parallels held between two vertical parallels, in the Mesha inscription one horizontal parallel vanishes, to appear again in the eighth and seventh centuries.[1]

This strange situation compelled the following surmise. "It would not follow that because the script [of Ahiram] is chronologically earlier than any other Phoenician writing ... it is also typologically earlier. There are some reasons to think that the Byblos style was eccentric in certain details."[2]

The defender of the earlier derivation of the Greek alphabet could point out that his opponent admitted that a few forms of the Ahiram inscription are "unaccountably" nearer the Greek than those of the Moabite stone.[3] But he himself had to concede that "our greatest trouble lies in explaining the lack of inscriptional material of any kind [in Greek] between 1200 and 700."[4]

The Linear B script first discovered on Crete and later in Greece, in Pylos, Boeotian Thebes, and Mycenae, was employed in Greece presumably until -1200. This script has been deciphered by Michael Ventris. Then came a period of almost five hundred years when no script was employed in Greece, or at least none has been found to have been employed. Perishable material (papyrus) was probably used for writing, say the defenders of the early derivation of the Greek alphabet from the Hebrew. But the Mycenaean writers used mostly clay until -1200, and the Greek inscriptions of the seventh century are also in clay or on stone, as are the Phoenician inscriptions of the period between. Had Greek inscriptions existed from -1200 to -700 "we must have found some traces of them."[5]

This problem also involves a further one: were the Homeric creations transmitted orally and recited from memory by the bards, or were they written down? They were created in the thirteenth or twelfth century, argue some scholars. They could not have been handed down orally for many centuries, argue others. The internal archaeological indications point overwhelmingly to the fact that the world of the *Iliad*

---

[1] See the comparative table in *Syria,* V (1924), 149, fig. 7.
[2] A. H. Gardiner: *Quarterly Statement of the Palestine Exploration Fund,* 1939, p. 112.
[3] Ullman: op. cit., p. 366.
[4] *Ibid.,* p. 376. But see supra, fn. 7.
[5] Carpenter: *American Journal of Archaeology,* XXXVII, 26-27.

and the *Odyssey* is the world of the late eighth century,[1] close to the time of the introduction of the Greek alphabet.

I shall stop here: the chain of problems carries us ever farther. The inscription of Ahiram belongs to the time of Ramses II, but the revision of chronology and history presented in this book implies that the time of Ramses II is not about -1300 but about -600. The Cyprian pottery that covered the floor of Ahiram's tomb was not brought in by robbers but is contemporaneous with the tomb, as its inscriptions are contemporaneous with Ramses II. The inscriptions in the tomb are of a later date than those of Abibaal and Elibaal by about one hundred years, and these, in their turn, are of a later date than the inscription of Mesha also by more than a hundred years. At the present time the inscription of Mesha is the oldest extant monumental inscription in Hebrew. The cuneiform Hebrew of Nikmed in Ugarit is of the same age as the Mesha inscription. This means that in the Carian-Ionian-Phoenician city of Ugarit, Hebrew was written in a cuneiform alphabet when a Hebrew alphabet was employed in Moab in Trans-Jordan,[2] and this would suggest the Hebrew, not the Phoenician, origin of the alphabet. Mesha says that he employed the Israelite captives in "cutting" – presumably ivory; very similar letters are carved on the ivories of Samaria and on the stele of Mesha.[3] It is probable that Hebrew captives from Samaria also carved his stele. In any event the Hebrew script was in use in Samaria at that time, and the characters were already well developed. The Hebrew alphabet may well have originated in the second millennium before the present era, but this cannot be asserted on the basis of the inscriptions of Ahiram.

The confusion of epigraphists is understandable. They are asked to explain the evolution of the Hebrew script, beginning with the time of Ramses II, about -1300, through the time of Abibaal and Sosenk in the tenth century, to the time of Mesha in the ninth century and the Shiloah inscription of Hezekiah of about -700, and finally to the time of the Lachish ostraca and Nebuchadnezzar, about -586. But the starting and the concluding points in the scheme are contemporaneous. The Hebrew script went through a normal process of development, without lapsing into archaisms. The scholars who compared the Greek letters with the Hebrew characters of presumably the thirteenth and

---

[1] G. Karo: »Homer«, in Ebert's *Reallexikon der Vorgeschichte*, XV (1926).
[2] See *Ages in Chaos*, Vol. I, »Ras-Shamra« and »El-Amarna Letters«.
[3] E. L. Sukenik in Crowfoot and Crowfoot: *Early Ivories* (London, 1938), pp. 6-8.

seventh centuries were comparing them with characters of practically one and the same age. Actually the letters in the sepulcher of Ahiram are one hundred years more recent than the letters Hezekiah cut in about -700.

The great gap of five hundred years in Greek epigraphy and history from -1200 to -700 does not exist in reality. The Minoan ages are reckoned in accordance with Egyptian chronology, and Greek ages according to the archaeological evidences of Greece. The Mycenaean Linear script was superseded by the Cadmean-Greek. If the Phoenician alphabet was introduced in Boeotian Thebes already in the ninth century, the Linear script was still used in Pylos and some other places in Greece for a century or more before being superseded by the Phoenician alphabet, which became the Ionian, later Latin, way of writing in use by us till the present.

After these assertions I should like to repeat a hypothesis I offered years ago.[1]

The introduction of Ionian (Greek) letters from the Phoenician shore is attributed to the legendary Cadmus, who came from Phoenicia (Tyre and Sidon vie for the honor of being his city) and built Thebes in Greece. The letters, when still written from right to left in Greece, were called Cadmean. Is it too bold to suppose that Nikmed, or Nikdem of Shalmaneser III's war records, who left Ugarit about -855 together with the Ionians and the Carians, is the legendary Cadmus?[2] He was a man of letters, a lexicographer, judging by his library with many dictionaries, and although he employed Hebrew in a cuneiform alphabet, he must have known the forms of Hebrew letters as he lived in the time of Mesha.

If Nikdem was the founder of Thebes in Greece he might have experimented there first with the cuneiform alphabet already used by him in Ras Shamra for writing Hebrew texts or he might have tried the Linear B script, making an alphabetic writing of it, before he found the best solution in using Hebrew letters for writing Greek. If a lengthy inscription contains only twenty to thirty repeated signs it may be concluded that an alphabetic script is employed.

In recent years in the ruins of the Cadmeion, the early palace in the Greek Thebes, roll cylinders with cuneiform signs on them have been

---

[1] *Oedipus and Akhnaton* (New York, 1960), p. 190.
[2] *Ages in Chaos*, Vol. I (1952), »The End of Ugarit«; *Oedipus and Akhnaton* (1960), p. 190.

discovered, the first cuneiform writings found on Greek soil.[1] The reading of some of them offered great difficulties.[2] An effort to read them
on the assumption that they are in cuneiform alphabetic Greek may,
perchance, prove successful.

Ithobaal, Son of Ahiram

Ithobaal, entombing his father at the time of the great struggle
between Ramses II and Nebuchadnezzar, when the armies of the
Egyptians and Chaldeans repeatedly swept over the Syrian shore,
warned in vain "whoever, king among the kings, or governor among
the governors," should enter the sepulchral chamber not to raise the
lid of the sarcophagus.

Nebuchadnezzar, the dreaded leader of "the terrible of the nations,"
who had already subdued Arvad, Byblos, and Sidon, laid siege to Tyre.
This great merchant center of the ancient world was inhabited by sea-
faring men. Their ships were made of the fir trees of Senir, the masts
of the cedars from Lebanon, and oars of the oaks of Bashan; with blue
and purple they tinted the embroidered linen from Egypt and spread it
out for sails. "The ancients of Gebal [Gwal] and the wise men thereof
were in thee thy calkers." The army of Tyre hung their shields upon its
walls round about and made its beauty perfect. Thus Ezekiel (Chapter
27) described the city of Tyre of his day.

The Assyrian king Esarhaddon, a hundred years before, had cursed
Tyre and its ships: "May gods let loose an evil wind upon your ships,
tear their riggings, carry away their masts; may a heavy sea swamp
them with its waves, may the raging floods break over them"[3] – and
still it stood, queen of the sea, and "the ships of Tarshish did sing of
[Tyre]"[4] in the faraway markets.

Tyre, like Jerusalem, allied herself with Egypt and when the resistance of Judah was broken the hour of Tyre had come. For thirteen
years, forsaken by its Egyptian ally, it withstood siege. Tyre could

---

[1] By N. Platon.
[2] Personal communication by J. Nougayrol, dated 29 March 1965.
[3] Luckenbill: *Records of Assyria*, Vol. II, Sec. 587.
[4] Ezekiel 27:25.

endure such a long siege because in antiquity it was an island city off the Phoenician coast. "Tyre ... [was] once an island separated from the mainland by a very deep sea channel 700 yards wide," wrote Pliny.[1]

Josephus Flavius quotes the *Phoenician Record,* the author of which is supposed to have been Menander of Ephesus: "Under king Ithobaal, Nebuchadnezzar besieged Tyre for thirteen years."[2] Josephus repeats the same information on the authority of Philostratos, who wrote a *History of India and Phoenicia.*[3]

Josephus does not mention the name of Ithobaal's father. But in the rabbinical literature[4] we are told that during the period when Nebu-chadnezzar was maneuvering for domination over the new empire he found a most stubborn adversary in the person of the Phoenician king Hiram (Ahiram).

In the Old Testament there is no special designation for Phoenicia as a country. However, the Scriptures apply the name Gwal not to Byblos alone but also, occasionally, to the Phoenician coast, and the "king of Gwal" entombed in Byblos may signify "king of Phoenicia." Tyre on the island had no cemetery of its own and Byblos was the sacred ground for all Phoenicia. Whether Ithobaal who built the sepulcher for Ahiram, king of Byblos, was Ithobaal who defended Tyre is an open question, but it was one and the same time and he had the same name.

King Ithobaal's defense of the last stronghold of Phoenicia against Nebuchadnezzar was terminated when Nebuchadnezzar concluded a treaty with him, the Phoenician becoming a vassal in the Babylonian Empire.[5] His ultimate fate is unknown.

"A Curious Fact"

The fragments of the alabaster vases with the name of Ramses II were not the only relics with his cartouches found by Montet in Byblos. He obtained from the builders of a modern house two pieces of a stele with cartouches of this pharaoh while two other pieces had already been used in the construction.

---

[1] Pliny: *Natural History,* V, 76.
[2] Josephus: *Against Apion,* I, 156.
[3] Josephus: *Jewish Antiquities,* X, 228
[4] Ginzberg: *Legends,* VI, 425-26.
[5] H. R. H. Hall: *Ancient History of the Near East* (London, 1913), p. 547.

When Montet left Phoenicia to dig in the Delta, his work at Byblos was continued by Maurice Dunand, who found on various sites a number of objects with the name of Ramses II incised on them. Among many other things he found parts of a large doorway or portal bearing Ramses II's cartouches.[1] The rock carvings of Ramses II at the mouth of the Dog River (Nahr el-Kelb), dated in the pharaoh's second, fourth, and fifth year, are not far away, on the coast between Beirut and Byblos. A portal with Ramses II's name in the latter city indicates that his passage through Byblos was also commemorated.

Among Dunand's other finds, the most important was a stele of King Yehimilk written in Hebrew characters. Some epigraphists have expressed the opinion that it is older than the Ahiram inscriptions, others kept to the view that the Ahiram inscriptions are earlier.

Dunand's pupil and assistant, Nina Jidejian, in her history of Byblos conveyed the surprise that bewildered her master, herself, and others. After describing the objects associated with Ramses II found at Byblos she opened the next chapter as follows:

> The results of excavations at Byblos have shown a curious fact which has been a source of discussion among scholars. In the excavated area at Byblos there is a complete absence of stratified levels of the Iron Age, that is for the period 1200 – 600 B.C.[2]

There was found no stratified level to bridge the time between Ramses II and Nebuchadnezzar, or more than six hundred years on the conventional timetable. "The excavators were unable to perceive any stratification of the Iron Age, a period which must have been one of prosperity and intense commercial activity."[3] It is known, for instance, that an emissary of Egyptian priests, named Wenamon, visited the place and the palace of the local king, supposedly in the eleventh century, but no vestiges of that palace have been discovered and only "large foundation stones of a building of the Persian period (550-330 B.C.) were unearthed to the east of the site."[4] "Apart from the tenth century royal inscriptions (referred to in the preceding section) there are only a few fragments from Byblos to cover the Early and Middle

---

[1] M. Dunand: *Fouilles de Byblos*, I (1937), pp. 53, 54, 56, 93, 339.
[2] N. Jidejian: *Byblos Through the Ages*, p. 57.
[3] *Ibid.*
[4] The true time of Wenamon's travel is examined in *Peoples of the Sea*, a volume of the *Ages in Chaos* series dealing with the Persian period: Wenamon visited Byblos under Darius II in the second half of the fifth century.

Iron Ages,"[1] or the said period from -1200 to -600. Such an imbroglio had to be expected.

All the difficulties of archaeological and epigraphic nature that have
bedeviled three generations of scholars and embroiled them in disputes and recriminations are only imaginary difficulties.

The events took this course: Ithobaal put his father to rest in the early
years of Ramses II. When Ahiram died, Ramses II sent mortuary gifts:
an example of such expression of condolence by an Egyptian monarch
at the occasion of the death of a king of Byblos was found in a nearby
tomb (marked by the archaeologists as number I) – rich mortuary gifts
sent by Amenemhet III of the Middle Kingdom were stored there.

After the battle of Kadesh-Carchemish in his fifth year, Ramses II
retreated from Phoenicia and also from Syria and Palestine. Once more,
between the eighth and the eleventh years of his reign, Ramses advanced and occupied Beth-Shan in northern Palestine and possibly
also reached the Phoenician coast; after his eleventh year Egypt for-
feited Syria and Phoenicia as spheres of influence.

It appears that Nebuchadnezzar, occupying Phoenicia after the battle
of Carchemish, may have violated the tomb of Ahiram, whose son had
sided with Ramses II.

This order of events explains why fragments of vases with Ramses II's
name were found in the tomb and in the shaft leading to it: why the
tomb was desecrated, the vases broken, the lid of the sarcophagus
moved sideways, all only a short time after Ithobaal entombed his father. The Cypriote vases that were found in the tomb are of the late
seventh century; the Egyptian vases are also of the last decade of the
same century; Ramses II is of the same time; the Hebrew letters on the
sarcophagus lid are also of the same time, and the desecration of the
tomb took place only a few years later and was the work of Nebuchadnezzar's soldiery.

---

[1] *Byblos Through the Ages*, p. 57.

A Recapitulation

In the first three chapters it has been shown that the fortress of Kadesh in northern Syria and Carchemish were one, as evidenced by the geographical position north of Bab and Arima, the topography of the site, the plan of fortifications in the records and pictures of Ramses II, and in the modern excavation; that the battle of Kadesh described in detail by Ramses and the battle of Carchemish described by Jeremiah were one and the same battle; that Tell Nebi-Mend conceals the fortress of Riblah; that the nineteen years' war between Ramses and the king of Kheta and between Necho and Nebuchadnezzar were one and the same war; that the treaty of peace signed by Ramses II and the provisions for extradition of refugees by Egypt were an agreement between the pharaoh and Nebuchadnezzar. The Hebrew idioms in the Egyptian language of the days of Ramses II were borrowed from the Judean population of the later period of Kings, while the ostraca written to the defenders of Lachish, besieged by Nebuchadnezzar, and the seals of Ramses II and the vase of the Nineteenth Dynasty found in that city are of the same age. Also the vases of Ramses II and the objects of the late seventh century unearthed in the sepulcher of Ahiram in Byblos are of one and the same period.

Hebrew letters on the tomb of Ahiram date from the very end of the seventh century or the beginning of the sixth, close to -600. These Hebrew characters, engraved on stone, are of later origin than the characters of Mesha or Hezekiah and of one age with the cursive characters of Lachish written in ink.

It appeared strange that a great pharaoh, who built a canal for communication between the basins of the Mediterranean Sea and the Indian Ocean, who sent an expedition around Africa, who waged great wars and impressed Greek authors and Jewish prophets and annalists, did not leave Egyptian records of his achievements. But we discovered that the great war and other activities of the pharaoh, known as Pharaoh Necho to the Jewish annalists and as Necos to the Greeks, were recorded by the pharaoh known to modern historians as Ramses II. However, we still do not have a complete picture of the great events that took place on the Middle Eastern scene at the close of the seventh and the beginning of the sixth centuries. Nebuchadnezzar was a powerful king too. He also impressed the Jewish annalists and Greek authors. Many building inscriptions and prayers were left by him. But where are the Babylonian historical records of this king? It seems odd that a great and long war between Egypt and Babylonia, recorded in such detail in the Scriptures, should have been non-existent in the records of the main participants. After having recognized the real nature of the records of Ramses II, we ought to trace some historical inscriptions of Nebuchadnezzar.

Chapter 4

The "Forgotten Empire"

Pictographic Script and the Cuneiform Archive of the "Hittites"

At the end of the eighteenth century bas-reliefs with peculiar pictographic inscriptions were noticed and pointed out by travelers passing near Ivriz, on the plateau of Asia Minor. Later travelers saw similar pictorial signs carved on stone that had been re-used in a building at the bazaar of Hamath in northern Syria. The same peculiar signs were observed on slabs in the area of Jerablus-Carchemish on the bank of the Euphrates, and later on the site of ancient Babylon and in other places. They are completely different from Egyptian hieroglyphics. It was not known which people had left these mysterious inscriptions.

On the other hand, mention of the Kheta in the texts accompanying the bas-reliefs of the battle of Kadesh, in the poem celebrating this battle, and in the Egyptian text of the peace treaty between Egypt and Kheta stimulated conjecture about the identity of the rivals of Ramses II in the struggle for dominion over the ancient world. Who were the Kheta?

In the 1870's a solution was offered and accepted: the Kheta were the Hittites, occasionally mentioned in the Scriptures. It was the phonetic similarity of the names that prompted this identification.

William Wright, a missionary in Damascus, came to this conclusion and also decided that the mysterious signs are Hittite writings. Since almost nothing was known of Hittite history, it was like resurrecting an empire from oblivion, and it was called "a discovery of a forgotten empire."[1] However, warning voices were also heard among scholars who were opposed to the idea, very strange to them, that the ancient

---

[1] Priority claims are shared by Archibald H. Sayce (*Transactions of the Society of Biblical Archaeology,* 1876), and William Wright, whose work, *The Empire of the Hittites* (London, 1882), became the sensation of the eighties. But compare also De Rougé: *Œuvres diverses,* Vol. V, *Cours de 1869*, pp. 104ff.

world of the empires of Egypt and Assyro-Babylonia should be increased by a newly discovered empire of the Hittites.

The Egyptian documents that mention Hatti are the war annals of Thutmose III (in a few lines only) and of Seti and Ramses II (extensively). The el-Amarna letters, written in cuneiform, refer frequently to Hatti. This period in the conventional chronology covers the time from about -1500 to about -1250. Merneptah, who followed Ramses II, said that Hatti was pacified. Ramses III, supposedly of about -1200 to -1180, wrote that Hatti was already crushed.[1]

A Babylonian chronicle mentions the Hatti in connection with an invasion of Babylon at the close of the ancient dynasty of Hammurabi, in the seventeenth or sixteenth century before the present era.

The Assyrian annals mention the Hatti for the first time in the days of Tiglath-Pileser I, who undertook a campaign against them, supposedly in -1107. These annals refer to the Hatti sporadically until -717, when Sargon II conquered them and reduced them to full dependence by occupying Carchemish. It is asserted by modern scholars that whatever remained of them was extirpated by Nebuchadnezzar when he occupied Carchemish shortly before the battle with Necho; he claimed to be the overlord of all the Hatti lands.

The biblical table of the descendants of Adam states that Canaan, son of Ham, begat Sidon his firstborn, and Heth, and the Jebusite, and the Amorite, and the Girgasite, and the Hivite, and so on (Genesis 10:15ff). The land between the Nile and the Euphrates, promised to the patriarch Abraham, is said to have been occupied by Kenites, Kenizzites, Kadmonites, Hittites, and six other tribes.[2] When the Israelites approached Palestine from the desert they found Hittites, Jebusites, and Amorites dwelling in the mountains, and Canaanites living by the sea.[3] David had a few Hittite soldiers in his army (I Samuel 26:6; II Samuel 11:3), and his son Solomon "loved ... strange women ... of the Moabites, Ammonites, Edomites, Zidonians, and Hittites" (I Kings 11:1) and also traded with the kings of the Hittites and the kings of Syria (I Kings 10:29). "Kings of the Hittites" are mentioned once more, in II Kings 7:6.

---

[1] See my *Peoples of the Sea* for the true time of Ramses III - Nectanebo I.
[2] Genesis 15:19–20; see also Genesis 25:9 and 26:34.
[3] Numbers 13:29; compare Joshua 1:4.

Figure 15: Pictographs from Carchemish

In a double identification the Kheta of the Egyptian annals and the Hatti of the Assyrian annals were said to be the Hittites of the Scriptures, and the monuments with the pictographic script were attributed to them. Among these monuments are pieces of sculptured work, especially relief cuttings in rocks. Hittite art and script are regarded as material witnesses of an empire that played a role as great as that of Egypt, Assyria, or Babylonia but that, for some reason, was forgotten so that only late in the nineteenth century of the present era was it reestablished in its historical place in the concert of ancient nations.

Monuments with "Hittite" sculptures and pictographic script were found in Asia Minor, mainly in its eastern part, and in the region around Carchemish, in Hamath, in northern Syria, but also in western Asia Minor, on Mount Sipylus and at Karabel, near Smyrna. They were not found in southern Syria or Palestine, though biblical references to the Hittites possessing land in ancient Palestine (Hebron)[1] should have made the discovery of some "Hittite" monument in these places quite probable.

Some scholars wondered why one of the many tribes enumerated in the Scriptures as inhabitants of the Holy Land before its conquest by Joshua should have occupied such an unexpectedly important role on the scene of the ancient East.[2]

It was expected that, if the pictographic inscriptions would divulge their secrets in an intelligible language, the history of the Hittites would no longer depend on Egyptian and Assyrian sources alone. This was the dream of the historians.

Then something happened of which they had not dreamed. Out of a steep slope facing a river bed beneath the ancient ruins of Boghazkoi crept tablets inscribed with cuneiform signs. They were moved by sand and debris and their own weight. Boghazkoi, a village in Turkey in the region of the evangelical Galatia, about one hundred and forty kilometers east of Ankara, occupies a site with a few steep hills on which ruins of ancient buildings, among them a palace, are found. The

---

[1] "The cave of Machpelah, in the field of Ephron the son of Zohar the Hittite, which is before Mamre" (Genesis 25:9). Compare E. Forrer: »The Hittites in Palestine«, *Quarterly Statement of the Palestine Exploration Fund*, 1936, pp. 190-203.

[2] "The Canaanite, the Amorite, and the Hittite, and the Perizzite, the Hivite, and the Jebusite" (Exodus 33:2). "It is surprising to find the great northern nation of the Hittites classed as a subdivision of the Canaanites." (J. Skinner: *A Critical and Exegetical Commentary on Genesis* (New York, 1910), p. 214.)

region is circumscribed by the large bend of the river Halys (now Kizil Irmak) that flows toward the Black Sea. The river of Boghazkoi is a confluent of the river Halys. Rock reliefs at Yazilikaya, a gorge within walking distance of the village of Boghazkoi, had long attracted the attention of travelers and scholars; they already occupied an important place among the Hittite monuments of art when the tablets of Boghazkoi came to light. Short pictographic legends accompany the figures on the rock reliefs.

Tablets found on the slope were sold by the peasants of Boghazkoi, piece by piece, to every traveler willing to pay a few piasters for them. In 1906 two scholars appeared on the scene looking for the source of the tablets.[1] In three weeks, excavating with the help of peasants and without taking proper precautions, they hurriedly carried from the slope two thousand five hundred tablets and fragments.

They tried to read the tablets while new ones were being brought in at the rate of more than a hundred a day. Some were inscribed in the Babylonian (Akkadian) language. Other tablets bore cuneiform signs, too, but they spelled out some unknown tongue or tongues.

The Boghazkoi tablets written in Babylonian were read without difficulty. In those hectic days when tablets by scores were brought in, the archaeologist Hugo Winckler was surprised to read by the light of a candle a Babylonian copy or draft of the treaty between Ramses II and the king of Hatti, already known from its Egyptian version inscribed on the walls of the Ramesseum and of the great hypostyle hall of the temple of Amon at Karnak. The silver tablet on which the original of the text was engraved is not extant, but both versions, the Egyptian and the Babylonian, were found, the one in Egypt, the other in Anatolia.

That the Kheta and the Hatti are the same was seen from the hieroglyphic and cuneiform versions of the treaty between Ramses II and Khetasar (Hattusilis of the cuneiform): in the hieroglyphic text the latter is called "the great chief of Kheta" and in the cuneiform text "the great king of Hatti."

It became evident that the royal archives of the so-called Hittite Empire had been brought to light. The theory of the "forgotten empire" seemed fully confirmed. Was not the originator of this idea farsighted

---

[1] Hugo Winckler and Makridi-Bey. A detailed record of the excavations was never published. Preliminary reports appeared in *Mitteilungen der Deutschen Orientgesellschaft,* No. 35 (1907), and in *Orientalistische Literaturzeitung,* IX (1906), 621-34. A posthumous sketch, *Nach Boghaskoi,* by Winckler, was published in 1913.

when he prophesied in his book, *The Empire* of *the Hittites:* "As regards the final acceptance of the views here advanced, I have no fear whatever"[1]?

The next year (1907) thousands more tablets and fragments were carried from the same slope in Boghazkoi, raising the number to about ten thousand.

There was, however, difficulty of a stratigraphic nature: the remains among which the tablets were found indicated a much more recent period than the age of these documents. But the existence of the treaty with Ramses II precluded even a consideration of the conflicting data, and a chronological place in accord with the time of Ramses II was allotted to Hattusilis, the king of Hatti, and to the entire period.

E. Forrer, a Swiss cuneiformist, recognized that in the archives of Boghazkoi at least eight different languages were represented, all using cuneiform signs. One of the languages was represented more often than all others except Babylonian and it was assumed to be the language of the Hittites. Through persistent efforts by F. Hrozny, a Czechoslovak cuneiformist, this language, dominant in the archives, was decoded. Initially, Hrozny met with much opposition among his colleagues but as years passed the opposition ceased and he triumphed. The tongue was recognized as belonging to the family of the Indo-European languages. However, in no text written in "Hittite" was it called by the name Hattish or Hittite.

When one more language of the archives was deciphered, it was found to be called in the texts Khattili, or the language of Hatti. It was too late to rename the other language, and the newly deciphered one was called Hattish, leaving the name Hittite for the language deciphered by Hrozny. Its true name, as given in the texts, was "Neshili".

Khattili (Hattish) was used in the palace and also in temple services, for litanies, prayers, and exorcisms.[2] The ritual texts either were written in Khattili alone or were bilingual, with a translation into so-called Hittite. Khattili is a rich language; in its inflections it employs prefixes but not suffixes; it is not Indo-European and bears no recognizable relation to any known linguistic group.

---

[1] Wright: *The Empire of the Hittites,* p. x.
[2] "Songs also were very frequently sung by the singers in the Khattish language during religious services. Khattish appears to have played an important role, especially in the religion of the Khatti land." F. Hrozny: »The Hittites«, *Encyclopaedia Britannica* (14th ed.), XI, 602.

A hypothesis was offered that the Hittites of Syria and Asia Minor were an amalgam of two peoples, one of which belonged to the Indo-European race. The Indo-European nation might have absorbed the culture and the religion of the older population, its language receiving many Babylonian and Khattili elements.

A system of at least three main languages and several secondary ones in the same archives complicates the problem for historians and philologists: Babylonian was used for diplomatic purposes (as in the treaty with Ramses II); some dialect, called Hittite by the researchers, was used in most of the domestic documents, sometimes also for diplomatic purposes; and the tongue called "the language of Khatti" in inscriptions was used for religious purposes and also employed in matters of etiquette at the palace. Four or five other tongues were read in the cuneiform tablets from Boghazkoi and were named appropriately by the decipherers. It appears that Hattusas (the ancient city at the site of Boghazkoi) was a capital with many international connections.

Removing the historical scene to where it belongs, namely, to the seventh and sixth centuries before the present era, we wonder which of these languages is Chaldean, which Phrygian, which Lydian, which Median, which perchance Etruscan, spoken by a people who came to Italy from Asia Minor. Phrygian is related to Luwian: The Phrygian kingdom ended about the time the Luwian-speaking Syro-Hittite states were subjugated by Assyria. The Cimmerians, an illiterate people from southern Russia, conquered Gordion, the Phrygian capital, in -687; to reach Gordion they had to pass through the bend of the Halys and engulf Boghazkoi. It is very questionable whether they acquired or adapted any alphabet to their use. The Cimmerian left little trace of any kind behind them. After -687, under Gyges, Lydia became the dominant power in western Asia Minor, contemporary with the expansion of the "Hittite" kingdom of East-Central Anatolia, centered on Boghazkoi. "Hittite" was the language most commonly used during the Empire period. Modern scholarship found that Lydian "seems to be Hittite"[1] – the Lydian and the "Hittite" kingdoms were contemporary, and used the same language. Hurrian, as we endeavored to show in the first volume of *Ages in Chaos*, is but a mistaken name for Carian.

The association of the languages of the Boghazkoi archives with the ethnic groups that occupied Asia Minor in the time the archives were brought together is a task for philologists.

The problem of the "Hittite Empire" was complicated by the strange pictographic signs found in many places in Anatolia, Mesopotamia, and northern Syria: these signs originally gave rise to the surmise of the historical existence of the Forgotten Empire.

The seals of the kings of Hatti found in Asia Minor bear both characters, the pictographic and the cuneiform. On a few cuneiform tablets of the Boghazkoi archives pictographic signs are also impressed. Similar signs are carved in the rock reliefs of Yazilikaya.

The unearthed documents of the archives provided material for many new chapters of history. Books and journals dealing with the "Hittites" and their inscriptions were published. The period from Amenhotep III to Ramses II, covering the fourteenth and thirteenth centuries of conventional chronology, was studied anew with the help of these inscriptions.

The royal annals found at Boghazkoi are composed in a manner that reveals a close relation to the Assyrian royal annals of Sennacherib, Esarhaddon, and Assurbanipal of the seventh century.[2]

Other texts of Boghazkoi establish that "Babylonian magic and medicine and astronomy were known and cultivated in Asia Minor. Also a translation of the Gilgamesh epos was found there."[3] The "Hittites" had in common with the Babylonians scholarly works, hymns, writings based on historical traditions, vocabularies, and other literary works.[4]

Assyrian justice, as far as civil laws were concerned, had much in common with the civil laws of the Boghazkoi archives.[5]

The Assyrian Empire is supposed to have begun its ascendancy after the fall of the "Hittite Empire." But in some ways the "Hittites" were

---

[1] J. G. Macqueen: *The Hittites* (London, 1975), p. 59.
[2] "Annalen treten zuerst in Boghazköi auf, und die Aehnlichkeit in Stil und Ausdrucksweise zwischen den hethitischen und assyrischen Werken ist so gross, dass man ohne die Annahme eines Zusammenhangs gar nicht auskommt." A. Götze: »Das Hethiter-Reich« in *Der Alte Orient*, XXVII, 2 (Leipzig, 1928), p. 44.
[3] *Ibid.*, p. 45.
[4] "Die Hethiter haben von den Akkadern neben Werken der Wissenschaft, wie Vokabularen, Omina and medizinischen Texten, und literarischen Werken im engeren Sinne, wie Götterhymnen und dem Gilgames-Epos, auch Stücke der historischen Traditionsliteratur übernommen." H. Güterbock: »Die historische Tradition und ihre literarische Gestaltung bei Babyloniern und Hethitern bis 1200«, *Zeitschrift für Assyriologie*, XLIV (1938), p. 45.
[5] L. Aubert: »Le Code hittite et l'Ancien Testament«, *Revue d'histoire et de philosophie religieuses*, IV (1924), 352-70.

more advanced than the Assyrians, and consequently it is assumed that the Assyrians regressed culturally as compared with the "Hittites." [1]

Scholars wonder about the unknown cause of this retrogression in cultural development when the age of the "Hittites" expired presumably about -1200, and was superseded by the Assyrian Empire, which rose presumably shortly before -1100. They wonder how it could be that the "Hittite" culture of the fifteenth to the thirteenth centuries, in all that concerns science, law, literature, royal annals, traditions, habits, and omens, so closely resembled the culture of the Assyrian Empire of the eighth and seventh centuries and of the Neo-Babylonian Empire of the seventh and sixth centuries.

In Boghazkoi treaties were found which had been concluded by the kings of Hatti (Kheta) with kings of other lands. Military annals of the father of Hattusilis were brought to light: his name is read Mursilis and he gives a description of his wars. An autobiography of Hattusilis, covering the time from his infancy until he came to the throne of the empire, was also unearthed.

The material of the preceding chapters has made it apparent that the "Great King of the Kheta," against whom Ramses II moved his legions, was the king of the Chaldeans, and that the signer of the peace treaty, Khetasar, or Hattusilis of the cuneiform version, was Nebuchadnezzar (Nabukudurri-usur). This conclusion is rich in consequences. Another great structure of the historians collapses, the "Hittite Empire."

Before we examine the annals of the father of Hattusilis we claim that they were written not by a "Hittite" king of the fourteenth century but by Nabopolassar the Great, whose history up to now has been only dimly illuminated.

An autobiography of Nebuchadnezzar! We have had numerous prayers of this king composed on the occasion of the erection of temples, but very few lines contain allusions to his political or martial rule, so rich in events; only a fragment of a small tablet mentions one event out of the complicated relations between the Chaldeo-Babylonian Empire under Nebuchadnezzar and Egypt, relations that endured for decades and to

---

[1] "Après les Hittites, commence l'empire assyrien, dont les mœurs temoignent par rapport à eux d'une véritable régression." G. Contenau: »Ce que nous savons des Hittites«, *Revue historique*, CLXXXVI (1939), 15.

which the Scriptures dedicated many chapters in the Books of Jeremiah, Ezekiel, Kings, and Chronicles. Pertinent material for writing the history of this great Neo-Babylonian period was drawn almost entirely from these texts of the Scriptures and from the Greek literature. In the preceding chapter it was shown that Ramses II was Pharaoh Necho and that an abundant hieroglyphic material dealing with the war of Egypt against the Babylonian Empire under Nebuchadnezzar exists.

The cuneiform material pertaining to the same period was unearthed at Boghazkoi in 1906. But by the same black magic that has distorted the past of mankind by five to eight centuries this firsthand material was ascribed to a wrong millennium and to a wrong people.

Mursilis the "Hittite" and Nabopolassar the Chaldean

Among the Boghazkoi texts two long inscriptions are versions of Mursilis' war annals. One version embraces the time from his first regnal year to his ninth or tenth year.[1] The other version, much more detailed, is found on fragments, the sequence of which is not always apparent. With the help of the "ten years' annals" the fragments were put in order. However, there remains an acknowledged uncertainty as to the correctness of this arrangement, for the detailed annals recount rather differently the same period of the first ten years.[2] It is believed that these fragments cover the time from the first to the end of the eleventh year and again from the nineteenth to presumably the twenty-second year of Mursilis. "A painful hiatus lies between."[3] The gap ap-

---

[1] Part of the tenth year of the annals is only the ninth year of Mursilis, as his accession to the throne took place during a calendar year. See E. Forrer: *Geschichtliche Texte aus Boghazkoi* II (Leipzig, 1926), p. 35: "... das letzte Jahr der Zehnjahr-Annalen also das neunte volle Jahr ist ..."

[2] "Da die Bruchstücke ihr gegenseitiges chronologisches Verhältnis in keinem Falle ohne weiteres zu erkennen geben, ist ihre Anordnung ein Problem für sich." A. Götze: »Die Annalen des Mursilis«, *Mitteilungen, Vorderasiatisch-ägyptische Gesellschaft*, XXXVII (1932), 2.

[3] "Dazwischen klafft eine schmerzliche Lücke." *Ibid.*, p. 9. In his original publication Götze hypothesized that the fragments might have extended to the twenty-seventh year of military activities of Mursilis. But further research led to a different conclusion: "The present parts of the annals of Mursilis justify the assumption that his reign covered ... not much more than twenty-two years." A. Götze in the *Cambridge Ancient History* (3rd ed.; 1975), Vol. II, Pt. 2, pp. 126-27. The last entries date from the *twenty-second* year.

parently conceals the climactic period of Mursilis' wars, as already in the ninth year the prolonged conflict was approaching a decisive stage. Mursilis clashed with the king of Assyria, who had the support of the king of Egypt, and the first years of the annals contain, in addition to records of various campaigns that Mursilis undertook in all four directions, the record of the preliminary stages of this major conflict.

In his second year Mursilis sent a military chief to Sarri-sin-ah, prince of Carchemish, who was his brother, with an order to resist the king of Assyria.

> When the Assyrian comes, you will battle with him.

In the seventh year of the annals mention is made of some agreement to which the king of Egypt was a party (" – Treaty – when the king of the land of Egypt – and when with – the king of the land of Egypt"), and though the lines are mutilated, it is evident that an alliance was concluded by the king of Assyria with the king of Egypt against Mursilis. Also, at the approach of the king of Egypt, some Syrian potentates swung to the side of Mursilis' enemies.

> As soon as tidings were brought about the arrival of the Egyptian troops, I moved against them.

Mursilis wrote to the garrison in Carchemish that if the Egyptian army entered Nuhasse (in Syria) he should be informed immediately.

> ... and I shall come and battle against them.

But the clash with the Egyptian army was postponed.

> Meanwhile the Egyptian troops did not come.

Two years later, in the ninth year of Mursilis, the war with the king of Assyria became active.

> The king of Assur conquered the land of Carchemish.

Mursilis turned to this region and freed it, and put his nephew, the son of Sarri-sin-ah, on the throne of Carchemish. In the same year he marched to the region of Harran.

> I moved toward Harrana; my army reached Harrana and I joined the army there.

Some important portions of the text are damaged, but its editor was able to reconstruct them, and this is his conclusion: "Mursilis in his ninth year met his adversary, on the Euphrates line."[1]

At the conclusion of his ten-year annals, Mursilis stressed that he had described only his own deeds and that the achievements of his princes and generals were not included.

The most important fact learned from the annals is that Mursilis battled for a number of years against a coalition of the king of Assyria and the king of Egypt. The war went on without decision. In the ninth year it was waged in Harran. There he met and fought Assuruballit, king of Assyria.

According to the reconstructed chronology, Mursilis, father of Hattusilis, was the Chaldean name of Nabopolassar, father of Nebuchadnezzar. I am therefore bound to compare the facts found in the annals of Mursilis with the facts known about Nabopolassar, king of Akkad (Babylonia) and Chaldea.

Until half a century ago there were at the disposal of the historians no Babylonian texts of historical content covering the rule of Nabopolassar. But in the 1920's cuneiform tablets, stored in the British Museum for years, were "unearthed" there and found to be fragments of Chronicles of the Chaldean (Babylonian) Kings written much later, probably in Persian times, on the basis of some surviving records.[2] In this respect they are akin to the Books of Chronicles of the Old Testament, also composed under the Persian rule. Among the tablets containing the Chronicles of the Babylonian Kings, one deals with the military campaigns of Nabopolassar.[3] It narrates the story of Nabopolassar's wars during the period starting with the tenth year of his reign and thus presents new and long-sought material on the fall of Nineveh and the eclipse of Assyrian might.

The Babylonian Chronicle (British Museum 21901) of Nabopolassar's wars begins with the tenth-year campaign:

> In the tenth year, in the month of Iyar, Nabopolassar called the Akkadian army and went along the shore of the Euphrates.

---

[1] *Ibid.,* XXXVIII, 248. While Assuruballit is not mentioned in the annals, it turns out that Götze's conclusion was correct. But the enemy of Mursilis was Assuruballit II.

[2] Earlier publications: C. J. Gadd: *The Fall of Nineveh* (London, 1923). Julius Lewy: »Forschungen zur alten Geschichte Vorderasiens«, Die Neubabylonische Chronik G, *Mitteilungen: Vorderasiatisch-ägyptische Gesellschaft,* XXIX (1925), 2. Newly edited and translated texts: D. J. Wiseman: *Chronicles of Chaldean Kings (626-556 B.C.) in the British Museum* (London, 1956). I followed Gadd's translation, checking it in Wiseman's version.

[3] Tablet B. M. 21901.

After a few months according to the Chronicles:

In the month of Tishri the Egyptian and Assyrian armies went to pursue the king of Akkad. ...

The next year "the king of Assyria mobilized his army and turned the king of Akkad back from Assyria." But he was unable to exploit his victory over Nabopolassar, for the Medes invaded Assyria and captured the city of Assur.

The year after that saw the Scythian king with his army coming to participate in the "battle of Assyria."

The king of Umman-Manda marched toward the king of Akkad [Nabopolassar].

But he was persuaded to take the side of the enemies of Assyria. Then came the great and famous assault on Nineveh and the great slaughter. The Assyrian Empire was nearing its final hour.

Sin-shar-ishkun, the heir of Assurbanipal, perished; the legend of self-immolation of Sardanapal in his palace at Nineveh seems to reflect the end of Sin-shar-ishkun. After the fall of Nineveh, Assuruballit, a younger brother of Assurbanipal,[1] whose residence was in Harran, proclaimed himself king of Assyria. According to the Chronicles,

Assur-uballit in Harran took his seat on the throne as king of Assyria. ...

For the next two years Nabopolassar continued to carry war to the Assyrian land.

The Umman-Manda came to the support of the king of Akkad and they united their armies and toward Harran, against Assuruballit, who sat on the throne of Assyria, they marched.[2]

The assistance Egypt gave to Assyria as long as Nineveh was its ally was not discontinued with the fall of the city but was given to Assuruballit in Harran.

The great army of Egypt ... crossed the river and marched against Harran. ...
The king of Akkad marched to the aid of his army.
In the 17th year[3] – the king of Akkad mobilized his army and –

---

[1] "I appointed Ashur-etil-shame irsitim-uballitsu, my younger brother, as high priest to the god Sin dwelling in Harran," wrote Assurbanipal. Dougherty: *Nabonidus and Belshazzar*, p. 24.
[2] Luckenbill: *Records of Assyria*, Vol. II, Sec. 1182.
[3] Wiseman, differing from Gadd, reads "In the 18th year."

Here the text of the Chronicles' tablet catalogued as British Museum 21901 ends.[1]

In no other period of history were Assyria and Egypt allies in a war. The two cases dealt with here are separated by seven centuries of conventional history, but they are really one and the same.

Mursilis' march along the Euphrates and his battles against the Assyrian troops, supported by Egyptian troops, and the military operations in Harran against Assuruballit are said to have occurred in the fourteenth century. The march of Nabopolassar along the Euphrates and his battles against the Assyrian troops, supported by the Egyptian army, and the military operations against Assuruballit in Harran are said to have taken place in the seventh century. Nabopolassar died in the twenty-second year of his reign. The last fragment of Mursilis' war annals is of his twenty-second regnal year.

The "painful hiatus" in the annals of Mursilis between the tenth and the nineteenth years is in large part filled by the Babylonian Chronicle covering the tenth to the seventeenth or eighteenth year of his reign.

During these years the king of the Scythians, the Umman-Manda, intervened, at first with the intention of helping the king of Assyria, but eventually as a partner in an alliance against him.

Nabonidus (-556 to -539), the last king of the Neo-Babylonian Empire, wrote of the downfall of Assyria under the joint impact of the Medes, Chaldeans, and Scythians: "The king of Umman-Manda, the fearless, ruined the temples of the gods of Assyria, all of them."[2]

Herodotus narrates how, when the king of the Medes besieged Nineveh, "there came down upon him a great army of Scythians, led by their king Madyas son of Protothyas. These had invaded Asia after they had driven the Cimmerians out of Europe: pursuing them in their flight, the Scythians came to the Median country."[3]

This epoch saw for the first time the invasion of the Scythians from the steppes of Russia. "Scythians came by the upper and much longer road, having on their right the Caucasian mountains," wrote Herodotus.[4]

---

[1] Tablet B. M. 22047, covering the end of Nabopolassar's reign and the accession of Nebuchadnezzar, is discussed in one of the following sections.

[2] S. H. Langdon: Die Neubabylonischen Königsinschriften, (Leipzig, 1912), »Nabonid«, p. 273; also L. Messerschmidt: »Die Stele Nabunaids«, Mitteilungen, Vorderasiatisch-ägyptische Gesellschaft, I (1896), 1-83.

[3] Herodotus, I, 103.

[4] Ibid., I, 104.

The participation of the Scythians in the war against Assyria is related in the Babylonian Chronicle for the fourteenth to the seventeenth year. The king of the Scythians is called king of Umman-Manda. As this period from the fourteenth to the seventeenth year is missing in the annals of Boghazkoi, we look for a reference to the Umman-Manda in some other documents of Boghazkoi and find it in juridical texts unearthed at that site. The "Hittite" laws refer to the warriors of the Umman-Manda.[1]

Is it correct to maintain that the Umman-Manda were already on the scene in the Middle East seven hundred years before they drove the Cimmerians from Europe and came after them by way of the Caucasus? This consideration alone should have been a warning that the centuries of history were disarranged.

Names and Surnames

For the sake of a better orientation among the personalities on the historical stage, it seems appropriate to point out a few facts. It was the custom in Babylonia as well as in Syria, and probably in other regions of western Asia, too, for the name of a deceased person to be taken by a survivor. It was believed that the blessing of the deceased would descend on his namesake, or it may have been a wish to keep alive the memory of the dead that gave rise to this custom. A son was named for his grandfather or father; or a boy was called by the name of his departed brother. When a king died, a number of citizens called themselves or their children by the name of their venerated monarch.

The royal princes of the ancient Orient, not different from royal princes of old European nations, gave several names to their children. Like the Egyptian pharaohs and Jewish kings, the princes and kings of Assyria and Babylonia had more than one name; the *Talmud* relates that Sennacherib had eight and Hezekiah seven.[2] In Egypt it was a statute

---

[1] See J. Friedrich and H. Zimmern: »Hethitische Gesetze« in *Der Alte Orient* (Leipzig, 1922), Pt. I, Sec. 55, p. 14; B. Hrozny: *Code Hittite* (Paris, 1922), p. 49, Par. 54; S. Smith: *Alalakh and Chronology,* p. 35; cf. also S. Langdon: *The Venus Tablets of Ammizaduga* (London, 1928), pp. 9, 31-32.

[2] *The Babylonian Talmud, Tractate Sanhedrin* 94a; Jerome on Isaiah 20:1 and 36:1. See Ginzberg: *Legends,* VI, 370. This custom survived till this century – in the princely houses of Germany in the nineteenth century and the British royal house still in the twentieth.

that the king should have five royal names and nomens, not all of them permanent. Occasionally they were replaced by other names; besides, the king had private names. Ramses III, for instance, had more than a dozen names.[1]

From the text of Hattusilis' autobiography, which will follow, one can learn that several personalities, such as Arma or Labash, are referred to by different names, each in the course of the same narrative. For the purpose of the identifications pursued in this work, it is fortunate that both Nergil (Nergilissar) and Labash, his son, are occasionally mentioned by the same names in "Hittite" and in Babylonian documents.

It was also quite regular that the same king, especially in Mesopotamia, should be called by different names in different provinces – thus Tiglath Pileser III (-745 to -727) of Assyria was called Pul in Babylonia, also a domain of his. "It had come to be established as almost a usual rule for the Assyrian king who reigned in Babylon to have another name than that used in Assyria."[2] Not only in Nineveh and Babylon but also in other parts of the empire the king bore different names. Hittite kings had Hurrian names beside their own throne names: thus the boy king known in history by his Hurrian name of Urhi-Teshub had the throne name Mursilis (III).

It was also very usual to change by a royal decree the name of a person so that it should sound more agreeable to the ears of foreign people. Eliakim's name was changed by Pharaoh Necho to Jehoiakim (II Kings 23:34), and Mattaniah's name was changed by Nebuchadnezzar to Zedekiah (II Kings 24:17); the names of Daniel and his friends were changed by Nebuchadnezzar (Daniel 1:7). Who would discover the biblical Daniel in a Belteshazzar if there were no direct indication of the change of name? It is known from the cuneiform inscriptions of the Assyrian kings of the seventh century, Sennacherib, Esarhaddon, and Assurbanipal, that they called the Egyptian kings, their vassals, by names that bear no resemblance to the names those vassals used in hieroglyphic texts.

The custom of changing names was very old: a pharaoh of the Middle Kingdom changed the name of Joseph to Zaphnaph-Paaneah (Genesis 41:45).

---

[1] See R. Gauthier: *Le Livre des rois d'Egypte* (Cairo, 1916), Vol. III.
[2] R. W. Rogers: *A History of Babylonia and Assyria* (6th ed., New York and Cincinnati, 1915), II, 483, note.

Not only different nations but different gods had to be satisfied. The name of Nebuchadnezzar invites the protection of the god Nebo, the planet Mercury. The planets Jupiter (Marduk), Mars (Nergil), Venus (Ishtar), and Saturn (Bel), and the Moon (Sin) and the Sun (Shamash) had to be appeased, too, because each of them could harm. Moreover, in various provinces the god-planets had other names, such as Enlil, Ninlil, Nana, and so on. The names of the gods of the planetary pantheon also had their equivalents in various languages, and many of these names were incorporated into the Akkadian tongue.

Besides all this, cuneiform can be read both ideographically and syllabically, and thus "Nergil" (Nergal) could become "Muwatallis."[1]

For these reasons it is not surprising that Greek authors called Nabopolassar "Belesys" (Diodorus, II, 24) and "Bussalossor" (Abydenus), and that in the Boghazkoi texts he is called "Mursilis" and "Bijasili", in Egyptian "Merosar", in Babylonian "Bel-shum-ishkun" and "Nabopolassar". As was brought out in preceding pages, Hattusilis was a Chaldean name of the king who is variously named Nebuchadnezzar and Nebuchadrezzar in the Scriptures, the name he himself preferred upon having achieved great fame as the builder of Babylon, under the aegis of Nebo, the protector god of his father and of the city the father conquered and the on built. In a different work I intend to bring out that what is known as the catastrophe of the Tower of Babel (Babylon) was caused by a close passage of Mercury, Nebo of the Babylonians (heard in the names Nabopolassar and Nebuchadnezzar), or Thoth of the Egyptians (heard in the name Thutmose). Nergilissar's name, however, reflects the cult of Mars, a planet that came much into prominence in the eighth century before the present era.[2]

Nabopolassar Becomes an Invalid

Berosus, the Babylonian historian, writing in Greek about events three and four centuries earlier, recorded the succession of the kings of the Neo-Babylonian Empire and described how Nabopolassar became sick,

---

[1] Delaporte: Les Hittites, p. 125: "Le nom de ce roi s'écrit tantôt Mouttalli, tantôt Mouattalli, Mouwatalli, dans les textes en langue akkadienne; dans les documents en langue hittite, il se présente en allographie sous la forme sumérienne Nirgal, idéogramme de l'akkadien Moutellou (seigneur)."

[2] Worlds in Collision, »Mars«.

and "being himself unequal to the fatigues of a campaign, committed part of his army to his son Nebuchadnezzar," and how Nebuchadnezzar subdued the rebellious provinces.[1] "Meanwhile, as it happened, his father Nabopolassar sickened and died in the city of Babylon, after a reign of twenty-one years."

Nabopolassar, the indefatigable warrior, when he first became stricken by illness, had to relinquish his post at the head of his army; later the state of his health worsened for a second time and he died.

The archives of Boghazkoi have preserved the authentic story of the illness of Mursilis, father of Hattusilis.

> I was on the road to Til-Kunnu. Stormy weather broke loose, the god of Storm did thunder dreadfully. Inside my mouth the word became scarce, and the word came out somewhat stumbling.
> And the years came and went and this condition began to play a part in my dreams. And god's hand struck me in the time of a dream, and the ability of speech I lost entirely.[2]

The king was crippled by the first paralytic stroke; unable to endure the hardships of military life, he retired as military chief. A few years later he became gravely ill, when he lost the power of speech; soon afterward he died. Judging by his annals – those found in Boghazkoi, and those discovered in the storeroom of the British Museum – Nabopolassar-Mursilis was an indomitable man of battle and an honest annalist without equal. The annals up to the tenth year, from the tenth year to the seventeenth, and from the nineteenth to the beginning of the twenty-second are masterpieces of veracity, relating victories and reverses alike, and are very different from the annals of Assyria, or those of any other king of the great empires of the ancient world.

---

[1] Berosus quoted in Josephus: *Against Apion,* transl. H. Thackeray (Loeb Classical Library, 1966), I, 135.

[2] A. Götze and H. Pedersen: »Mursilis Sprachlähmung, ein Hethitischer Text«, *Det Kongelige Danske Videnskabernes Selskab* (Copenhagen), *Historisk-Filogiske meddelelser,* XXI, I (1934), p. 5.

109

The Order of Succession to the Throne of Babylon

Berosus, upon telling of Nabopolassar's death after a twenty-one-year-long reign, continued:

> Being informed ere long of his father's death, Nahuchodonosor [Nebuchadnezzar] settled the affairs of Egypt and the other countries. The prisoners – Jews, Phoenicians, Syrians, and those of Egyptian nationality – were consigned to some of his friends, with orders to conduct them to Babylonia, along with the heavy troops and the rest of the spoils; while he himself, with a small escort, pushed across the desert to Babylon. There he found the administration in the hands of the Chaldaeans and the throne reserved for him by their chief nobleman.[1]

Of the events that followed the reign of Nebuchadnezzar, Berosus told the following:

> Nabuchodonosor [Nebuchadnezzar] fell sick and died, after a reign of forty-three years, and the realm passed to his son Evilmaraduch. This prince, whose government was arbitrary and licentious, fell a victim to a plot, being assassinated by his sister's husband, Neriglisar, after a reign of two years. On his death Neriglisar, his murderer, succeeded to the throne and reigned four years. His son, Laborosoardoch, a mere boy, occupied it for nine months, when, owing to the depraved disposition which he showed, a conspiracy was formed against him, and he was beaten to death by his friends. After his murder the conspirators held a meeting, and by common consent conferred the kingdom upon Nabonnedus, a Babylonian and one of their gang.[2]

Berosus wrote that Cyrus, the Persian, conquered Babylonia in the seventeenth year of Nabonidus.

The *Talmud* and the *Midrashim* agree in general with Berosus on the length of Nebuchadnezzar's reign, assigning to it from forty to forty-five years.[3] In the Scriptures as in Berosus he was succeeded by Evil-Merodach.[4] The Scriptures, however, do not mention that Evil-Merodach was followed by Nergilissar, and he in turn by his son, who was still a boy. The capture of Babylon by the Persians is described in the Book of Daniel, and the feasting king, who drank from the vessels

---

[1] Josephus: *Against Apion,* I, 136-38.
[2] *Ibid.,* I, 146-49.
[3] See Ginzberg: *Legends,* VI, 427, n. 114. According to the Scriptures (cf. II Kings 24:12, 25:27), Nebuchadnezzar reigned forty-four years as king of Babylon.
[4] II Kings 25:27; Jeremiah 52:31.

of the Temple of Jerusalem and who saw the handwriting on the wall the night the kingdom fell, is called Belshazzar. Belshazzar, according to an inscription of Nabonidus, was his heir and co-ruler.[1]

Nabonidus, remembered as the king-archaeologist who dug for old foundation inscriptions, in an inscription of his own wrote of the events that led to his reign in these words:

> Unto the midst of the palace they brought me and all of them cast themselves at my feet. I am the powerful representative of Nebuchadnezzar and Nergilissar, my royal predecessors. Amil-Marduk, the son of Nebuchadnezzar, and Labash-Marduk, the son of Nergilissar, they distorted the ordinances.[2]

This narrative seems to confirm perfectly the second part of Berosus' account. The first part of it, concerning the ascension of the throne of Babylon by Nebuchadnezzar, finds its confirmation in a cuneiform tablet of the British Museum, first published in 1956.[3] It tells:

> In the twenty-first year the king of Akkad stayed in his own land, Nebuchadrezzar his eldest son, the crown-prince, mustered [the Babylonian army] and took command of his troops; he marched to Carchemish which is on the bank of the Euphrates, and crossed the river [to go] against the Egyptian army which lay in Carchemish ... fought with each other and the Egyptian army withdrew before him. He accomplished their defeat and to non-existence [beat?] them. As for the rest of the Egyptian army which had escaped from the defeat [so quickly that] no weapon had reached them, in the district of Hamath the Babylonian troops overtook and defeated them so that not a single man [escaped] to his own country. At that time Nebuchadnezzar conquered the whole area of the Hatti-country. For twenty-one years Nabopolassar had been king of Babylon. On the 8th of the month of Ab he died [lit. "the fates"]: in the month of Elul Nebuchadrezzar returned to Babylon and on the first day of the month of Elul he sat on the royal throne in Babylon.

For some time we have also been in possession of a well-preserved votive stele of the mother of Nabonidus, a priestess who reached the venerable age of one hundred and five years. The stele gives the names of the kings under whom she lived, having been born in the twentieth year of Assurbanipal: The succession of the kings and the length of their reigns are the same as in Berosus, who flourished three hundred

---

[1] Langdon: Die Neubabylonischen Königsinschriften, »Nabonid«, Inscription IV.
[2] R. P. Dougherty: Nabonidus and Belshazzar (Yale Oriental Series, 1929), p. 72.
[3] Tablet B. M. 21946, D. J. Wiseman: Chronicles of Chaldean Kings.

years after Nebuchadnezzar. The stele only omits the boy, son of Nergilissar.

With all this evidence at hand there should be no difficulty. However, the building inscriptions of Nergilissar conceal a problem. Already in the opening sentence of both these tablets, Nergilissar proclaims:

I am the son of the King of Babylon, Bel-shum-ishkun.[1]

Nebuchadnezzar reigned in Babylon over forty years, and before him his father Nabopolassar reigned for more than twenty years. So who was the king of Babylon, Bel-shum-ishkun, if Nergilissar reigned after Nebuchadnezzar? There was no answer to this question. "In Nergilissar's most important inscription he calls his father Bel-shum-ishkun, of whom nothing is known."[2] Nergilissar applied "lofty titles to Bel-shum-ishkun, viz. sar Babili, king of Babylon. With the data now at our disposal identification of Bel-shum-ishkun with any known sovereign is difficult"[3]

Yet a possible clue to the identity of the king of Babylon whom Nergilissar claimed as his father is in Diodorus of Sicily, who, in telling the story of the fall of Nineveh, calls the Chaldean Nabopolassar by the name of Belesys: "this man's name was Belesys."[4] "Belesys" could easily be a Greek version of the cuneiform name Bel-shum-ishkun.

Nergilissar recorded that he found Esagila, the great temple in Babylon, in a state of decay:

Esagila ... its walls were ruined, its joints did not hold together, its sills were no more firm.
I put its foundation on its old base stone, I built high its wall.[5]

If he really reigned two years after Nebuchadnezzar, it is odd that Esagila should have fallen into such a ruinous state in so short a time. Nebuchadnezzar is renowned for his building activities as not many kings of antiquity are; he built and repaired temples all over the country; but more than of any other sacrarium he took care of Esagila, the great temple. His religious inscriptions often begin like this:

Nebuchadnezzar, the king of Babylon, the caretaker of Esagila and Esida, the son of Nabopolassar, the king of Babylon, am I.[6]

---

[1] Langdon: Die Neubabylonischen Königsinschriften, »Neriglissar«, Inscriptions I and II.
[2] Rogers: A History of Babylonia and Assyria, II, 547.
[3] Dougherty: Nabonidus and Belshazzar, p. 61.
[4] Diodorus: The Historical Library, transl. Oldfather, Bk. II, 24.
[5] Langdon: Die Neubabylonischen Königsinschriften, »Neriglissar«, Inscription II.
[6] Ibid., 23, 24, and in many other instances.

He mentioned his office of guardian of Esagila even before the fact that he was the son of Nabopolassar. Again and again he wrote:

Esagila and Esida I made shine like a star-adorned sky, I made them radiant like a bright day.[1]

According to his inscriptions, Nergilissar made repairs to the ruined temple structure and also covered the gates with silver, but Nebuchadnezzar rebuilt it from the foundation to the roof and covered it all around with gold.

How, then, could it be that two years after his death – and no enemy ravished Babylon in the meantime – the joints of the temple of Esagila did not hold together, its sills were no longer firm, and its foundation needed complete repair?

A look at a photograph of the excavation of Esagila with "its enormous wall structures composed of millions of bricks inscribed with the name of 'Nebuchadnezzar, the caretaker of Esagila,'"[2] is sufficient to make one realize the weakness of any suggestion that after Nebuchadnezzar's death the walls and foundations of Esagila were found in a ruinous state.

In the other inscription Nergilissar recounted how the king's palace in Babylon became ruined and was no longer habitable.

The palace ... ruined over the shore of Euphrates; its joints burst. Its crushed walls I demolished and I reached the ground water. In sight of the ground water I put its foundation firm with asphalt and burned bricks. I built it and accomplished it.[3]

This was the palace Nebuchadnezzar occupied as king of Babylon. "The residence of Nergalshar-usur was in the same palace as that of Nebuchadnezzar, and in this he carried on extensive alterations and improvements. The first of them concerned its foundations."[4] Nebuchadnezzar wrote of remodeling and enlarging it, a work done thoroughly:

Its foundation upon the bosom of the abyss I laid down deeply.[5]

[1] *Ibid.*, »Nebuchadnezzar«, Inscriptions 27a, 27b, and many others.
[2] R. Koldewey: *Das wiedererstehende Babylon* (1st ed.; Leipzig, 1913), pp. 205-6.
[3] Langdon: *Die Neubabylonischen Königsinschriften,* »Neriglissar«, Inscription I.
[4] Rogers: *History of Babylonia and Assyria,* II, 547.
[5] Langdon: *Building Inscriptions of the Neo-Babylonian Empire,* Inscription »Nebuchadnezzar« XXXI, also XXXVI

Figure 16: Excavations of the Esagila at Babylon. From *Das Wieder-erstehende Babylon*, J. C. Heinrichs, R. Koldewey, Leipzig (1925)

Nebuchadnezzar wrote also:

A great wall of mortar and burnt brick as a mountain I threw about it, and beside the brick wall a huge wall of immense stones, material from the great mountains I made and like a mountain I raised its top. ...
For the beholding (of) all men I filled it with costly furnishings. Majestic, fearful and awful things of my royal splendor were scattered throughout it. ... This house, may it grow old unto distant time. ... May I receive in it the heavy tribute of kings of all quarters, yea of all mankind... Within it may my descendants forever rule. ...[1]

How could it be that the palace of Nebuchadnezzar, built to endure for many generations, fell into ruin, its mighty walls crushed, its foundation shattered, a few years after his death?

But we also have archaeological evidence. The ground about the foundation of the palace was excavated, and a wall of square stones was found, immense blocks held together by wooden clamps covered with asphalt. The structure stands in the ground water, on the rock formation in the depth, "the breast of the nether world." Every block in the third row above the ground water bears the inscription, "Nebuchadnezzar ... am I. The foundation of the Palace of Babylon I made with mountain blocks."[2] Not only did the blocks remain in their place for the two years following the death of Nebuchadnezzar, but even today they are in perfect order, over twenty-five hundred years after they were set and joined.

The archaeological data given here concerning the condition of the palace and the temple of Esagila do not accord with the accepted succession of the kings of Babylon. This is a most serious situation. In the contradiction brought to light here, on one side there are the following pieces of evidence: (1) the statement on the tablet British Museum 21946[3] that says on which day Nabopolassar died and on which day, soon thereafter, Nebuchadnezzar, summoned to return to Babylon, mounted the throne; (2) the tomb plates of the mother of King Nabonidus[4] that name Nergilissar (but not his son Labash-Marduk)

---

[1] *Ibid.*, Inscription »Nebuchadnezzar« XV.
[2] R. Koldewey: *Babylon*, p. 175.
[3] D. J. Wiseman: *Chronicles of Chaldean Kings*, p. 69.
[4] James B. Pritchard, ed.: *Ancient Near Eastern Texts Relating to the Old Testament* (Princeton University Press, 1950), pp. 311–12; James B. Pritchard, ed.: *The Ancient Near East, Supplementary Texts and Pictures Relating to the Old Testament* (Princeton University Press, 1969), pp. 560-62.

as following Nebuchadnezzar and his son Evil-Marduk, but do not name a Nergilissar or a Labash-Marduk before Nebuchadnezzar; (3) the throne statement of Nabonidus,[1] who does not enumerate the predecessors, but refers only to Nebuchadnezzar and his minor son Evil-Marduk, and to Nergilissar and his minor son Labash-Marduk; and, finally, (4) the record of Berosus,[2] which coincides all the way with the statement on the tomb plates of the mother of Nabonidus, with the exception that he places Labash-Marduk, son of Nergilissar, after him, and she does not.

Of these four bits of testimony, that on the British Museum tablet 21946 dates most probably from Persian time (-538 to -331). Berosus dates from post-Persian, or Hellenistic, times. The mother of Nabonidus, who was born under Assurbanipal and lived for a hundred and five years, on her self-composed eulogy in her ninety-fifth year, let Nabopolassar follow Assurbanipal, though we know the royal heir of Assurbanipal was Sin-shar-ishkun, who perished in his palace in Nineveh in -612, and then came Assuruballit – and against all three of them Nabopolassar successively carried on a protracted war. She refers to Nebuchadnezzar as coming after Nabopolassar without anybody reigning in between. The statement of Nabonidus that he was "the real executor of the wills of Nebuchadnezzar and Nergilissar, my royal predecessors," could be read either in descending (Nebuchadnezzar and then Nergilissar) or ascending fashion (Nergilissar and then Nebuchadnezzar). Since his mother does not mention Labash-Marduk after Nergilissar, as he does, it is Berosus who solves the question for modern historians, by letting the boy Labash-Marduk follow Nergilissar. Berosus presents Nabonidus as "one of the gang" and a drinking boon companion of the boy emperor. However, when Nabonidus was proclaimed king he was already advanced in years. Berosus, it seems, committed a mistake here; considering that he was writing after -300, and the events he was describing took place in the later part of the seventh century (death of Nabopolassar, and his being followed by Nebuchadnezzar returning from pursuing the beaten Egyptians), he must have relied on some earlier testimony. An interesting fact is that, in giving the reigning years of the succession of the Neo-Babylonian kings, Nabopolassar (twenty-one years), Nebuchadnezzar (forty-three years), Evil-Marduk (two years), Nergilissar (four years), Berosus' figures coincide, without de-

---

[1] Pritchard, ed.: *Ancient Near Eastern Texts*, p. 309.
[2] Flavius Josephus: *Against Apion*, I, 146-49.

viation, with the figures of Nabonidus' mother. Such exact correspondence of figures in two sources, some two hundred and fifty years apart, is unusual in archaeological literature. The commemorative plate of the mother of Nabonidus, found in Harran in 1906, was defective because of many broken signs, and the figures of royal reigns inserted in the published text were actually borrowed from Berosus. But then, in the second commemorative or tomb plate, found in 1956 and in perfect condition, the figures were all there and were the same as in Berosus. Upon reading the text, the thought must have arisen – is not perhaps the new plate a counterfeit or the product of scholarly forgery? Many inscriptions in cuneiform, when offered for sale, have been rejected by museums, recognized or assumed to be fakes. But in the case of Nabonidus' mother we can trace the report of the finding of the second commemorative stele, and the suspicion of forgery loses ground. Yet a certain wonder has persisted in scholarly circles since the discovery of the second plate: why should one person have two commemorative tablets, planned as funerary plates?

The enumerated testimonies for the order of kings of the Neo-Babylonian Empire, with Nebuchadnezzar following immediately upon Nabopolassar, can be safely reduced from four to two – Nabonidus does not discuss the throne sequence following Nabopolassar's death, and Berosus seems to have had the tablet of Nabonidus' mother as his main source. On the other hand, the existence of King Nergilissar after Nebuchadnezzar and Evil-Marduk is well established, first of all on the testimony of Nabonidus' mother.

In what follows, the other set of archaeological testimonies, which comes now to a judicial summation, will offer a case for the royal succession according to which, after Nabopolassar and before Nebuchadnezzar, another Nergilissar (in such a case Nergilissar I) reigned. If such evidence is strong, what should we think of the most direct statement of the British Museum tablet? We have, first, to counterweight the opposing statement and then look for a solution.

As earlier brought out, Nergilissar found the royal palace of Babylon in a most ruined state, and he rebuilt it and put in new foundations. Yet the foundations of the same palace were found in perfect shape when Koldewey[1] reached them, all the way to the rock, or, in Nebu-

---

[1] R. Koldewey: Das wiedererstehende Babylon.

chadnezzar's phrase, the "breast of the Netherworld." Theoretically, this argument can be disposed of by disagreeing with modern scholars, who make Nergilissar occupy the same palace as Nebuchadnezzar, yet no other palace, whose foundation could be ascribed to Nergilissar, was discovered, and why should he improve on a ruined palace if Nebuchadnezzar left him a magnificent palace on firm foundations? But any such argument could not be applied to the Esagila. There was only one Esagila. The temple of Esagila in Babylon was the apple of Nebuchadnezzar's eye; in his great building activity he paid to no other place so much attention nor spent so much effort nor lavished such munificence as on the Esagila. The foundations of Esagila, as built by Nebuchadnezzar with bricks carrying his name, are perfect even today, and should have been so in the days of his successors, a few years after his death. Here the archaeological evidence is uncompromising: Nergilissar must have written his building inscription before Nebuchadnezzar wrote his, and this means that he must have reigned *before,* not after, Nebuchadnezzar.

The third piece of evidence, also coming from Nergilissar's building inscriptions, is his reference to himself as a son of the king of Babylon, Bel-shum-ishkun – but if Nebuchadnezzar reigned for forty-three years in Babylon, and his son Evil-Marduk reigned for two years after him and before Nergilissar, the latter's claim is in complete conflict with the facts and dates; but it is easily compatible with the situation if he reigned following Nabopolassar and before Nebuchadnezzar. Moreover he called his father by the name similar to that used by the Greek authors for Nabopolassar.

The fourth piece of evidence, not yet discussed by us, is a tablet preserved in the British Museum (25124) describing a war waged by Nergilissar in his third year at the western confines of Asia Minor, on the border of Lydia.

> In that year from the pass leading to the city of Sallune as far as the boundary of the city of Ludu he burned with fire.[1]

The Nergilissar who reigned subsequent to Nebuchadnezzar must have mounted the throne after the Lydians and the Medes had agreed, whether in -615 or in -585, on the division of spheres of domination

---

[1] D. J. Wiseman: *Chronicles,* pp. 74-77, commentary on pp. 39-42. Wiseman's contention that the "Ludu" of the *Chronicle* is not Lydia but Pamphylia, under Lydian control, does not follow from the text.

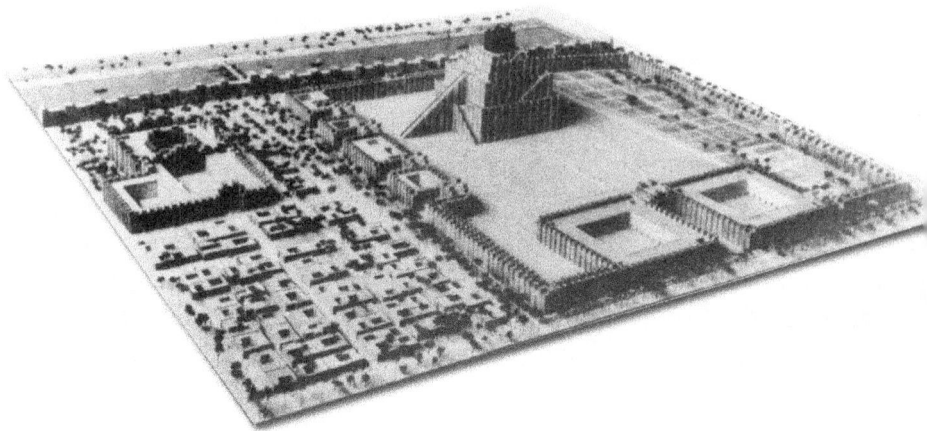

Figure 17: A reconstruction of the central area of Babylon at the time of Nebuchadnezzar. From *Ancient Near East in Pictures Relating to the Old Testament*, Princeton University Press (1950)

in Asia Minor – and there was no opportunity and no historical vrai-semblance for weak occupants of the Babylonian throne, successors of Nebuchadnezzar, to move across Asia Minor to the Lydian border. This campaign had in itself an element of surprise that greeted the historians who read the document.[1] But in the third year of Nergilissar, reigning before Nebuchadnezzar, a thrust toward Lydia is in harmony with the balance of power in Asia Minor at that time.

The evidence of one set of four testimonies is in conflict with the evidence of a second set of an equal number of testimonies. Some of the evidence on both sides of this summation has been shown to be circumstantial, or open to dispute. Yet there remain data that are irreconcilable as long as only the material we could muster from the Neo-Babylonian history was presented in the dispute.

With the knowledge that the Chaldean (Neo-Babylonian) dynasty of Babylon had its origin in the region of Boghazkoi in east central Anatolia, we have good reason to expect that a solution to an apparently unsolv-able problem will be found there, and even the reason for a purposeful disfiguring of history will be disclosed.

---

[1] *Ibid.*, p. 39: "The new Chronicle now gives us a very different picture of Neriglissar."

The Autobiography of
Nebuchadnezzar

Climbing the Throne

The autobiographical record of Hattusilis was prepared to be kept in a temple of Ishtar. It is a confession and justification of his behavior in coveting the imperial crown. The autobiography[1] covers the period of his life from childhood to his accession to the throne of the empire.

When a child, Hattusilis fell dangerously ill, and because of his feeble health he was thought to be doomed. His brother dreamed a dream in which Ishtar appeared and advised his father:

> The years which remain for Hattusil are only few. His health is poor. Give him to me: he shall be my priest, and he will return to health.

His father heeded the advice and gave "the small boy to the goddess in divine service." He grew up as a priest in the temple of Ishtar.

Already the beginning of the autobiography casts light on four or five facts we know about Nebuchadnezzar. All through his life he had a feeble constitution and the appearance of a dwarf. In the talmudic tradition he is called Nebuchadnezzar the Dwarf ("nanas").[2]

His childhood, spent in a temple, must have been responsible for Nebuchadnezzar's ecstatic religious character, which is clearly mirrored in his building inscriptions. All his life he called himself priest.

Nebuchadnezzar, the novice in the temple of Ishtar, remained her worshiper as king. When building Babylon he erected or restored and rebuilt the famous Gate of Ishtar, excavated at the site of the old Babylon.[3] "I built the gate of Ishtar of blue glazed bricks."[4] He also built and repaired many temples of Ishtar and memorialized his acts for future

---

[1] Götze: Mitteilungen, Vorderasiatisch-ägyptische Gesellschaft, XXIX (1925); and »Neue Bruchstücke zum grossen Texte des Hattusilis«, ibid., XXXIV, Heft 2 (1930).
[2] Sources in Ginzberg: Legends, VI, 422. Is his epithet "nanas" also an allusion to his being dedicated to Ishtar-Nana?
[3] R. Koldewey: Das Ischtar-Tor in Babylon (Leipzig, 1918).
[4] Langdon: Die Neubabylonischen Königsinschriften, 22.

generations in his building inscriptions. "I rebuilt ... Eanna, temple of Ishtar in Erech."[1] He called himself "regardful of the sacred places of Ninib and Ishtar."[2]

In other creeds Ishtar was called "Nana", "Nin-karrak", "Gula", and "Zarpanith". It was the planet Venus that was deified by all the Orient, in fact by all the ancient world. In his building inscriptions Nebuchadnezzar invoked the great goddess under her various names. He was grateful to her who had restored his health: "To Gula, the queen, who makes my body healthy," he built temples.

Hattusilis' autobiography, too, ascribed his recovery to the care of the goddess.

The boy remained in the temple apparently until the end of his father's life. When his father died – "when he became a god" – his brother Nergil became the "Great King"; Nergil made Hattusilis the chief of the army and also put him at the head of a part of the empire.

> AUTOBIOGRAPHY SEC. 4 My brother Nir-gal [Nergil] sat on the throne of his father, and I became before his face the commander of the army. ... My brother ... let me preside over the Upper Land, and I put the Upper Land under my rule.

The Upper Land was apparently either Assyria or some part of Anatolia; the Lower Land was Babylonia.

While still a lad, he led his troops against the enemies who invaded the country.

> AUTOBIOGRAPHY SEC. 5 My brother Nirgal used to send me into war. ... And whatever enemy land I faced I was victorious. ... I shall make a true memorial tablet about the lands I overcame when I was a youth.

Various districts rebelled against the Chaldean yoke and the lad on the Assyrian throne.

> AUTOBIOGRAPHY SEC. 6 All the lands of Gasgas, Pishukus, Ishupittas did rebel and took the strongholds. And the foe went over the river Massandas and pressed into the country.

In this chapter of the autobiography of Hattusilis again may be found some three or four allusions to events and circumstances described in the texts concerning Nebuchadnezzar. Berosus wrote in his lost *His-*

---

[1] Langdon: *Building Inscriptions of the Neo-Babylonian Empire.*
[2] *Ibid.*, p. 101.

tory of Chaldea, in a passage preserved verbatim by Josephus Flavius, that the king of Babylonia, on hearing of the defection of the provinces, "committed part of his army" to Nebuchadnezzar

> ... still in the prime of life, and sent him against the rebel Nebuchadnezzar engaged and defeated the latter in a pitched battle, and placed the district under Babylonian rule.[1]

In the first series of wars Nebuchadnezzar headed the army, although he was not king; in this, we see, Berosus was correct. For a chief of the army he was very young: this detail also is true. He subdued the rebellious provinces, and here again Berosus was correct. But in one detail Berosus and other later sources were wrong, and it is possible to check and correct it now, after more than two thousand years. It concerns the question of who sent Nebuchadnezzar against the rebels, his father or his brother. The matter of succession received special attention in a previous section. The event itself – the revolt of the provinces and its suppression – is truly depicted by Berosus, and is repeated at length in the autobiography:

> The Gasgas Lands rebelled. ... My brother Nirgal sent me, giving me but a small number of troops and charioteers. ... I met the foe ... and gave him battle. And Ishtar, my Lady, helped me, and I smote him. ... And this was the first act in the prime of manhood.

Both Hattusilis' autobiography and Berosus' writing about Nebuchadnezzar stress the extreme youth of the commander of the army. As soon as the youth was made governor of the Upper Land, even before he had earned his laurels in his first encounter with rebels, he met opposition in the person of the former ruler of that province.

> AUTOBIOGRAPHY SEC. 4 Before me it was governed by Sin-Uas, the son of Zidas. ... And Sin-Uas, the son of Zidas ... wished me evil. ... And accusations became loud against me. And my brother Nirgal set action against me. Ishtar, my Lady, appeared in a dream: "I shall trust thy care to a god. Be not afraid." And thanks to the Divinity I justified myself.

The proceeding in which Hattusilis was apparently charged with plotting to seize the throne marked a painful period in the life of the youth. But sufficient evidence was not produced, and the king ignored the admonitions of his father's adviser.

---

[1] Josephus: *Against Apion,* I, 135.

AUTOBIOGRAPHY SEC. 5 When my brother Nirgal obtained his insight of the matter, he gave me not the slightest punishment, and he took me again into his favor, and gave into my hands the army and the chariotry of the Hatti Land.

From the building inscriptions of Nebuchadnezzar (Inscription XVII) we know that he used this term for the land under his rule west of the Euphrates: "the princes of the Hatti land beyond the Euphrates to the west, over whom I exercised lordship."

Then came the time of his great and victorious battles. He was raised from governor of the Upper Land (either Assyria or a part of Anatolia) to king. The king of the Upper Land was subordinate to the Great King of Hatti, but it was the second most important position in the empire.

AUTOBIOGRAPHY SEC. 8 He made me king in Hakpissas.

Nergil also gave him a number of provinces to govern.

We have here the solution of the riddle as to why in the Second Book of Kings it is said that "Pharaoh-Necho king of Egypt went up against the king of Assyria to the river Euphrates," whereas in the parallel chapters of Second Chronicles reference is made to the "king of Babylon" or the "king of the Chaldees." At that time Nebuchadnezzar was still king of Assyria. In the autobiography there follows this passage:

AUTOBIOGRAPHY SEC. 9 It came to pass that my brother made war with Egypt. ... And I led for my brother the army and the charioteers against the land of Egypt.

The autobiography gives only a few lines to this campaign. Hattusilis promised to describe his wars on a special tablet; this has not yet been found, except for one mutilated fragment which is recognized[1] as narrating the story of the battle Hattusilis fought for his brother Nergil against Ramses II at Kadesh-Carchemish. For our purposes the short reference to that campaign suffices; the full story was told in the chapter dealing with the records of Ramses II concerning his wars with Kheta, and the material has already been contraposed to the biblical data on the war of Nebuchadnezzar against Egypt.

It is known[2] that Nebuchadnezzar, pursuing the beaten Egyptian army,

---

[1] D. D. Luckenbill: »Hittite Treaties and Letters«, *American Journal of Semitic Languages and Literatures,* XXXVII (April 1921), Document No. 7, pp. 192-93.

[2] Cf. Berosus in Josephus: *Against Apion,* I, 135ff.

came to the border of Egypt and then returned to Babylon. Actually the autobiography states:

> AUTOBIOGRAPHY SEC. 9 I returned from the land of Egypt and brought offerings to the Goddess.

Ramses II did not disclose that the army of Kheta, after the battle of Kadesh, pursued him through Syria and Palestine, but he did not conceal the fact that these provinces fell away after the battle: the biblical sources, too, substantiate this fact, here revealed by the autobiography.

It is frequently related that Nebuchadnezzar fought the battle on the field of Carchemish while he was still a prince but returned from the Egyptian frontier because of the urgency connected with the succession to the throne.[1] The truth appears to be that he returned because he was accused of coveting the throne of the empire; apparently he was called to give an explanation in the inquiry, which seemed to have been already settled. On his march through Syria and Palestine his behavior gave his adversaries new ground to accuse him of craving supreme power in the state. Head of the army and victor at Kadesh-Carchemish, conqueror of the Syrian and Palestinian provinces which only a few years before had been subjugated by Egypt, he seemed to have attained too much acclaim and power. But his return was necessitated by another reason too: he had to defend the Upper Land against an invasion that took place when the army moved into Syria.

> AUTOBIOGRAPHY SEC. 9 When Sin-Uas the son of Zidas saw the favor of Ishtar and also of my brother, he and his sons tried to bring imputations upon me. ...
> Hakpissas revolted, but I drove out the Gasgas people and subjugated it again.

Soon after his return he was called to answer the accusation and brought before his brother, the emperor. At the trial he reversed the roles and accused his accuser.

> AUTOBIOGRAPHY SEC. 10 Ishtar brought the case again into action.

He was able to prove religious wantonness in his adversary, and finally the emperor, his brother, decided in his favor and delivered Sin-Uas into the hands of Hattusilis.

---

[1] Cf. L. Delaporte: *Die Babylonier, Assyrer, Perser und Phöniker*, p. 288.

AUTOBIOGRAPHY SEC. 10 Because he was a royal prince, and also an old man, I did nothing to him. ... His sons I sent to Alasia (Cyprus).

In a variant, which preserves the same portion of the autobiography, it is written:

And because Arma was a relative and also a very old man, and also sick, I let him be.[1]

Obviously Sin-Uas and Arma were two names for the same person. Soon we shall see whether this old relative was right or wrong when he warned the emperor against his young brother. Meanwhile, Hattusilis bided his time. The day would come when he would sum up his life to date, stating:

AUTOBIOGRAPHY SEC. 13 I became the Great King. Then Ishtar, my Lady, gave unto me for trial my ill-wishers, my begrudgers and my opponents. Some died by arms, the others died on the day which was fixed for them.[2]

But we are ahead of the story. We shall read that by arms in the field a son of Arma died; Arma himself was apparently put to death.

Hattusilis' ambition, the opposition he met in Arma, the trial, his vindication, and the ultimate victory over his opponent occupy a prominent place in the autobiography, which covers the period to the end of Hattusilis' struggle for the crown of the Great King.

That Nebuchadnezzar was anxious not to let his father's crown rest with a brother of his is common knowledge in history as it has been written over the centuries. The autobiography of Hattusilis sheds a clear light on all phases of the drama.

It is interesting to note that talmudic tradition as well as the Fathers of the Church have retained some memory of the personality of Arma, a magnificent old prince, a relative of Nebuchadnezzar, his antagonist. He lost his life at the hand of Nebuchadnezzar after years of dispute and strife. His name is handed down as Hiram, king of Tyre and Sidon. This name was hereditary among the kings of Tyre and Sidon.

Hiram "was a contemporary of Nebuchadnezzar, and in many respects resembled him. ... The end of this proud king was that he was conquered by Nebuchadnezzar, deprived of his throne, and made to suffer a cruel death."[3] According to the *Midrash*, Hiram was a very old

---

[1] Götze: *Mitteilungen, Vorderasiatisch-ägyptische Gesellschaft,* XXXIV, Heft 2 (1930), 19.
[2] *Ibid.*
[3] Ginzberg: *Legends,* IV, 335-36.

man[1] and was slain "by Nebuchadnezzar, who was closely related to him."[2]

The next passages in the autobiography are preserved in damaged condition. Then these words follow:

> AUTOBIOGRAPHY SEC. 10 My [deceased] brother had no grown-up son. I took Urhi-Tesupa and put him on the throne of his father in the city of Hatti.

This means that Nergil (Nergilissar) died and that his minor son was placed on the throne of the empire. It is this situation which is described by Berosus: "His son ... a mere boy, occupied it [the throne]. ..."[3] In the text of Hattusilis' autobiography the boy is also called Labash.[4]

King Nabonidus wrote: "When the days were fulfilled, and he [Nergilissar] met his fate, Labash-Marduk, his young son, who did not understand how to rule, sat on the throne, against the will of the gods."[5]

In his autobiography Hattusilis said that out of respect for the memory of his brother he crowned the latter's son. Probably Nergil had sworn his brother to be faithful to his son. Such an oath, accompanied by many curses in the event of violation, was often attached to agreements of that time; the treaty with Ramses II had a special oath-and-curse clause; in other documents of Boghazkoi a "Great King of Hatti" often demanded from his vassal kings a vow of allegiance and protection for his heir, invoking the curse of a thousand gods. Berosus wrote that after nine months the reign of the boy came to a violent end.

Judging from the text of the autobiography, probably only some months passed before Hattusilis refused obedience to his nephew. The period of his loyalty to his brother and to his brother's son is given as seven years, the larger part of which was under his brother's rule. Hattusilis found fault with his nephew and accused him of curtailing the power vested in him, Hattusilis. He wrote a letter challenging the boy emperor.

---

[1] S. G. Bernstein: *König Nebucadnezar von Babel in der jüdischen Tradition* (Berlin, 1907), p. 24.

[2] Ginzberg: *Legends,* VI, 424ff. Hiram was related to Nebuchadnezzar through his marriage to Nabopolassar's widow. *Midrash Rabba* on Leviticus 18.

[3] Josephus: *Against Apion,* I, 20.

[4] Götze: *Mitteilungen, Vorderasiatisch-ägyptische Gesellschaft,* XXXIV, Heft 2 (1930), 33 (IV, 62). The Babylonian language has the sounds "m" and "b" ("v") expressed by the same character; thus "Yaman" can be read "Yavan" (Greece), or "Amel-Marduk" (son of Nebuchadnezzar) as "Awel (Evil)-Marduk".

[5] Messerschmidt: *Mitteilungen, Vorderasiatisch-ägyptische Gesellschaft* I (1856), 29; also Langdon: *Die Neubabylonische Königsinschriften,* p. 277.

A letter of Hattusilis addressed to the king of Karaduniash (Babylon) is preserved in the Boghazkoi archives. "The latter, a minor, seems to be under the thumb of an old grand vizier who is not inclined to be friendly" toward Hattusilis.[1] The indication that the minor was at Babylon is, of course, important.

In this letter Hattusilis wrote: "When thy father went to his fate, as a brother I mourned the death of thy father."[2] At that time he promised loyalty: because of love for his brother, the son of his brother he would guard. Had they not been faithful brothers? "When the king of Egypt and I were angry," he had written to the father of his present addressee: "'The king of Egypt has made war against me.' And thy father replied, '... I will go with thee.'" Further on in the letter he calls his brother Muatalli (Nergil)[3] by his name. This letter confirms the fact that Nergil (Nergilissar), brother of Hattusilis, was king of Babylon.

Hattusilis proceeded: "But Itti-Marduk-Balatu (the vizier), whom the gods have allowed to grow old beyond limits, in whose mouth evil words have no end, thus he spoke: 'Thus dost not address us as brothers, as thy slaves thou art subjecting us.'"

The letter was a challenge to the boy emperor in Babylon. This letter, mentioned in the autobiography, manifests an open rift with the boy emperor.

Feeling the necessity of justification, Hattusilis wrote:

AUTOBIOGRAPHY SEC. 11 If anyone should ask: Why didst thou make him king, and why writest thou him now about thy falling off? – so it will be replied: He should not have started a quarrel with me.

In the next sentence Hattusilis revealed that the old prince Arma was right in his accusations:

AUTOBIOGRAPHY SEC. 12 Because already before, Ishtar, my Lady, did promise me the King's power; Ishtar, my Lady, appeared at that time to my wife in a dream:

I will help thy spouse. The whole Hattusas (Hatti) I will convert to the side of thy husband. Because I esteem him, at no time did I give him an evil trial, [neither committed him] to an evil god. And now again I shall raise him. ..."

---

[1] Luckenbill: *American Journal of Semitic Languages and Literatures,* XXXVII (1921), Document No. 13.

[2] *Ibid.* The translator wrote: "I fail to grasp the meaning of a number of sections of the correspondence." The addition "as (though we had been) brothers," in parentheses, seems unnecessary.

[3] *Ibid.,* p. 204.

And Ishtar, my Lady, cared for me, and what she told, did happen. And Ishtar, my Lady, showed her protection in full measure.

During his years as commander of the army, when earning the laurels of victory over Ramses II, he had secured the support of the army for the days of dispute to come. The army and the land followed him. And again in a dream apparition Ishtar said:

> AUTOBIOGRAPHY SEC. 12   The lands of Hatti, in their entirety, I, Ishtar, turned to Hattusil.

He took hold of the boy whose throne was in Babylon (Karaduniash); "out of respect for my brother's memory" he did not hurt him: "I led him like a prisoner with me." Here again Hattusilis refers to Nergil, the father of Labash, as to his brother. He placed the boy "in Nuhasse," probably in Baalbek. But Hattusilis (Nebuchadnezzar) was not the man to sleep quietly while he left the legitimate heir to the throne nearby. Hattusilis had to suppress his feelings of gratitude toward his brother, who had shown him affection and had trusted him so much. He had again to find fault with the boy. Nuhasse was too near; a coup d'état could set the boy free.

> AUTOBIOGRAPHY SEC. 12   And as I found out the situation, I took hold of him and sent him to the seaside.

It was either some island in the Persian Gulf or the maritime region of the Black Sea.

The conjecture of some scholars that the boy king received asylum in Egypt does not seem to be based on sufficient grounds. Now Hattusilis could write his apotheosis:

> AUTOBIOGRAPHY SEC. 13   I was a prince and I became a Great Mesedi, I was a Great Mesedi and I became the king of Hakpissas, I was the king of Hakpissas and I became the Great King.

He condemned all his opponents to death. It is not stated whether the boy king was also killed. "Who entered the prison never left it alive during the lifetime of Nebuchadnezzar," Hebrew tradition relates.[1]

In his building inscriptions Nebuchadnezzar wrote: "The kings of the remote district which is by the upper sea and ...the region by the nether sea, the princes of the land of Hatti beyond the Euphrates to the west, over whom I exercised lordship ..."[2]

---

[1] Bernstein: *König Nebucadnezar von Babel in der jüdischen Tradition*, p. 32.
[2] Langdon: *Building Inscriptions of the Neo-Babylonian Empire*, Inscription »Nebuchadnezzar«, XVII.

The empire, which had grown under his father and brother, acquired under his rule such power as never before. "I received tributes, more than my father and ancestors," stands in the autobiography. All the kings paid respect to him, and "he who behaved like an enemy, him I conquered. To the countries of Hatti I added region after region." The reference to the "Hatti lands" is the same in the texts originating from Boghazkoi and from Babylon.

These concluding sentences of the autobiography are no vain boast: Nebuchadnezzar in truth brought the Chaldean Empire to a greatness never before attained by any other historical state. Tribute was paid, enemies were conquered; Jerusalem testified to that.

The war between Hattusilis and Ramses II is narrated in detail in the Egyptian sources, and everything in the previous chapters that serves to identify Ramses II with Pharaoh Necho serves also to identify Nebuchadnezzar with Hattusilis, and this in addition to the material of the present chapter. The course of the battle at Kadesh-Carchemish, the numerous events of the nineteen years' war in their precise succession, and the treaty with its clauses have a bearing on both identifications. A subsequent chapter will tell of peaceful relations between Nebuchadnezzar and Ramses.

The Personality of Nebuchadnezzar

The spirit in which the autobiography of Hattusilis is written is that of a man arrogant toward others, unscrupulous, treacherous, thirsty for power, but humble before his deity, full of fear, ecclesiastic, looking for omens, and paying with psalmody and sacerdotal offerings for the guidance and protection of his heavenly mistress. He felt himself chosen to be king over many kings. In ecstatic devotion he conjured up apparitions and heeded his dreams. He did not call himself "Sun," as did his father and grandfather: "And when thou, vassal king so-and-so, will guard the Sun, the Sun will guard thee"; nor did he adopt the style of the Egyptian kings, who deified themselves in bombastic terms in the opening and concluding passages of their annals and decrees. It may be said that the autobiography of Hattusilis has no parallel in the cuneiform or hieroglyphic writings of any other king except the Baby-

Ionian inscriptions of Nebuchadnezzar. Here and there one finds the same spirit of haughtiness and the same humble attitude toward the protecting deity, a mystical obsession, a fear of magic spells, a preoccupation with dreams, an ecstatic chanting. If there were no proof that Hattusilis and Nebuchadnezzar were the same person, the similarity of their spiritual makeup would appear to be most singular.

In the autobiography it is related that the Heavenly Queen appeared in a dream to warn that the boy was approaching death and asked that he should be dedicated to her "and he will become well."

Nebuchadnezzar thanked the Heavenly Queen "who makes my body healthy."[1] He wrote: "Beloved Lady who watches over my life and gives me good visions ... a token to drive away sickness."[2] "My Lady took me by my hand and was my patron," wrote Hattusilis repeatedly.[3] "Beloved Lady, protectress of my soul, Grand Mistress," "Patron of life, my Lady, who favors my soul,"[4] wrote Nebuchadnezzar. "My Lady kept guard and protection over my head permanently," "My Lady saved me on every occasion," wrote Hattusilis.[5] "When it was ill with me and I was sick; I saw clearly the vision of the Goddess' action." "The Goddess, my Lady, on all and every occasion holds me by her hand." The goddess appeared on days of trial to encourage Hattusilis, "Don't be afraid," and again she appeared in a dream to prophesy Hattusilis' success in the struggle for the crown.

"My beloved Mistress who watches over my life and gives me good visions," wrote Nebuchadnezzar.[6] "Make clear my visions," he asked again.[7] "In fear without ceasing,"[8] "I was tremblingly obedient,"[9] Nebuchadnezzar wrote in the same spirit in which he composed his autobiography.

In his later years Nebuchadnezzar showed profound devotion to the father-god Marduk; in middle age to the god Nebo;[10] and, as we see here, in his younger years to the "Mother Compassionate."[11] But nei-

---

[1] Langdon: *Building Inscriptions of the Neo-Babylonian Empire*, p. 129.
[2] *Ibid.*, p. 67.
[3] Götze: *Mitteilungen, Vorderasiatisch-ägyptische Gesellschaft*, XXIX, 3; Sec. 3, p. 9.
[4] Langdon: op. cit., p. 107.
[5] Götze: op. cit., p. 11.
[6] Langdon: op. cit., p. 67.
[7] *Ibid.*, p. 69.
[8] *Ibid.*, p. 67.
[9] *Ibid.*, p. 103.
[10] *Ibid.*, pp. 17, 22.
[11] *Ibid.*, p. 131; see p. 77.

ther was he faithful to his gods. An illness, a story of some wondrous healing, led him to seek another deity; the story of Daniel, and that told by Egyptian priests, which will be cited below, are illustrations. Even the very god or goddess who was helpless to cure in one temple might be more powerful and benevolent in another holy place. The favors of Ishtar of Agade, Ishtar of Arbela, Ishtar of Uruk, the favors of Gula, of Nana, were solicited and repaid by sacrifices, by repairing their buildings, by religious ceremonies, by money, by prayers and liturgies, by prostration, by magic.

The feeling of being guided time and again gave way to terror, and the traits of a paranoiac personality are revealed alike by the autobiography, by the "building inscriptions," and by the Scriptures.

Prayers for exorcising evil spirits from the royal palace were found among the Boghazkoi texts. "They show that the Hittites, like the Babylonians, used [wax and clay] statuettes representing dogs to ward off evil demons."[1]

The elder daughter of Hattusilis became mentally ill, and Hattusilis wrote a prayer: "If thou, O god, my lord, wish to do something evil to my elder daughter, then do it to this adorned figure of a lady, and turn thy face in kindness to my elder daughter and cure her of this sickness."[2] He offered fat animals to the evil spirit that entered his daughter.

Talmudic sources say that a daughter of Nebuchadnezzar, being mentally ill, consulted two false prophets, who gave her wrong advice, suggesting sexual intercourse with themselves: they were put to death by Nebuchadnezzar.[3]

In Egyptian literature there is preserved the story of the mental sickness of a daughter of a foreign king (probably Hattusilis). A stele (called the Bentresh stele), inscribed presumably about eight to nine hundred years after Ramses II, during the Persian age in Egypt,[4] records the

---

[1] J. Friedrich: »Aus dem hethitischen Schrifttum«, II, *Der Alte Orient,* XXV, 13.

[2] *Ibid.,* »Gebet der Gasehulijawiasch«.

[3] *Tractate Sanhedrin* 93a; Origen: *Epist. ad Africanum;* Jerome on Jeremiah 29.

[4] A. Erman: »Die Bentresh Stele«, *Zeitschrift für ägyptische Sprache und Altertumskunde* XXI (1883), 54ff, thought that the stele originated in the late pharaonic period. J. Wilson in Pritchard, ed.: *Ancient Near Eastern Texts,* p. 29, relates the stele to the Persian or Greek period. The stele, Louvre C 284, actually speaks of the land of Bakhtan, and some scholars have presumed that Bakhtan is Bactria (e.g., Constant de Wit: »Het Land Bachtan in de Bentresjstele«, *Handeligen van het XVIIIe Vlaamse Filologencongres* (Gent, 1949), pp. 80-88). It may be that Babylonia is meant. It is generally agreed that the king of Bakhtan was in fact the king of Hatti, Hattusilis. The name given to the daughter of the king of Bakhtan

miracle of a healing of the mentally ill Princess Bentresh, the elder daughter of the king of "Bakhtan." The priests of Khonsu in Egypt ascribed this healing to their god. The story took place in the time when Pharaoh Ramses II (Usermare-Setepnere), after the conclusion of the long war, was maintaining peaceful relations with the "chief of Hatti."

It was not explained why the priests of Khonsu, well versed in the art of writing, should have handed down the story orally for so many centuries before they wrote it down. But there is no real difficulty here. Between the end of Ramses' reign and the Persian conquest of Egypt only decades elapsed, not centuries.

The fact that Hattusilis wrote a spell to pacify the evil spirit that had entered his daughter lends credibility to the story written by the Egyptian priests. According to the stele of the priests of Khonsu, when a daughter of the king of "Bakhtan" became ill, "possessed of spirits," a physician was sent from Egypt, but he found himself unable to contend with him. The image of the god Khonsu was then brought from Egypt that she might become well immediately," and the spirit left her. The king honored the evil spirit with a farewell feast. He decided to keep the wonderful image in his land, and delayed sending it back for more than three years.

Then, the Bentresh stele narrates, "while the king was sleeping on his bed, he saw this god coming to him, outside of his shrine; he was a falcon of gold, and he flew (up) to the sky and (off) to Egypt. [The king] awoke in a panic."[1] Terrified by the dream, he ordered the priests of Khonsu to depart with the chariots of Khonsu.

The incident of a king awakening in a panic is found twice in another literary work, also set down in writing in the Persian or early Greek time in Babylonia – the Book of Daniel. Both times it refers to the king of the Chaldeans, Nebuchadnezzar.

"Nebuchadnezzar dreamed dreams, wherewith his spirit was troubled, and his sleep brake from him" (Daniel 2:1).

Nebuchadnezzar attached exceedingly great importance to his dreams, and the second and fourth chapters of the Book of Daniel bear witness

---

(cont'd) whom Ramses II took for his chief wife (Nefru-Re) is the same as that of the daughter of Hattusilis whom Ramses married in his thirty-fourth year (see below, section »Nebuchadnezzar Visits Ramses II«).

[1] J. Wilson: »The Legend of a Possessed Princess« in Pritchard, ed.: *Ancient Near Eastern Texts*, pp. 29-31. Cf. G. Lefebvre: *Romans et contes de l'époque pharaonique* (Paris, 1949), pp. 221-232.

to this.[1] Even in a decree, according to the Book of Daniel (4:5), he wrote: "I saw a dream which made me afraid, and the thoughts upon my bed and the visions of my head troubled me."

Tortured by dreams, he used to consult "the magicians, and the astrologers, and the sorcerers" and "was troubled to know the dream" (Daniel 2:2-3).

Although frightened by dreams, Hattusilis nevertheless conjured up visions. In his younger years the visions of Ishtar appearing to him and to his wife in dreams predicted good fortune for him.

The inscription in the sun temple in Sippar, built by Nebuchadnezzar, reads: "Thou, O Shamash, in vision and dream answer me right."[2]

Superstitious rather than religious, he would give praise and offer worship to the most antagonistic deities, and in this he denied them all. He built an "image of gold" and "set it up in the plain of Dura" (Daniel 3:1), and was converted to praising the "high God" of Daniel (Daniel 4:2), and kept in his land the statue of the Egyptian deity Khonsu.

The man in whose lifetime nobody dared to smile[3] was himself a defenseless prey to nightmares. The evil spirit was drawing near him. An experienced psychiatrist may recognize in the autobiography of Hattusilis the schizothymic personality that may easily develop into a paranoid schizophrene.

Nebuchadnezzar's illness, dissimulated for a long time by his split personality, finally broke through. He could no longer hide his feeling of alienation and asked: "Is not this great Babylon, that I have built?" (Daniel 4:30).

> DANIEL 4:33 ... and he was driven from men, and did eat grass as oxen, and his body was wet with the dew of heaven, till his hairs were grown like eagles' feathers, and his nails like birds' claws.

For about seven years Nebuchadnezzar suffered from this mental disorder and was unable to rule the country or to take care of himself.

This scriptural narrative of the mental illness of Nebuchadnezzar bears all the signs of veracity.

---

[1] Dougherty ascribes an early origin to the Book of Daniel, especially to the fifth chapter. "The view that the fifth chapter of Daniel originated in the Maccabaean age is discredited. ... A narrative characterized by such an accurate historical perspective as Daniel 5 ought to be entitled to a place much nearer in time to the reliable documents which belong to the general epoch with which it deals." Dougherty: *Nabonidus and Belshazzar,* p. 200, note.

[2] H. Winckler: *Inschriften Nebukhadnezar's,* Keilinschriftliche Bibliothek, III, 2 (1890), p. 65. Langdon: *Building Inscriptions,* p. 99.

[3] *The Babylonian Talmud, Tractate Shabbat* 149b.

Nebuchadnezzar was unquestionably a man of great ability. A gifted military leader, he introduced new weapons, new tactics of quick movement and lightning attacks; a shrewd politician, he knew how to weaken the spirit of the nations with whom he was at war, destroying their unity in order to undermine their resistance (Book of Jeremiah). He gave full attention to the productive capacity of his war industry, and in each country that came under his domination his first step was to remove to Babylon all the skilled workers, artisans, and smiths. He transferred whole populations of defeated countries from their homes to faraway lands, hurriedly and with total disregard for human suffering. He was utterly cruel to his victims; he kept many in prison, mutilated many, and was ingenious in his atrocities. He patronized science and especially sponsored the education of youth (Daniel 1:4). He was superstitious and conferred with astrologers. He indulged in perverted sexual practices,[1] suffered from a split personality, was harassed by nightmares, and finally sank into insanity. After a number of years he regained his mental balance, only to see his daughter overcome with a similar affliction.[2]

When building his capital, "Babylon the Great," he implored the god Marduk that from there his descendants should rule mankind forever and ever.

A generation later, on a night of feasting and visions, the empire of Nebuchadnezzar disappeared.

Changing History

From the very beginning of the reign of Nergil (Nergilissar), his younger brother Hattusilis (Nebuchadnezzar) was suspected of coveting the crown of the empire. After the battle of Carchemish the campaign was interrupted because Hattusilis was called to exonerate himself. When Nergil died after a reign of a few years, he was survived by a child, a son, Labash, who was crowned emperor of Babylon. But soon Hattusilis revolted against his nephew, the boy emperor, and banished him. Shortly thereafter the boy seems to have been killed. The rule of Nergil and his young heir together lasted seven years.

---

[1] See *Tractate Shabbat* 149b and Jerome, Commentary on Habakkuk 2:16, concerning Nebuchadnezzar's practice of pederasty.
[2] The Bentresh stele.

This sequence of events is revealed in the autobiography of Hattusilis (Nebuchadnezzar).

It appears that Nebuchadnezzar, after having mounted the throne, was plagued by the thought that his achievement had been effected through treachery and breach of a solemn oath. The oath imposed on him by his brother, the king, to keep faith with the latter's minor son and heir was accompanied, as in similar cases of that time, by a string of self-imposing curses in case of a breach of the oath. Gods were invoked one by one, each of them being invited to act in wrath against the oath-taker in case of a breach. Most horrible punishments were pronounced to keep the swearing man from faithlessness, especially from faithlessness against one deceased who, being now in communion with the gods, could urge them to mete out punishment to the oath-breaker who had solemnly invoked their names as a guarantee against such base action.

To justify himself before his subjects and to be able to live with his own conscience, Nebuchadnezzar accused his nephew of the very thing of which he was guilty: treachery. The king could deceive his subjects, or members of the royal houses abroad, or even the historians; but he could not deceive himself. Even if he could talk himself into believing in his accusations against his nephew, the guilt feeling that seeped from the frightened subconscious mind might have contributed to his mental illness. He did not honor his oath of loyalty. Thus the throne was erected on a shaky foundation as far as the internal security of the king was concerned.

As years passed by, a desire grew in Nebuchadnezzar (Hattusilis) to obliterate the past and to have it appear that he was, from the beginning, a legitimate heir to the throne of his father, Nabopolassar, and that Nergilissar, his elder brother, who followed their father and then died while king, and Labash-Marduk, the boy son of Nergilissar, whom Nebuchadnezzar removed from the throne, were not rightful kings. Adulterating history, Nebuchadnezzar claimed that his reign followed that of his father, actually that he was crowned as soon as his father died. Dynastic histories know quite a few such "changes"; kings, with the loss of the throne, often lose also their place in the history of their nations.

In Egyptian history, Akhnaton and the epigoni of the Eighteenth Dynasty (Tutankhamen included) were later omitted from the dynastic lists.

Nebuchadnezzar changed the dynastic order and the history of the years following the death of his father – he eliminated his brother and brother's son as kings preceding his own reign as if they were illegitimate occupants of the throne. Documents were composed in which he was again and again called "first-born," though he was not. Doing so, he could find justification in the oriental custom according to which "the father had the right to disregard the law of primogeniture and choose the son to be designated 'first-born.'"[1] This practice, known from literary evidence in the archives of Ugarit and Nuzi, is familiar also from the patriarchal age of the Israelites: Abraham annulled Ishmael's primogeniture on the birth of Isaac, and Jacob chose Joseph instead of Reuben, and Ephraim instead of Joseph's eldest son Manasseh.[2] But Nabopolassar did not elect Nebuchadnezzar over Nergilissar – the primogeniture was usurped when the father was no longer alive.

Sennacherib did not need to claim that he was the first-born of Sargon, nor Esarhaddon that he was the first-born of Sennacherib, which he was not; Esarhaddon killed his brothers, who were parricides, and he needed neither justification nor concealment of the facts; Assurbanipal had no need to stress his being the first-born of Esarhaddon, though he carried on a war against his brother, Shamash-shum-ukin, king of Babylon: in this war neither of them insisted on his first-born rights, the domain having been divided between them by their father in his will. But Nebuchadnezzar continuously stressed his being the first-born and, therefore, the rightful successor to the throne of the Babylonian Empire. He had to falsify history in order to validate his claim to a rightful succession to the throne.[3]

Nebuchadnezzar claimed to have been first-born, and the immediate successor of Nabopolassar. This deceit succeeded and historians took the statement for truth; but the very fact of Nebuchadnezzar's stressing his being the "first-born" and therefore a rightful heir to the throne should raise suspicion.

---

[1] D. Wiseman: "Alalakh" in *Archaeology and Old Testament Study* (Oxford, 1967), p. 127.
[2] Genesis 21:10ff; 48:14, 22; 48:13; 49:3ff; cf. I Chronicles 5:1ff.
[3] Even the one tablet inscribed in the name of Nabopolassar, in which he refers to Nebuchadnezzar as to his first-born, may not be genuine; no other such references to a son as a "first-born" are known from the royal inscriptions of Assyrian and Babylonian houses.

His version of his accession has him returning from the pursuit of the Egyptian army because he received the news that his father had died; actually he returned to Babylon from the border of Egypt because he was summoned by his brother, who got the news that Nebuchadnezzar in his march across Syria and Palestine was behaving as if he were the emperor.

The historians of subsequent generations – the composer of the Babylonian Chronicle who lived in the Persian period (-538 to -332) and Berosus who lived at the beginning of the Hellenistic time – were misled. Trusting in the official government source dating from Nebuchadnezzar's long reign, they accepted his version of history.

Thus Nebuchadnezzar not only removed his brother's son from the throne and then banned him and, probably, murdered him but also eradicated both of them from their places in history.

The events in their proper order are so momentous that another look at them is justified.

Hattusilis reached the throne of the empire and kept the scepter securely in his grip. In the lifetime of his brother who trusted him so much and even in the lifetime of his nephew – better to say in the few short years of his nephew on the throne – Hattusilis never raised, not even in his own mind, the question of the legitimacy of his nephew's or his brother's succession as emperors. He must have known his own ambitions when young in years: taken out of a temple where he grew up as a novice, he showed his military prowess; his aspirations were recognized through his behavior when in Syria and Palestine; equally endowed to stand a trial and meet his accusers, he turned the scales of justice, was grateful to his brother – and to Ishtar, his protectress – but never questioned the legitimacy of his brother's being the supreme arbiter. And later, when the brother, still in his young years, was gone (and we will never know whether there was foul play[1]), Hattusilis praised himself that he, in loyalty to his brother, had placed the latter's son, a minor, on the throne of the empire – still raising no argument as to the legitimacy of the nephew's rights to the throne.

Next, he wished to present the story of the wars of the past as if he had been an ally of his now deceased brother in the campaign in which

---

[1] G. Bruno Meissner: »Die Beziehungen Ägyptens zum Hattireiche nach hattischen Quellen«, *Zeitschrift der Deutschen Morgenländischen Gesellschaft,* 72 (1918) p. 42.

the Chaldean (Babylonians) opposed the pharaoh of Egypt. He wrote to his nephew in Babylon:

> When the king of Egypt and I were angry, to thy father ... I wrote: "[The king of Egypt] has made war against me." And thy father replied as follows: "[As–] went against the king of Egypt, so will I go with thee – I will go. ..."[1]

Actually, as we learned from his own autobiography, he was put by his brother Nergil at the head of the army that fought the pharaoh, but he was not an ally. Here he palpably lied to his nephew.

Before long he started a campaign of degradation of the boy emperor, and though only a few missives of the exchange have survived, there must have been truth in the words of the old vizier who wrote from Babylon:

> Thou dost not address us as brothers, as thy slaves thou art subjecting us.[2]

Then came the baleful words in the autobiography (Sec. 11):

> If anyone should ask: Why didst thou make him king, and why writest thou him now about thy falling off? – so it will be replied: He should not have started a quarrel with me.

Of course the boy king, the son of his brother, did not start a quarrel, for he was not in a position to do so. Soon he was banned from Babylon to some fortified place in Syria – it could have been Tell Nebi-Mend (the ancient Riblah); it could have been Palmyra, or Baalbek. But he did not remain long there. Hattusilis himself wrote: "I took hold of him and sent him to the seaside." And he raised the question of the legitimacy of his nephew's claim to the throne. Labash-Marduk, called also Urhi-Teshub, whom he removed from the throne, had no legitimate rights. He was born to his brother Nergil not by his chief wife but by a secondary wife.[3]

The son of Nergil was not only proclaimed to have been an illegitimate son, his reign unlawful – he was immured in prison, or already dispatched from this life.

Next Hattusilis raised the question of the legitimacy of his late brother Nergil's occupation of the throne. In a treaty with a king of Syria

---

[1] D. D. Luckenbill: »Hittite Treaties and Letters«, *American Journal of Semitic Languages and Literatures,* 37 (1921), p. 202.
[2] *Ibid.,* p. 201.
[3] Autobiography, III:41. The expression used by Hattusilis is "son of a concubine."

(Amurru), years after his brother Nergil's death, he wrote that, upon the death of their father, "Muwatalli (Nergil), my brother, seized the royal throne."[1] By saying so, Hattusilis clearly intended to convey the impression that his brother occupied the throne not by right but by an illegal act of seizure, and thus was a usurper. Of himself, Hattusilis wrote: "When Nergal had snatched the great king to his fate,[2] I, Hattushili, sat on the throne of my father"[3] Here Hattusilis makes a clear distinction, by way of phrasing, between the usurpatory reign of his brother and his own legitimate mounting the throne. In addition, he not only omits to mention the reign of his nephew[4] but clearly refers to himself as a successor to his father, not his brother or nephew.

As testimony we have only fragments of clay that have survived many centuries, even millennia, but they carry with them the almost complete story of a dynastic crime. To cover up this crime, Nebuchadnezzar forged history.

At last we know which of the two sets of evidence for and against Nebuchadnezzar's mounting the throne upon Nabopolassar's death tips the scales. In Boghazkoi, the old capital of the Chaldean kingdom, we have found the answer in a confession written by the culprit himself – in his autobiography and in his letters and treaties. Naturally, proclaiming his brother Nergilissar and his nephew Labash-Marduk to have been unlawful occupants of the throne was part of the scheme not only to deprive the lawful king of his throne and freedom but also to disfigure history. He succeeded in both.

After the battle of Carchemish he was called to Babylon from pursuit of Ramses II (Pharaoh Necho) not because of the death of his father – Nabopolassar had already been dead for some time – but because his own behavior in Syria-Palestine made him suspect of striving for imperial power: he acted as if he were already the emperor. In years to come it would become a state crime to refer to Nergilissar and Labash-

---

[1] Luckenbill: op. cit., p. 198.
[2] Of this expression Meissner (op. cit., p. 42) comments: "Whether a violent death can be assumed from this fact alone is not clear to me."
[3] Luckenbill: op. cit., p.198.
[4] That Hattusilis counted the years of his nephew as his own has already been concluded by H. G. Güterbock. Cf. Ph. H. J. Houwink Ten Cate: »The Early and Late Phases of Urhi-Tesbub's Career«, in Anatolian Studies Presented to Hans Gustav Güterbock (Istanbul, 1974), p. 137, note 49. J. D. Schmidt draws attention to the fact that in the treaty that Hattusilis concluded with Egypt the reign of his nephew "is completely ignored." Ramesses II (Baltimore, 1973), p. 125.

Marduk as his legal predecessors. They were not permitted to be referred to as former kings. His own reign has been reported as of various durations – forty, forty-three, forty-five or more, up to forty-eight years. In rabbinical sources, as well as in medieval Arabic ones, the length of the reign of Nebuchadnezzar is given usually as forty, but also, equally consistently, as forty-five years.[1] The true duration of Nebuchadnezzar's reign, given in many sources in varying figures, can be clarified if it is understood that some calculations start counting from the time Nebuchadnezzar occupied the throne of the empire, some count from the death of his brother, some from his occupying the position of the vice-king of Assyria, and some from the death of their father. The latter was the figure he preferred on documents, as we shall see, in the later part of his reign.

The depersonification of Nergilissar and his son that went on for several decades of Nebuchadnezzar's reign must have become so ingrained that Nabonidus' mother omitted to mention them on her votive plate.

It is quite possible that the usurper of the throne after Evil-Marduk, son of Nebuchadnezzar, called himself purposely Nergilissar, the name of the elder brother of Nebuchadnezzar. In those times the mysticism, necromancy, and beliefs in resurrection or reincarnation were so strong that several would-be usurpers maintained that they were reincarnations of Nebuchadnezzar, and claimed his throne, one such Nebuchadnezzar having started a movement in -522 upon the death of Cambyses.[2]

It is possible that Nergilissar II called his son "Labash-Marduk" by the name of the son of Nergilissar I. But as I said earlier, Nabonidus' mother did not mention him and Nabonidus might have been referring to Nergilissar I – a more venerated figure than Nergilissar II – and to his son Labash-Marduk. In view of these plots and disfigurations, the Labash-Marduk mentioned by Berosus might have been a non-existent figure. Whether a Labash-Marduk II ruled Babylon for nine months or not is a very minor problem – a boon friend and drinking companion of the past-middle-age Nabonidus he was not.

---

[1] S. Bernstein: *König Nebucadnezar von Babel,* pp. 69-79. The figure of forty-five years is also found in Maçoudi: *Les prairies d'or* (Paris, 1861-77). From statements in II Kings 23:29; 23:36; 24:8 and 25:27 a reign of at least forty-eight years may be inferred.

[2] Hermann Bengston: *The Greeks and the Persians from the Sixth to the Fourth Centuries* (New York, 1965), pp. 357-58.

The main problem of the royal succession, unsolvable with evidence from Babylon alone, was solved here with the help of the Boghazkoi archives. The British Museum tablet 21946 dating from Persian (or possibly even Hellenistic) times, but describing the story of the death of Nabopolassar and the accession of Nebuchadnezzar, belongs to the same group as a few other possessions of the museum, like the Pilt-down skull – only the forgery was initiated in the days of Hattusilis the Chaldean, known to us from the Scriptures as Nebuchadnezzar.

Chapter 6

The "Forgotten Empire": Testimony of Art

Yazilikaya: "The Inscribed Rock"

The "Hittite" history reveals itself as the history of the Chaldean dynasty, especially of the period of the Neo-Babylonian monarchy. The documents of Boghazkoi, the ancient Hattusas, reflect the political life of the seventh century and the early part of the sixth. This conclusion is reached upon reconstruction of Egyptian history. The written documents from Asia Minor do not contradict the chronological order presented in this reconstruction; on the contrary, they add their own testimony to the same effect.

Will the collections of "Hittite" art present contradictory testimony? Art has its own way of development; influences may be traced in motifs and in the manner of execution. Wings dedicated to "Hittite" art have been opened in museums; will a strong opposing voice rise out of these halls?

Just the opposite.

It is interesting to follow the question over more than one hundred and forty years of research, from the 1830's, when the ruins of Boghazkoi were first described, to the present day. Three stages may be marked in this period: the time before the theory about the "Hittite Empire" was launched in the 1870's; the years from the 1870's to the discovery of the "Hittite" archives in Boghazkoi in 1906; and the time from 1906 to the present.

The ruins of Boghazkoi and the rock bas-relief of Yazilikaya ("the inscribed rock") two miles away were made known for the first time in 1834.[1] A few years later a scholar, exploring Asia Minor, was impressed by the rock reliefs – "one of the most curious and remarkable monuments" – and wrote: "The composition seems to represent the meeting of two kings, each of whom holds emblems of royalty in his

---

[1] By C. Texier: *Description de l'Asie-Mineure* (Paris, 1839), I, 214ff.

hand, and is followed by a long train of soldiers or attendants, dressed in similar costumes. The principal figure on the left-hand side ... is dressed in a tight close-fitting dress, with a high conical cap and beard; while the other principal figure is dressed in loose flowing robes, with a square turreted headdress and is without a beard.

"I am rather inclined to think," he proceeded, "that it represents the meeting of two coterminous kings, and that it was intended to commemorate a treaty of peace concluded between them. The [river] Halys, which is not many miles distant, was long the boundary between the kingdoms of Lydia and Persia and it is possible that in the figure with the flowing robes we may recognize the king of Persia, and in the other the king of Lydia, with his attendants, Lydians and Phrygians, for their headdress resembles the well-known Phrygian bonnet. This spot may have been chosen to commemorate the peace.

In the same hollow is another figure ... sculptured upon the rock, but detached from the above-mentioned procession. Curious emblems are in his hand also."[1]

Guided by the appearance of the royal figures approaching each other and by that of their attendants, the quoted scholar thought that the bas-relief depicted the conclusion of an armistice after the great battle fought by Croesus and Cyrus in about -550 somewhere nearby.[2] One group wears Phrygian caps, the other Persian tiaras.

Another early scholar,[3] investigating the ruins of Boghazkoi and the rock bas-relief of Yazilikaya, interpreted the figures on the rock as those of Lydians and Medes. Cyaxares, king of Media, who together with Nabopolassar conquered Nineveh, later became involved in a five years' war with Alyattes, the Lydian king, father of Croesus. During the battle near the river Halys the sun was eclipsed as Thales of Miletus had predicted.[4] The armies broke off fighting. Through the efforts of the king of Babylonia and the king of Cilicia a peace was negotiated

---

[1] W. J. Hamilton: *Researches in Asia Minor, Pontus and Armenia* (London, 1842), I, 393-95.

[2] Herodotus, I, 76.

[3] H. Barth: »Versuch einer eingehenden Erklärung der Felssculpturen von Boghaskoei im alten Kappadocien«, *Monatsberichte der Königlichen Preussischen Akademie der Wissenschaften* (Berlin, 1859), 128-57.

[4] See Herodotus, I, 74. Thales lived perhaps from -640 to -550. The famous eclipse is ascribed to May 28, -585, by F. K. Ginzel: *Specieller Kanon der Sonne und Mond Finsternisse* (Berlin, 1899). He quotes ten other suggested dates, from February 3, -626, to March 16, -581.

Figure 18: A relief sculpture from Hattusas:
an example of Chaldeo-Hittite art of the late
seventh or early sixth century.
From *Die Hethiter* by Johannes Lehmann, C.
Bertelsmann Verlag, Munich.
Credit: Flirmer Fotoarchiv, Munich

and signed.[1] They "brought it about that there should be a sworn agreement and exchange of wedlock: they adjudged that Alyattes should give his daughter Aryenis to Astyages, son of Cyaxares."[2]

On the rock relief of Yazilikaya a new moon or an eclipsed sun is carried by two figures: this seems to give support to the interpretation

---

[1] Herodotus, I, 74.
[2] *Ibid.*

of the Yazilikaya rock scenes as a memorial to the peace treaty between Cyaxares, king of Media, and Alyattes, king of Lydia.

The Babylonian king who acted as mediator is thought to have been either Nabopolassar or Nebuchadnezzar, depending on the date of the eclipse: the eclipses of September 30, -610, and of May 28, -585, are rivals for the honor of having been the one predicted by Thales.[1]

Herodotus calls the Babylonian king who helped arrange the peace Labynetus. I am inclined to think that the peacemaker was Nergilissar, and if such was the case the earlier of the two dates would be the one predicted by Thales. In the Boghazkoi texts Nergil, or Muwatalis, carries also the name Labarnas.[2]

The rock reliefs bear a few signs in the pictorial script, but as long as they were undeciphered, they could not guide the scholars in defining the time when they were carved; the style, the garments, characteristic as they are, and certain details, such as clubs and battle-axes, speak for the end of the seventh or the first half of the sixth century. "The club and the battle-axe appear for the first time on the Assyrian sculptures in the war pictures of the grandson of Sennacherib, who probably was the last king of Nineveh, and therefore the contemporary of Cyaxares."[3]

The ruined palace of Boghazkoi also impressed this scholar with its "greatest resemblance to the ground plan of the Northwest Palace of Nineveh" built by Sennacherib in -700.[4]

When, in the 1870's, the theory of the "Hittite Empire" was put forth, the pictographic signs found in Hamath and Carchemish and on the rock bas-relief of Boghazkoi were held to be "Hittite" hieroglyphics contemporary with Ramses II. This meant an increase of six to seven hundred years in the age of the reliefs. Though caution was voiced not to be too hasty in placing this particular monument in the period before Esarhaddon, son of Sennacherib,[5] it went unheeded: the historians, influenced by the presence of the pictographic characters on the

---

[1] In the days of Mursilis an eclipse of the sun occurred, which he described in the following words: "While I marched towards the land Azzi, the sun became obscured." See E. Forrer: »Die astronomische Festlegung« in *Forschungen*, II (Berlin, 1926), p. 2.

[2] J. Friedrich: »Staatsverträge des Hatti-Reiches in Hethitischer Sprache«, *Mitteilungen, Vorderasiatisch-ägyptische Gesellschaft*, XXXIV (1936).

[3] Barth, op. cit., p. 139. Assurbanipal, grandson of Sennacherib, was the next to last king of Nineveh.

[4] *Ibid.*, p. 129.

[5] G. Hirschfeld: »Die Felsenreliefs in Kleinasien und Das Volk der Hettiter«, *Philosophisch-historische Abhandlungen der Königlichen Preussischen Akademie der Wissenschaften*, 1886 (Berlin, 1887), II, 23ff.

bas-reliefs, assigned the bas-relief and other monuments of the same style to the time of the "Hittite Empire," or to the age of Seti and Ramses II, in the fourteenth and thirteenth centuries. To insist that the "Hittite" sculptures could not have originated in the second millennium was equivalent to denying the theory of the "Hittite Empire," and as the style of the art monuments is a visible fact and theory is only theory, a noted art expert (O. Puchstein) took his stand with a clearly expressed opinion.[1]

The motifs of these sculptures and many details of execution speak in favor of identifying this art as belonging to the time between the tenth and sixth centuries and not the fourteenth and thirteenth centuries.

All those sculptures show clear signs of a much later time of origin; therefore their being creations of the Egyptian Kheta is excluded.
In any case, there is neither here [in Asia Minor], nor in northern Syria, evidence that the so-called Hittite sculpture existed already in the tenth century B.C. This fact seems to me incompatible with the views of Sayce. For him, the greatest expansion of power of the Hittite Empire, and with it also the prime of Hittite art, lies almost half a millennium before the time in which the extant monuments of ancient Commogene and Asia Minor were created.
Therefore the art which has produced these and similar works does not have to be ascribed to the enigmatic Hittites of the second millennium B.C., but should be regarded as a remarkable sign of the then highly developed culture of the population of Asia Minor and Commogene in the time from 1000 to 600 B.C.[2]

The best-developed motifs in "Hittite" art of Asia Minor and northern Syria point to the seventh century all the way to -600; to evaluate them as products of even the eighth century appears to be a violation

---

[1] O. Puchstein: *Pseudohethitische Kunst* (Berlin, 1890).
[2] "Weisen alle jene Bildwerke deutliche Kennzeichen einer viel späteren Entstehungszeit auf; es ist daher ausgeschlossen, dass sie Schöpfungen der ägyptischen Cheta sein könnten."
"Jedenfalls gibt es weder hier [Asia Minor] noch in Nordsyrien ein Zeugnis dafür, dass die sogenannte hethitische Plastik schon in dem 10. Jahrhundert v. Chr. existierte. Diese Tatsache scheint mir mit den Ansichten von Sayce unvereinbar zu sein. Für ihn liegt die grösste Machtentfaltung des Hethitischen Reiches und damit auch die Blüte der hethitischen Kunst fast um ein halbes Jahrtausend vor der Zeit, in der die erhaltenen altkommagenischen und kleinasiatischen Denkmäler entstanden sind."
"Es braucht daher die Kunst, die diese und ähnliche Werke hervorgebracht hat, nicht den rätselhaften Hethitern des 2. Jahrtausends v. Chr. zugeschrieben werden, sondern sie ist als ein merkwürdiges Zeichen der ehemals hochentwickelten Kultur der kleinasiatischen und kommagenischen Bevölkerung in der Zeit von 1000-600 v. Chr. zu betrachten."
Ibid., pp. 13, 14, 22.

Figure 19: "Procession of gods" from Yazilikaya.
From *Die Kunst der Hethiter*, Ekrem Akurgal (1967)

of sound judgment. The late Assyrian influence is unmistakably obvi-ous. The "Hittite" monuments have been adjudged as being of a time at least five centuries too early and therefore could not be of the "For-gotten Empire." As to the Yazilikaya reliefs, "the divine figures (partici-pating in the procession) received their form not before the seventh century, under the influence of the Assyrian concepts.

> Only then, that is, in the seventh century B.C., had Assyrian life style in Cappadocia settled and influenced the artists of the reliefs of Boghazkoi. ... From differences of such kind we may draw the conclusion that in Boghazkoi we are dealing with local gods whose images were not fash-ioned before the seventh century B.C. under the influence of Assyrian conceptions, as we see it. They can indeed be brought into harmony with the gods that, according to Greco-Roman sources, were venerated in Cappadocia in later time.[1]

---

[1] "Erst damals, d.h. im 7. Jahrhundert v. Chr., assyrisches Wesen in Kappadokien sich eingebürgert and die Künstler der Reliefs von Boghazköi beeinflusst haben."
"... Aus derartigen Abweichungen dürfen wir den Schluss ziehen, dass es sich in Boghazköi um einheimische Götter handelt, deren Bilder erst im 7. Jahrhundert v. Chr. unter dem Einfluss assyrischer Vorstellungen, so wie wir es sehen, ausgeprägt worden sind. Sie lassen sich tatsächlich mit den Göttern in Übereinstimmung bringen die nach griechisch-römischen Quellen in späterer Zeit in Kappadokien verehrt wurden." *Ibid.*, pp. 13, 21.

The art expert insisted that the specimens of art of Asia Minor and northern Syria, which bear the undeciphered hieroglyphic signs, cannot be ascribed to Kheta, the enemy of Ramses II. Why not? For the reason that Kheta or the "Hittites," together with Seti and Ramses II, must have belonged to the fourteenth-thirteenth centuries, whereas the specimens of art of Asia Minor ascribed to these "Hittites" are products of the seventh century. The time of Seti and Ramses was not challenged, and the chronology of history was not brought under suspicion.

But when, in 1906, the soil of Boghazkoi yielded the archives of the kings of Kheta (Hatti), and among them the cuneiform copy of the treaty of Hattusilis (Khetasar) with Ramses II, all objections to the theory of the "Hittite Empire" were silenced. The same art expert who gave his splendid style analysis wrote a large work on the "Hittite" architecture of Boghazkoi and, stressing the discovery of the cuneiform copy of the treaty of the king of Kheta (Hatti) with Ramses II, omitted to mention his former objections. "The chief archaeological gain of this first excavation was, however, the realization, arrived at by Winkler from the clay tablets, that the old city layout at Boghazkoi had once been the capital of the Hatti Empire. How far it certainly reached back in time has been determined through the fragments of the letter exchanges carried on around 1300 B.C., between Ramses II and the Hittite king Hattusil."[1]

A fact that seemed to be more compelling than style and motifs was before the eyes. No artistic expertise could stand up against such obvious evidence. Mute monuments cannot compete with eloquent tablets. When the opinion derived from contemplating the objects of art was abandoned, no doubt remained that the culture of Boghazkoi had

---

[1] "Der archäologische Hauptgewinn dieser ersten Grabungskampagne war aber die von Winkler den Tontafeln entnommene Erkenntnis, dass die alte Stadtanlage bei Boghasköi einst die Hauptstadt des Hatti-Reiches gewesen ist. Bis in welche Zeit sie sicher zurückreichte, bestimmte sich durch Stücke des Briefwechsels, den um 1300 v. Chr. Ramses II mit dem Hethiterkönig Hattušil geführt hat." O. Puchstein: *Boghasköi, Die Bauwerke* (Leipzig, 1912), p. 2. See also Hall: *The Ancient History of the Near East*, p. 329: "It may eventually appear that some of the actual remains at Boghaz Kyoi are of later date than the archives found by Winkler, but it is improbable that they can be much later." Before the discovery of the archives, Hall had been one of the principal opponents of the theory of the "Hittite Empire." In 1901 he advocated an eighth-century date for the monuments of Boghazkoi because of what he recognized as Assyrian influence on the sculptures. Five years later he completely reversed his stand. See his *The Oldest Civilization of Greece: Studies of the Mycenean Age* (Philadelphia, 1901), pp. 115, 124, 273.

been contemporaneous with the end of the Eighteenth and the beginning of the Nineteenth Dynasties in Egypt and had been a product of the second millennium before the present era.

On the cuneiform written treatises and annals of the kings of Hatti, there were seal impressions in pictographs, and identical seal emblems are a part of the reliefs of Yazilikaya. As we shall see, this fact sufficed to compel the archaeologists who have continued for the last half century to dig at Boghazkoi and to study the reliefs of Yazilikaya to hold to the opinion that these are products of the Hittite Empire that existed before -1200.

Archaeology and "Hittite" Monuments

"Hittite" monuments were found in Babylon, the most important one being discovered in the palace of Nebuchadnezzar. It is a bas-relief stele with a deity holding lightning in his hand in low relief. The back of the dolerite is inscribed with "Hittite" hieroglyphs excellently preserved.[1] The stela apparently comes from Aleppo and dates from the first half of the ninth century.[2] It has now been translated.[3]

In the course of excavations in Anatolia and northern Syria, perplexing facts were gathered, and nearly every "Hittite" find could be interpreted as belonging in two different ages.

In Gordion of the Gordian knot legend were found Phrygian mound tombs with antiquities, which their discoverers" assigned to the seventh and sixth centuries. They judged the age of their finds by comparing them with well-known Greek antiquities. "Since the find of numerous Greek vases in the necropolis together with strongly hellenized terracotta, the cultural dependence of Phrygia upon Hellas in the sixth century is proved beyond doubt."[5] The archaeologists ascribed many of these objects to a time after the expulsion of the Cimmerian and before the fall of Croesus, or between -630 and -546.[6]

[1] R. Koldewey: *Die Hettitische Inschrift gefunden in der Königsburg von Babylon am 22. August 1899* (Leipzig, 1900).
[2] Written communication from J. D. Hawkins: dated March 18, 1977.
[3] P. Meriggi: *Manuale di Eteo Geroglifico*, II/1 (Rome, 1967), no. 13, p. 37ff.
[4] G. and A. Körte: *Gordion* (Berlin, 1904).
[5] *Ibid*, p. 218.
[6] *Ibid*.

However, a protest came from a scholar who studied the finds of Gordion in their relation to the "Hittite" age: "It seems highly probable that the interment (Tumulus III) belongs to the last centuries of the second millennium or the last period of the Hittite Empire:"[1]
The difference in estimate is more than six hundred years.
The last-quoted opinion seemed to be verified by the excavations at Alisar[2] (fifty miles southeast of Boghazkoi), where the archaeologists assigned a stratum with similar finds to the fourteenth and thirteenth centuries, on the basis of seals bearing "Hittite" pictographs together with ceramics painted in geometrical designs, found also in Gordion.
But evaluation of the age of the finds at Alisar was in its turn criticized. Fibulae or metal buckles of a definite form were found there, and it is "so impossible ["unmöglich"]" that the sole explanation thinkable would make them come "only by chance into a much older stratum."[3] The earliest fibulae appeared well after the thirteenth century. "It is excluded ['ausgeschlossen'] that the better-developed fibulae could belong to a stratum at least ["allermindestens"] four hundred years too old."
This last opinion and the criticism of the Alisar results came from the new excavators of Boghazkoi.[4] But they, in their turn, were baffled by the reversed stratification at Boghazkoi. They wrote of their own work on the citadel that "the mere statement about the depth at which a find is made is worthless," and tried to draw consolation from the experience of the excavators at Jericho,[5] one of whom, incidentally, had to publish a repudiation of his age evaluation of Jericho, to which matter I shall turn my attention at an appropriate place.
The excavators at Boghazkoi assigned the buildings (Stratum II) to the period of the "Hittite Empire" in the second millennium, but they were compelled to admit that these buildings "must have been still occupied in the seventh century." At least there appears in great quantity east-Greek late-geometrical ceramics, and "it would be difficult to date these in an earlier age."[6] This means that the buildings were occu-

---

[1] H. Frankfort: *Studies in Early Pottery in the Near East* (London, 1927), p. 158. See K. Bittel and H. Güterbock: »Bogazkoy«, *Abhandlungen der Preussischen Akademie der Wissenschaften, Philosophische-historische Klasse,* 1935 (Berlin, 1936).
[2] H. H von der Osten and E. Schmidt: *The Alishar Huyuk,* 7 vols. (Chicago, 1930-37)
[3] Bittel and Güterbock, op. cit., 1935, p. 22.
[4] *Ibid.,* p. 22.
[5] C. Watzinger: *Die Denkmäler Palästinas,* 2 vols. (Leipzig, 1933-35), I,5.
[6] Bittel and Güterbock, op. cit., p. 26.

pied for at least six or seven centuries, and that the last occupants kept in their rooms, besides the ceramics of their own age, the seventh century, objects belonging to the earlier occupants of these rooms, among other things "Hittite" seals of the "Hittite Empire," presumably of the second millennium. Is it reasonable to suppose that anyone who occupies a house would keep in his rooms things left in them by those who dwelt there six hundred years earlier?

The excavators of Boghazkoi found it necessary to establish once more the age of the Yazilikaya rock relief, in view of a scholarly skepticism that again began to lower the time of its origin. Whereas one scholar thought it possible to assign the rock relief to the "Old Hittite Empire" of the nineteenth-eighteenth centuries before this era,[1] and others attributed it to the thirteenth century,[2] sometimes even specifying the decade, or explaining the rock relief as the wedding of Hattusilis, a number of scholars took more and more into consideration parallels with other excavated antiquities, and ascribed the rock relief to the period following the downfall of the "Hittite Empire,"[3] and some of these brought the date of the rock relief down to the tenth or to the ninth century.[4] There was even advanced a hypothesis ascribing one part of the rock relief to the fourteenth or thirteenth century and the other to the tenth or the ninth century.[5]

This chaos of opinion impelled a scholar to write: "Everyone who compares the time estimates of the scholars knows how widely these evaluations differ. Not decades or centuries, but often whole millennia separate the time reckonings of divers scholars."[6]

The excavators at Boghazkoi decided to put an end to this old question. They wrote: "Since Winckler [the discoverer of the archives] unriddled the name and the significance of Boghaz Keui, no one should have seriously questioned the age of Yazilikaya, which is before -1200. ... Moreover, the architectural features of Yazilikaya also point to the

---

[1] Herzfeld: »Hettitica«, in *Archäologische Mitteilungen aus Iran*, 2 (1930), 132-203. See Bittel: *Die Felsbilder von Yazilikaya* (Bamberg, 1934).
[2] Sayce, J. Garstang, V. Müller.
[3] H. H. von der Osten, Albright.
[4] V. Christian: *Archiv für Orientforschung*, IX (1933), 25ff
[5] F. W. von Bissing: »Untersuchungen über Zeit und Stil der 'chetitischen' Reliefs«, *Archiv für Orientforschung*, VI (1930-31), 159-201.
[6] T. Bossert: »Das hethitische Pantheon«, Archiv *für Orientforschung*, VIII (1932-33), 297

time of the New Hatti Kingdom,"[1] or the New Empire of Suppiluliumas, Mursilis and Hattusilis. "A final decision" they found in hieroglyphic seals unearthed at Boghazkoi and in identical cartouches on the rock relief of Yazilikaya, nearby.

But the excavators, Bittel and Güterbock, found in Boghazkoi "hieroglyphic seals in higher strata," too,[2] and could not explain them. They also found quite a few Greek inscriptions of the late Phrygian and post-Phrygian periods,[3] but since, at the outset, they had decided that a "mere statement about the depth at which a find is made is worthless," they ascribed the Phrygian objects to a date four or five hundred years more recent than the end of the "Hittite Empire" in conformity with their preconceived chronology.

"In the Deepest Darkness"

The criticism of the Alisar excavation by the excavators of Boghazkoi in the matter of the buckles (fibulae) made a greater impression than had been intended. The archaeologists of Alisar made a public revocation of all their estimates, already published in monumental volumes.

"A definite change has to be made" with respect to the archaeological level "which we formerly called Period IV and attributed, on account of the frequent occurrence of seals with "Hittite" hieroglyphs, to the time of the New Hittite Empire (about -1500 to -1200). ... Furthermore, studies based on more extensive material, especially that from the 1931 season at Alisar, reveal a close affinity between our Period IV pottery and the later Phrygian ware of Gordion. The appearance of the so-called 'Hittite' hieroglyphs in this building level, and in this building level only [italics in the text], demands explanation. ... The beginning of hieroglyphic writing in Asia Minor has been put much too early, and its connection with the Hittites of the two empires seems rather questionable."[4]

---

[1] Bittel and Güterbock: *Abhandlungen der Preussischen Akademie der Wissenschaften,* 1935, p. 46.
[2] *Ibid.,* p. 58.
[3] *Ibid.,* pp. 84ff
[4] H. H. von der Osten: *Discoveries in Anatolia, 1930-31,* Publications of the Oriental Institute of the University of Chicago (1933), pp. 9-10.

This statement that the "Hittite" hieroglyphic seals were found in the later Phrygian stratum, and in this stratum only, and that, consequently, the "Hittite" hieroglyphs may not belong to the "Hittites" is tantamount to a signature on a declaration of bankruptcy. These peculiar hieroglyphic signs were the alpha of the theory of the "Hittite Empire." W. Wright, a missionary at Damascus, made the hieroglyphic stone in the corner of an Arab building in Hamath the cornerstone of the structure of the "Forgotten Empire."[1] This theory was brilliantly confirmed by the find of the archives of Boghazkoi, the archives of the Hatti Empire. And now, after all these triumphs, this capitulation?

"It seems most probable that these hieroglyphic-writing people played an active part in the destruction of the Hittite Empire, perhaps in association with the Phrygians."[2]

The level of the hieroglyphic inscriptions was named anew the "first post-Hittite level,"[3] and correspondingly with Level IV all levels were reduced in age by a number of centuries.

This turns light into darkness. "In spite of all the advances of the last twenty-five years in 'Hittitology' we are, from the archaeological point of view, in the deepest darkness as to the Hittite question."[4]

This *testimonium paupertatis* could have been elicited only because of some basic entanglement.

Gordion's necropolis was declared to belong to the seventh-sixth centuries because of the geometric designs of eastern Greek vases. Alisar IV yielded the same ware. But this stratum also contained hieroglyphic seals. These are contemporaneous with the seals of Boghazkoi and the cartouches on the bas-relief of Yazilikaya, and also with the archives of Boghazkoi: on some cuneiform tablets from these archives there are impressions of (pictograph) seals made when the clay was soft, before firing.

At a later date the excavator at Alisar submitted a piece of wood found under the wall of the Acropolis in Level III, first labeled Old Bronze, to a radiocarbon test. The result had it that the wood was seven hundred years more recent than expected on the basis of the accepted historical chronology.[5]

---

[1] Wright:*The Empire of the Hittites.*

[2] Von der Osten: *Discoveries in Anatolia,* p. 10.

[3] *Ibid.*

[4] H. H. von der Osten: *Four Sculptures from Marash,* Metropolitan Museum Studies, II, 1929-30 (New York, 1930), 115.

[5] W. F. Libby: *Radiocarbon Dating* (Chicago, 1952), p. 71.

The same repentant author who revoked his estimate of Alisar IV and ascribed it to the post-Phrygian time had written a few years earlier: "There are no historically known circumstances which would adequately explain a general use of hieroglyphics in the very center of the Hittite Great Empire during its existence."[1]
Everything became confused.

"Now as before we must build the Hittite chronology upon the Egyptian chronology," since "Hittite" history has no chronology of its own, wrote one of the leading Hittitologists.[2] How fatal this dependence is we learn to understand.

Gordion

The Phrygian kingdom was crossed by the river Sangarius (modern Sakarya); its eastern frontier was along the Halys River (modem Kizil Irmak). Gordion's ruins are about fifty miles southwest of Ankara and eighty-five more miles from Boghazkoi (Hattusas). It was the seat of King Gordias, the founder of the dynasty, and of King Midas of legendary fame – everything he touched turned to gold.
The Greek tradition has it that the Phrygians came from Thrace, crossing the Bosphorus. The time of their arrival is not known and there is nothing of archaeological nature to support the view sometimes expressed that they had already arrived in Anatolia in the thirteenth century: the only argument for such an early date is in the circumstance that Homer refers to the Phrygians as the allies of King Priam of Troy. Yet the opinion is expressed, too, that such an early dating should be disregarded, Homer's reference to the Phrygians being in the nature of an anachronism. No Phrygian antiquities from before the first half of the eighth century (-800) have been found.[3]
The end of the Phrygian kingdom is known – it fell before the invasion of the Cimmerians in -687 or a year or two later.

---

[1] Von der Osten: *Four Sculptures from Marash,* p. 115.
[2] "Nach wie vor müssen wir die hethitische Chronologie auf die ägyptische aufbauen." Götze: *Mitteilungen, Vorderasiatisch-ägyptische Gesellschaft,* XXXVIII (1933), 9.
[3] E. Akurgal: *Phrygische Kunst* (Ankara, 1955), p. 112: "Die Phrygische Kunst erst am Beginn des 8. Jahrhunderts entstanden ist."

The Cimmerians came from the north, traversing the coastal routes of the Caucasus; their original home is often thought to have been in Crimea. Although the literary tradition of the invasion of the Cimmerians and the fall of Gordion is persistent, nothing was found by the archaeologists that could be ascribed to their presence in that city or in Phrygia in general. It appears that they did not tarry for any length of time in Phrygia and, like the Scythians who soon followed them on the coastal roads of the Caucasus, were but transient conquerors. The date they came from their native land (in -687 or soon thereafter) makes it quite certain that they were started on their migration by the natural events of that year, described at some length in *Worlds in Collision*. This was also the year that Sennacherib met his famous debacle as described in Herodotus and also in the books of Isaiah, II Kings, and II Chronicles, while threatening Jerusalem with capture and its population with eviction and exile.

After the passing of the Cimmerians, Phrygia was exposed to occupation by the neighboring states, west and east. To the west was Lydia with its capital at Sardis; east was the Chaldean kingdom. We, however, recognized the "Hittite Empire" with its capital at Hattusas as the Chaldean kingdom and its time as the seventh century and the first half of the sixth. The rock relief with the peace procession at Yazilikaya dates from the same age.

After the brothers Körte excavated at Gordion in the beginning of this century, no further exploration took place through the two World Wars and the interval in between. But in 1950 Rodney Young, sponsored by the University of Pennsylvania Museum, led a team there and then returned over many seasons of excavation.

If the conventional scheme of history is true, the level of the "Hittite Empire" should be found at Gordion *beneath* the Phrygian level; but if the reconstructed scheme is true, what goes under the name of the Hittite Empire must have left some of its relics *above* the Phrygian layer. And here is what Dr. Young and his team uncovered at Gordion:

The Phrygian stratum is covered by a layer of clay. "For purposes of dating the sherds from this layer of clay are of little use; they are almost entirely Hittite." The abundant presence of "Hittite" relics qualifies it, in the opinion of the excavator, as "clearly a deposit already in the clay when it was brought from elsewhere to be laid down over the surface of the Phrygian city mound."[1]

Young goes on to say that if this clay layer was spread over the mound during the Persian period, as he sees himself forced to conclude, "it would have been necessary to carry it up over the Persian gate [of the city wall] before it could be dumped over the mound at the west."[2] He calls this "a procedure evidently highly extravagant of labor."

This would indeed have been highly extravagant if it were true. But is it true that the Persians removed the clayey soil from somewhere in the east and then carried this layer of soil, with Hittite pottery in it, over hilly terrain and spread it evenly all over the capital of Phrygia to build on top of it? The layer is on the average four meters thick and, considering the expanse of Gordion, the enterprise, if it took place, must have involved a transfer of millions of tons of clayey soil over a considerable distance.

Even were this the solution of the remarkable sequel of strata, then, between the Phrygian and the Persian layers, besides the clay layer, there should be some other stratum to fill the gap between the end of the Phrygian kingdom in about -687 and -548, the year Cyrus conquered Asia Minor, taking the Chaldean kingdom, the Phrygian Gordion, and Sardis of Lydia, where he made Croesus his captive. But only the "Hittite" layer separates the Phrygian stratum from the Persian.

"The new city built over the clay layer dates from the second half of the sixth century. There is thus a lacuna of about a century and a half in the stratification and history of the site; the clay layer was not accumulated but dumped, apparently all at one time; the clay, brought from elsewhere, contains almost exclusively pottery of the Hittite period."[3]

The reason for saying that the stratum had not accumulated but had been dumped all over the mound is obviously the fact that the pottery in it dates almost exclusively from the period of the "Hittite Empire."

Let us follow for a little while this trend of logic: The layer containing things of the "Hittite Empire" is all foreign to Gordion, having been carried from a distance to be spread over the Phrygian city. The Phrygian city fell, overrun by the Cimmerians in -687, but they did not stay

---

[1] R. S. Young: »Gordion: Preliminary Report, 1953«, *American Journal of Archaeology*, Vol. 59 (1955), p. 12.

[2] *Ibid.*

[3] Young: »The Campaign of 1955 at Gordion: Preliminary Report«, *American Journal of Archaeology*, Vol. 60 (1956), p. 264.

there. Persian rule started in -548. About one hundred and forty years separate these two events. There must have occurred some accumulation of refuse, pottery, and other relics of the occupants of the place for these one hundred and forty years. But discounting the "Hittite" layer as not belonging, we are left with a "lacuna."

The Persians are thought by Young to have covered the Phrygian capital with the "Hittite" layer as a base for new construction. Did they also remove an equal layer that accumulated during almost a century and a half so as to create a lacuna in the stratification of the mound? Young writes: "The Gordion of the Lydian period between ca. 690 and 550 has evaded us thus far, though it seems unlikely that the main site was entirely deserted over this long period."[1]

After the passage of the Cimmerians, the Phrygian kingdom was divided between the Lydians and the Chaldeans. The presence of the "Hittite" layer above the Phrygian and below the Persian is in its proper place. The earth was not carried from a distance.

Young found also that the construction of the Phrygian Gate at Gordion had its "closest parallel in the wall of the sixth city at Troy." But supposedly a span of many centuries lay in between. "Though separated in time by five hundred years or thereabouts the two fortifications may well represent a common tradition of construction in northwestern Anatolia; if so, intermediate examples have yet to be found."[2] The sixth city of Troy, however, belongs not in the thirteenth century but in the eighth, the exact time when the fortifications of Gordion were erected.

The Dark Age of Anatolia

"Despite the industrious digging of the last decades, the period from -1200 to -750 for most parts of Anatolia still lies in complete darkness."[3] These are the words of Ekrem Akurgal, a prominent Turkish archaeologist, who carefully surveyed large regions of Asia Minor. The area

---

[1] Ibid.

[2] R. S. Young: »Gordion: Preliminary Report, 1953«, American Journal of Archaeology, 59 (1955), p. 13.

[3] E. Akurgal: Die Kunst Anatoliens (Berlin, 1961). "Trotz der eifrigen Spatenforschung der letzten Jahrzehnte, die Zeitspanne von 1200-750 für die meisten Teile des anatolischen Raumes noch in völliger Dunkelheit liegt."

contains no relics of art or industry, no remains of human culture or even habitation, for a full span of four hundred and fifty years.

"It follows that any relics of a culture between -1200 and -750 in central Asia Minor, especially in the highlands, are lost for us beyond retrieving.[1]

"It is also striking that till now in central Anatolia not only no Phrygian but generally no cultural relics of any people whatsoever have turned up that could be dated between 1200 and 750.[2]

"Also in the southern part of the peninsula the early Iron Age, or the period between -1200 and -750, is enshrouded in darkness."[3]

To come to such a conclusion and still to adhere to the accepted chronological timetable, a scholar needed to be completely convinced that in no excavated place of so large a region any artifact or any inhumed body from four to five consecutive centuries could be found. How utterly depopulated must have been the area which in the time of the "Hittite Empire" was populated by many nations that carried on intercourse in commerce and in diplomatic relations, had cultural exchange and manufactured goods in abundance.

In a projected volume on the archaeology and chronology of Greece, I shall deal with the so-called *Dark Age of Greece* which, like that in Asia Minor, covers on the accepted timetable the same period from -1200 to -750. These centuries, between the Mycenaean and the Ionic (Greek) periods, are unreal: they resulted from the dependence of the Mycenaean timing on Egyptian chronology – the same situation that we found in Asia Minor. There the treaty with Ramses II in Hattusas (Boghazkoi) brought the world of historians to conclusions similar to those occasioned by the scarabs of the Eighteenth Dynasty kings and queens found in the tombs of Mycenae.

The Dark Age of Anatolia (Asia Minor) was seen by H. Frankfort, an art historian, as extended toward the countries in the East.[4] Akurgal, however, pointed toward Carchemish on the Euphrates as the place

---

[1] "Demnach scheinen die Kulturreste der Zeit zwischen 1200-750 im mittleren Kleinasien, vor allem im Hochland, für uns fast unwiderbringlich verloren zu sein." *Ibid.*

[2] "Auffallend ist ferner, dass bis heute in Zentralanatolien nicht nur keine phrygischen, sondern überhaupt keine Kulturreste irgendeines Volkes zutage getreten sind, die in die Zeit 1200-750 datiert werden können." *Ibid.*

[3] "Doch ist auch hier [im Süden der Halbinsel] die frühe Eisenzeit, d. h. die Periode zwischen 1200 und 750, in Dunkelheit gehüllt." Ibid., p. 7.

[4] H. Frankfort: *The Art and Architecture of the Ancient Orient* (Baltimore, 1954), pp. 164-66.

where a continuous occupation could be traced, bridging the centuries unbridged in Anatolia to the west.

The "Gold Tomb" of Carchemish

The "Gold Tomb," so called for the golden objects, mainly figurines, found in it, was discovered beneath the floor of a room (room E) in the Northwest Fort of Carchemish, the only one found within the city walls. It yielded "the finest small objects that came to light during the whole expedition."[1] It was a cremation burial. The urn with the calcined bones, a little lapis lazuli, and four gold tassels was placed in a krater and covered by a smaller krater. All was enveloped in a mass of wood ash; in this mass was found a set of thirty-nine small figures carved in relief in lapis lazuli or in steatite set in gold cloisons. There were also lumps of molten bronze made shapeless by fire, fragments of ivory from furniture, also burned, a great number of minute gold beads and gold nailheads, and a couple of disks of gold, one of them in a damaged state, with designs of human and animal figures. Some of the objects had suffered greatly from the cremation, others were obviously put in the ashes when still hot, poured from the pyre into the pit in which the urn had already been placed.

The thirty-nine small figurines – not all of them survived well – attracted attention. Woolley wrote: "These little figures are the jeweller's reproduction in miniature of the great rock-cut reliefs of Yazilikaya. Not only is the general subject the same – a long array of gods, royalties, and soldiers – but the individual figures are identical in type, in attitude, in attribute, and in dress. The central figure wearing a long cloak, with the winged disk above his head, grasping a reversed lituus; the figure with conical head-dress, open kilt, and caduceus-like staff; the female figure with the pleated skirt reaching to the feet; the soldiers with their pointed helmets, short kilts, and upturned shoes – all are derived directly from Yazilikaya."

But this meant a problem:

> The close relation between the rock carvings and the Carchemish jewellery cannot be mistaken. The difficulty is in the first place one of date; the

---

[1] Sir Leonard Woolley: *Carchemish III* (London, 1952), pp. 250ff.

Figure 20: One of the small gold figurines from the "Golf Tomb" of Carchemish. From *Die Kunst der Hethiter*, Ekrem Akurgal (1967)

Figure 21: Relief of a Hittite king from Yazilikaya. From *Die Kunst der Hethiter*, Ekrem Akurgal (1967)

carvings are of the thirteenth century B.C. and the grave is of the last years of the seventh century. Either then the jewels are themselves much older than the grave in which they were found and had been handed down as heirlooms through very many generations, or they are relatively late in date and of Syrian manufacture (the Hittites of Anatolia having disappeared hundreds of years before) but preserve unbroken the old Hittite tradition. It must be admitted that the 'heirloom' theory is far-fetched in view of the fact that Carchemish is far removed from Hattusas and any family continuity bridging that gulf of space and time is most improbable.

However, this view was not shared by other authorities. Güterbock,[1] who for many years dug at Hattusas (Boghazkoi) and studied the nearby rock reliefs of Yazilikaya, wrote:

"There is no doubt that both in style and in subjects these figures ... are Hittite in the sense of the Hittite Empire of Bogazköy. How did carvings of the thirteenth century get into a tomb of the seventh?" Güterbock continued: "Two possibilities offer themselves: either the figures were made before 1200 and handed down as 'heirlooms' until

---

[1] H. G. Güterbock: »Carchemish«, *Journal of Near-Eastern Studies*, 1954, pp. 113ff.

they were deposited in the tomb, or they were made in the Late Hittite period but in a style that survived from the Empire. Sir Leonard seems inclined to favor the second alternative, but his argumentation is in part based upon his dates for the Water Gate and Herald's Wall sculptures with which I cannot agree. I would rather prefer the 'heirloom' theory ... The objection to the 'heirloom' theory, that there was no family continuity between the kings of the Empire and the Late Hittite rulers of Carchemish, is correct." He tried to overcome this objection, offering this hypothesis: It could have happened that "the Late Hittites who established themselves on the Euphrates after 1200 took them [the golden figurines] as booty when they sacked the Empire"; or, they were heirlooms from the days "Suppiluliuma and his successors brought these ornaments to Carchemish, where they were kept in the treasury in spite of the change of domination.

The only third possibility would be to doubt the age of the tomb itself, but this is not possible in view of the clear description of the find-circumstances."[1]

Is this the only other possibility?

The reliefs of Yazilikaya are not of the thirteenth century but younger by six to seven centuries. And this is the answer to the question quoted above: "How did carvings of the thirteenth century get into a tomb of the seventh?"

The Herald's Wall

Ekrem Akurgal in his archaeological survey of Asia Minor could point to no single relic from the Dark Ages (-1200 to -750); only in Carchemish, the city-fortress on the Euphrates, on the eastern fringe of Asia Minor, did he believe he was able to trace an uninterrupted history covering both the final centuries of the second millennium and the opening centuries of the first millennium.

As we came ever closer to the realization that there have not been blank centuries in Anatolia, the central plateau of Asia Minor, so we also perceived ever more clearly that the history of Carchemish, in the conventional history, is being written not in an orderly fashion but with

---

[1] *Ibid.*

centuries all confused. The battle of Carchemish (the battle of Kadesh) fought between Ramses II and Nebuchadnezzar took place in -605. It follows that any placement of this battle as having occurred in the fourteenth century or at the beginning of the thirteenth cannot but entail a disarray of historical sequences. The Balawat Gate of Shalmaneser III of the mid-ninth century with a bronze relief of the fortress towers of Carchemish preceded, not followed, Ramses II's design of the outer defenses of Carchemish.

We have already discussed the outer defenses of Carchemish. The mound was never completely explored, but certain areas of its inner part were brought to light – a temple complex and parts of the inner defenses of the fortress, among them a gate, an adjacent wall, called the "Herald's Wall," ornamented with sculptures in low relief, and, connected with this wall, another one, ending at a gate, called the "Water Gate", because it was partly submerged in the Euphrates.

One of the weathered figures on the sculptured slab of the Herald's Wall is a female with an "elaborate head-dress consisting of three bands across the base, from which rises a high crown divided by vertical grooves into three uprights which seem to be joined half-way up by cross-lines – it is the mural head-dress of the goddess in the large recess at Yazilikaya, to which indeed the figure as a whole bears a striking resemblance."[1]

Of this slab of the wall, as of a number of others, actually "of the majority of the stones, at least one can say that the style of the carvings is archaic" and this is baffling if the palace dates from "the latest phase of art at Carchemish." The conclusion is self-contradictory, and a solution is sought in the alternative: "either the whole wall was a survival from an earlier period incorporated in the late Palace, or the individual reliefs had been from an older building and re-used." Woolley continued: "In the King's Gate, on the contrary, there is unmistakable evidence showing that the series is of late date, although the Herald's Wall and the King's Gate are continuous, and form part of the same building. ..."[2]

Of a stone sculpture, Woolley wrote: "The statue certainly has an archaic look ... our first impression when we found it was that the figure was an early one, re-erected when the building was being re-

---

[1] Sir Leonard Woolley: *Carchemish III* (1952), p. 187.
[2] *Ibid.*, pp. 190-91.

modelled. But this archaism must be due simply to religious conservatism." The analogy was made both ways: with what was thought early and what was thought late, and the last consideration ("the analogy of the Zinjirli figure") "is conclusive for a late date."

Writing twenty years after Woolley, M. E. L. Mallowan concluded that the Herald's Wall was built in the early ninth century, a little later than the Long Wall of Sculpture.[1]

This view was also taken by J. D. Hawkins, one of the pioneers of the decipherment of the Hittite pictographic inscriptions, who based his dates principally on epigraphic evidence.[2]

The Syrian City States

The city states of northern Syria and eastern Anatolia – Carchemish, Malatya, Senjirli, Karatepe, Marash – grew up around the turn of the first millennium before the present era, and flourished until almost the end of the eighth century, when the last of them lost their independence to Assyria.

These city states never developed enough cohesiveness to form a unified empire, though in an emergency they did join forces against a common enemy. When in the ninth century Shalmaneser III marched his armies as far as the Upper Sea (the Mediterranean) and made inroads northwestward, into the Anti-Taurus region of Anatolia, the city states joined in a wide confederacy that included Ahab of Israel and, under the leadership of Biridri, the Egyptian commander in chief, succeeded in stemming the Assyrian advance.

The history of the city states is rather obscure, and what is known has to be reconstructed almost solely from references in annals of Assyrian kings; the inscriptions of the native princes written in the pictographic script, which by now can be read with some confidence, provide but sparse information on the political history of these principalities, consisting, as they do, mostly of dedicatory inscriptions. Increasingly, archaeological evidence provides a view of the daily life, religion, and cultural achievement of the city states.

---

[1] »Carchemish«, *Anatolian Studies*, 22 (1972), pp. 63-86.
[2] »Building Inscriptions of Carchemish«, *ibid.*, p. 106.

There is every indication that their culture was indigenous, that it grew from its own roots and matured in a slow process. The script, cumbersome and impractical; the primitive style of the bas-reliefs; the form of political organization in city states – all speak for slow regional growth.

Yet the proponents of the accepted scheme of ancient history assert that these states were successors to the great "Hittite" Empire of the second millennium; that after this empire went down under the wave of migratory hordes, remnants of its former greatness attached themselves to the isolated mountain fastnesses of northern Syria, where they continued to linger for centuries. At last they became vassals to Assyria, and were extinguished by the Chaldeans in the time of Nebuchadnezzar.

When the cultural remains of the Syro-Hittites are examined, it is unavoidable that strong doubts should be raised regarding this sequence of events. In the archive of Boghazkoi in east-central Anatolia the most frequently used language with Babylonian and the script that was employed was almost exclusively cuneiform – only in monumental inscriptions and on royal insignia did the old pictographic script survive. However, the Syro-Hittites, who lived at much greater proximity to Mesopotamian (Assyrian) culture, supposedly reverted to the pictographic script, which already in the Empire period had fallen out of common use. In fact, the pictographic script is now said to be a distinguishing feature of the Syro-Hittites.

Syro-Hittite art, as shown in the primitive bas-reliefs, does not bespeak the monumental antecedents of Yazilikaya. While some motifs are similar, it is nevertheless difficult to conceive of the bas-reliefs of Malatya and Karatepe as being merely degenerate imitations of monumental works of the Empire period. The art of each city state has its own flavor. It is in no way degenerate or formalistic: It is primitive, vital art rooted in the local soil.

The political organization of the Syro-Hittites is other strong evidence for local development that owes nothing to a great "Hittite Empire" in the previous millennium. As in early Greece, a city-state period preceded the development of a unified imperial state.

These three kinds of evidence, from writing, art, and political organization, confirm the conclusions already implicit in the revised scheme of chronology that the Great Empire of the Hittites, that is, the Chaldean

Empire, succeeded the Syro-Hittite states. Under it, in the late seventh and early sixth centuries, the old pictographic script dropped out of daily use, art flowered into a monumental and unified style, and the city-state political organization gave way to a monolithic empire.

The Lion Gate of Malatya

Malatya lies at the very center of the mountainous region of eastern Anatolia where the early Chaldean ("Hittite") states flourished at the beginning of the first millennium. Ever since it was first excavated by a French expedition led by Louis Delaporte between the years 1928 and 1930, the scholarly literature has abounded with ongoing disputes about the correct chronological placement of its chief monuments. The re-liefs of the Lion Gate, especially, caused much discussion. They were obviously closely related to the "Hittite" art of the Empire period: Delaporte in his report devoted several pages to a detailed comparison of many features of the Lion Gate reliefs with those of Yazilikaya and Alaca Huyuk, the two principal sites of the Empire period;[1] the pecu-liar conical hair style of the chief deity is found only at Malatya, Yazilikaya, and Alaca Huyuk; the form of the god's robes and other details, such as the winged disk above the heads of the figures in relief, are very nearly identical. To Delaporte it seemed manifest that such resem-blance of artistic details points to a close sequence in time, and his first conclusion was that Malatya was a city belonging to the time of the Empire. "At the time of the discovery of the Lion Gate the obvious connection of its sculptures with those of Yazilikaya made us estimate that it had been built a little after the neighboring Hittite sanctuary of Hattusas; since the downfall of the Hittite Empire took place at the beginning of the XIIth century, we then attributed the monuments of Malatya to the end of the XIIIth century."[2]

But as excavations continued and the stratification of the site could be established, it became clear that the level of the Lion Gate was in fact the last of the "Late Hittite" strata, immediately below the Assyrian stratum. Delaporte correctly recognized that the Assyrian occupation

---

[1] L. Delaporte: *Malatya, Fouilles de la Mission Archéologique Française*, Fascicule I, »La Porte des Lions« (Paris, 1940), pp. 31-38 et seq.
[2] Delaporte: *Malatya*, p. 39.

Figure 22: The lion gate of Hattusas.
From *Die Hethiter*, Johannes Lehmann, C. Bertelsmann Verlag, Munich.

Figure 23: The lion gate at Malatya.

of the site, which he recognized irr the archaeology, must reflect the campaign of Sargon of the year -712, in the course of which the Assyrian king claims to have occupied Malatya and taken its ruler captive. Thus the archaeological evidence indicated that the Lion Gate was built in the mid-eighth century, shortly before the Assyrian occupation of the city, while the evidence from art indicated that it was contemporary with the other monuments of the "Hittite Empire," which in turn were dated to the thirteenth century. Those scholars who reasoned chiefly from artistic evidence generally preferred an early date. Thus Henri Frankfort wrote: "The lions guarding the gate show a number of peculiarities which link them with the art of Boghazkeuy; their manes are rendered by connected spirals ... the small round marks between their eyes occur in the lions from Boghazkeuy."[1] Listing several more "striking" resemblances, Frankfort concluded that the Lion Gate could not have been built later than the early twelfth century.

A similar view was expressed by G. Hanfmann, who agreed that the Lion Gate sculptures "are still quite close in iconography and style to the latest sculpture of the Hittite Empire,[2] and also suggested an early date (-1050 to -900).

Historians who took into account the evidence of archaeology were unable to accept this dating. H. T. Bossert, especially, was adamant in arguing that an early date went counter to what was known of the stratigraphical situation at Malatya.[3] Even Hanfmann, who championed an early date, recognized the archaeological difficulties that this view raised, for it implied that the stratum in which the Lion Gate was found "would have lasted at least 250 years, thus equalling in duration all five earlier Neo-Hittite levels":[4] These five levels together would then have lasted less than 200 years. Bossert found this unacceptable and placed the structure squarely in the middle of the eighth century.

William F. Albright made a comparison with nearby Carchemish and concluded that the Malatya reliefs could not be later than the tenth century, because the Carchemish reliefs of the same period had already lost the influence of imperial Hittite art. He opted for a date

---

[1] H. Frankfort: *The Art and Architecture of the Ancient Orient* (Baltimore, 1954), p. 129.
[2] G. Hanfmann: »Remarques stylistiques sur les Reliefs de Malatya; Ankara Universitesi Dil ve Tarih-Cografya, No. 53, Arkeoloji Entstitüsü, mo. 3, by Ekrem Akurgal«, *American Journal of Archaeology*, 51 (1947), p. 329.
[3] H. T. Bossert: *Altanatolien* (Berlin, 1942), p. 69.
[4] Hanfmann, op. cit., p. 329.

Figure 24: Syro-Hittite art: Relief sculptures from the Lion Gate at Malatya. The upper slab shows a libation to a god, the scene of the lower slab presents a fight with a coiled dragon. These crude art forms later developed into the monumental sculptures of Yazilikaya.

between -1150 and -1050.[1] We, however, would not expect tenth-century reliefs from Carchemish to show influences from Yazilikaya, for the famous rock had yet to be carved. The art of which Yazilikaya is a prime representative arose only in the eighth and flourished in the seventh and early sixth centuries.

Albright's solution was rejected by O. W. Muscarella, who proposed an alternate scheme: Malatya was "a Hittite site with later re-use of the reliefs along with later ninth and eighth century reliefs. There is no evidence for an eleventh century date, which seems merely convenient. ..."[2] Muscarella thought to solve the problem by making Malatya both early and late, but not in between. Albright before him had sought

---

[1] W. F. Albright: »Comment on Recently Reviewed Publications«, *Bulletin of the American Schools of Oriental Research*, 105 (1947), p. 14.

[2] O. W. Muscarella: »Hasanlu in the Ninth Century B.C., and Its Relations with Other Cultural Centers of the Near East«, *American Journal of Archeology*, 75 (1971), p. 263.

a solution by putting the structure in between the opposing views of Bossert (eighth century) and of Delaporte, Hanfmann, and Frankfort (thirteenth or twelfth century).

Now the solution is at hand. The Lion Gate was built sometime in the second part of the eighth century, before the Assyrian occupation of the city, as the stratigraphical situation quite clearly indicates. It preceded by several decades the carvings at Yazilikaya, which quite possibly were made in the same artistic tradition, dislodged by Assyrian pressure from Malatya to the more westerly site. In the early years of the reign of Assurbanipal the pressure came from the other direction: The "Hittites" were moving eastward, occupying Carchemish in the time of Suppiluliumas, and Babylon a few decades later. Not long after that, Nineveh itself fell, and the great Chaldean Empire was in control of most of the Ancient East.

"The Land of Their Nativity"

"The lands of Hatti" must have been a geographical term for a very large area indeed; Hattusilis (Nebuchadnezzar), when achieving supreme power throughout the Neo-Babylonian Empire, wrote: "The lands of Hatti, in their entirety, Ishtar turned to Hattusilis." In the building inscriptions found in Babylon, Nebuchadnezzar similarly refers to the entire region west of the Euphrates, of which he became overlord, as Hattiland. It comprised eastern Anatolia, Syria, and other countries. It was a geographical term; in the same way we use terms like Asia Minor, Fertile Crescent, Near East, or Middle East.

Until rather recently "Ur of the Chaldees," on the southern flow of the Euphrates, was regarded as the birthplace of the patriarch Abraham;[1] archaeologists who dug in Tell al Mugaiyir found there an inscription which confirmed them in their belief that the place was ancient Ur. Great physical disturbances that occurred in the second millennium and huge deposits of alluvium that covered the city in some sudden catastrophe[2] must have driven the survivors from their homeland.

Cyrus H. Gordon, however, has argued that Ur in the south was not Abraham's birthplace: the scriptural description of his peregrinations

---

[1] Genesis 11:31.
[2] C. L. Woolley: *Ur of the Chaldees* (London, 1929).

before he went to Canaan to make his domicile there points to a different Ur, northwest of Babylonia, and this Ur, to differentiate it from the
southern city, was called Ur of the Chaldees.[3]
The Chaldeans changed their homeland more than once in large-
scale forced migrations. About -728 Tiglath-Pileser III, after a long war
with the Chaldeans (Kaldu), deported them to the northern region,
and at the end of the eighth century there were Chaldeans scattered in
Uruk, Nippur, Kish, Kutha, and Sippar.[1]
Merodach-Baladan, the rival of Sargon II, Sennacherib, and Assurbanipal, was called "king of the Chaldeans." His main territory was in
Beth-Yakhin, probably near the Persian Gulf; for a time he occupied
Babylon. Assurbanipal exterminated the Chaldean population at Beth-
Yakhin.
In the region of Ararat, east of Ur of the Chaldees, on the upper
Euphrates and around Lake Van, there lived a people who worshiped
the god Chaldi. Modern scholars, beginning with Lehmann-Haupt,
called them "Chaldians" on the assumption that their tribal name reflected the name of their chief deity (similarly the Assyrian nation took
its name from its chief god Assur), choosing this form of the name to
distinguish them from the Chaldeans of Babylonia. The dynasties of
these "Chaldians" were engaged in defensive wars against the Assyrians.[2] They were also called Urartu, a name that survives in the scriptural Ararat.
Scholars have noted "striking" similarities between Urartian (Chaldean)
and "Hittite" culture.[3]
In the light of the persistent pressure the Assyrians under Esarhaddon
and his son Assurbanipal exerted on the population around Lakes Urmia
and Van, which resulted in the involuntary resettlement of these populations farther and farther to the west, there is some ground to suppose that the worshipers of Chaldi earned the name "Chaldeans" ("Cas-
dim" in Hebrew) because they were one of the branches of the ancient
Chaldean people.
The Chaldeans under Nabopolassar occupied Babylonia, but Babylonia
was not their native land. They came from Chaldea and transferred

---

[1] »Abraham of Ur«, *Journal of Near Eastern Studies*, 17 (1958), pp. 97-89.
[2] Sennacherib's prism, I, 37f.
[3] Boris B. Piatrovsky: *The Ancient Civilization of Urartu* (New York, 1969).
[4] M. N. van Loon: *Urartian Art: Its Distinctive Traits in the Light of New Excavations* (Istanbul, 1966), p. 170.

their capital to Babylon. Ezeldel called them "Babylonians of Chaldea, the land of their nativity" (Ezekiel 23:15).

Where was "the land of their nativity"? From where did Nabopolassar come?

Judged by the remnants of the strange culture ascribed to the "Hittites," which I identify as Chaldean, the land of the Chaldean nativity in the eighth and seventh centuries was in Cappadocia and Cilicia, between the Black Sea on the north, the region of Ararat and the upper Euphrates on the east, the big bend of the Mediterranean on the south, and the river Halys on the west. Boghazkoi, Alisar, Senjirli, and Carchemish are situated in this area.

Xenophon,[1] the Athenian soldier (ca. -435 to -335) who fought in the army of Cyrus the Younger of Persia and traversed with the famous "ten thousand" mercenaries the length of Asia Minor, wrote about the Chaldeans as a tribe living in Armenia that stretched from Ararat to south of the Black Sea. One hundred forty years earlier Cyrus the Great, at war with Croesus, referred to Chaldeans as "neighbors" of Annenians. He also said of the land which modern scholars assign to the Hittites: "These mountains which we see belong to Chaldaea."[2] Strabo, a native of Amasia in Pontus, who knew Asia Minor at first hand, located the Chaldeans next to Trapezus (Trebizond) on the Black Sea coast: "Above the region of Pharnacia and Trapezus are the Tibareni and the Chaldaei, whose country extends to lesser Armenia"[3] It is asserted that these "Black Sea Chaldeans" of Xenophon and Strabo are not the real Chaldeans but "Chaldians," or that Xenophon used the wrong name for the bellicose tribe of that region. But Xenophon and Strabo were not wrong. Though under Nabopolassar and Nebuchadnezzar the Chaldeans entered the melting pot of the Neo-Babylonian Empire, many of them surived in Cappadocia: Xenophon met them there at the close of the fifth century and Strabo records their presence in the area as late as the first. Soon we shall also bring archaeological evidence to bear on the question and will show that Chaldean ("Hittite") pictographs were in use in this very region in the time of Strabo, and even beyond.

---

[1] Xenophon: *Anabasis*, IV, iii, 4; V, v, 17. *Cyropaedia*, III, i, 34ff. See also Strabo, XII, iii, 18-19; Plutarch: *Lucullus*.
[2] Xenophon: *Cyropaedia*, III, ii.
[3] Strabo: 12:3,18-20, 28, 29.

The Secret Script of the Chaldeans

Attaining supreme power in the extensive region from the shores of the Persian Gulf to the Black Sea and to the Mediterranean and the Red Seas, the Chaldean Empire embraced many nations, religions, and tongues. In the subjugated provinces the local languages were respected. "O people, nations, and languages," called Nebuchadnezzar in the Book of Daniel. The language in daily use in Babylon was Akkadian-Babylonian; in the provinces this was the language of official and diplomatic documents; these documents were often translated into the local tongues. The system was not bilingual but trilingual. Besides Babylonian, the official international language, and the native speech of the various localities, Chaldean was used in sacred services for liturgies and prayers and also in the solemn festivities of the palace. In the Book of Daniel it is written that King Nebuchadnezzar ordered training for certain Judean youths of aristocratic origin who were "skillful in all wisdom, and cunning in knowledge, and understanding science, and such as had ability in them to stand in the king's palace, and whom they teach the learning and the tongue of the Chaldeans"[1]

For many centuries and down to modern times scholars thought that Chaldean was the language in which a part of the Book of Daniel, as well as the *Talmud*, was written. For this reason there exist "Chaldean" dictionaries. However, it has subsequently been shown that the language of these books was not Chaldean but Aramaean or Syriac. In the same Book of Daniel (2:4) it is said that, besides the tongue of the Chaldean and Babylonian, Syriac was used in the palace. "Then spake the Chaldeans to the king in Syriac."

The absence of inscriptions in the Chaldean tongue conflicted with the reference in the Book of Daniel to a language the Chaldeans used in their secret teachings and for sacred purposes. It was finally stated that the "language of these Chaldaeans differed in no way from the

---

[1] Daniel (1:4). The view that Daniel is a product of the second century before this era is shaken, and Dougherty (*Nabonidus and Belshazzar,* pp. 196-200) demonstrates that "of all non-Babylonian records dealing with the situation at the close of the Neo-Babylonian Empire the fifth chapter of Daniel ranks next to cuneiform literature in accuracy" and that "the total information found in all available chronologically fixed documents later than the cuneiform texts of the sixth century B.C. ... could not have provided the necessary material for the historical framework of the fifth chapter of Daniel."

ordinary Semitic Babylonian idiom"[1] and was practically identical with the Akkadian language of Babylonia and Assyria.

The Akkadian population of Babylon was merged with the Chaldean stock, but the land of origin of the Chaldeans was not Babylon. The Chaldeans retained for themselves the position of a caste of priests and astrologers,[2] and it would have been only natural that, in their sacerdotal invocations and mysteries, they should have used the tongue of their ancient traditions, not known to the common people. They recorded their secret knowledge, not to be divulged, in a script not understandable to the profane abecedarians.

It is often asserted that no secret writing has been discovered in the countries along the Euphrates. Even modern books on ancient history maintain this in the chapters dealing with Chaldea; and in the chapters on the discovery of a strange pictographic script in Carchemish on the Euphrates, in Babylon, in Assur on the Tigris, in Hamath, in Boghazkoi, and in other places, the new statement is made that this writing must have been left by a people of "a forgotten empire" and, centuries later, by the so-called Syrian Hittites.

But since at least some of the monuments with this pictographic script are unanimously assigned to the sixth century,[3] the "Hittites" who supposedly wrote these hieroglyphics (pictographs) when under the later kings of the Chaldean dynasty in Babylon must have escaped not only the memory of subsequent generations but also the notice of their contemporaries.

A Dagger and a Coin

Although the Chaldean Empire came to an end with the capture of Babylon by Cyrus in -539 (or -538), and Chaldean ceased to be a state

---

[1] J. D. Prince: »Chaldaea«, *Encyclopaedia Britannica* (14th ed.), V, 195 It is sometimes supposed that the language of the wise men was non-Semitic Sumerian. Compare E. Renan: *Histoire générale et système comparé des langues sémitiques* (7th ed.), p. 65.

[2] "The Chaldeans, belonging as they do to the most ancient inhabitants of Babylonia, have about the same position among the divisions of the state as that occupied by the priests of Egypt." Diodorus of Sicily, transl. Oldfather, I, 29.

[3] The royal stele of Marash, the stele of Bor, the statue of Palanga, all of them with pictographic inscriptions. See Von der Osten: *Four Sculptures,* pp. 112-32.

language, the Chaldeans as a tribe in mountainous Cappadocia and Cilicia and as a class of priests did not cease to exist. One might expect, therefore, that the Chaldean pictographic script would have been used in the centuries following the fall of Babylon. The lead strips inscribed with pictographs from Assur were found to be similar to the strips inscribed with exorcisms in Greek in the third and second centuries. One might expect also that Chaldean pictographs would have been employed as long as cuneiform was used. Cuneiform survived mainly because the Persians adapted it to their language as syllabic characters. The latest extant cuneiform inscription dates from the year 75 of the present era, in the reign of the emperor Vespasian.

Very soon after the announcement of the discovery of the empire of the "Hittites" a bilingual inscription in cuneiform and pictographs drew the attention of the scientists. A. H. Sayce wrote in his *The Hittites: The Story of a Forgotten Empire* (1888): "Within a month after my paper had been read before the Society of Biblical Archaeology which announced the discovery of a Hittite Empire and the connection of the curious art of Asia Minor with that of Carchemish, I had fallen across a bilingual inscription in Hittite and cuneiform characters. This was on the silver boss of King Tarkondemos." The boss is an engraved disk which was attached to a dagger handle. Sayce continued: "The reading of the cuneiform legend offers but little difficulty. It gives us the name and title of the king whose figure is engraved within it – 'Tarqu-dimme king of the country of Erme.' The name Tarqu-dimme is evidently the same as that of the Cilician prince Tarkondemos or Tarkon-dimotos," who lived in the days of Augustus, in the very first years of the Christian Era. "The name is also met with in other parts of Asia Minor under the forms of Tarkondas and Tarkondimatos; and we may consider it to be of a distinctively Hittite type. Where the district was over which Tarqu-dimme ruled we can only guess; it may have been the range of mountains called Arima by the classical writers, which lay close under the Hittite monuments of the Bulgar Dagh. In this case Tarkondemos would have been a Cilician king."

Since the very beginning of the "Hittite" studies the boss of Tarku-dimme has been an outstanding object of investigation, as for a long time it was the only known bilingual inscription in pictographs and another script. The pictograph inscription on the boss was not deciphered – it did not appear to be an exact equivalent of the cuneiform.

But the author quoted above (Sayce) considered that the dagger might have belonged to a prince in Cilicia whose name was Tarkondemos; he further brought out that a prince of the same name lived in Cilicia in the days of Augustus Caesar. The question, Was there a nation of "Hittites" in the days of Augustus? was avoided. No Roman author, historian or geographer, said anything of Hittites, yet Asia Minor was under Roman domination.

In the first pre-Christian century the Chaldeans and the Persian magi were regarded as possessors of a secret and ancient knowledge. A charm in Chaldean letters on the handle of a dagger may have been designed to protect its owner against his enemies. One of the originators of the idea of the "Hittite Empire" unwittingly provided proof that the pictographic characters were used at least until the beginning of the Christian Era.

Subsequent authors who dealt with the pictographic script of the "Hittites" were quite unanimous in their expressed views that this script, which continued in use till the sixth century in the Syrian cities among the so-called "Syrian Hittites," had already come into complete disuse in Asia Minor in about -1200, with the fall of the Hittite Empire. If, however, the script is Chaldean, not "Hittite" then it is only reasonable to expect its survival through Greek and into Roman times in the Near East.

In 1950 a Swiss numismatist published in a local numismatic magazine a communication telling of a coin with some pictographs and a Greek version printed next to it. The world of the orientalists did not become aware of this find until late in 1952 when H. T. Bossert wrote a paper drawing attention to the coin.[1] Sometime thereafter Theresa Goell, the excavator of Nemrud-Dag in the Commogene district, west of the Euphrates, purchased a similar coin in Samosata, the ancient capital of the Commogene kingdom.[2] Both coins have the same "Hittite" pictograph reading "Gal-Lugal" ("Great King") and in Greek, next to it, "Basileus Megas", or "the great ruler." The coins were minted by Antioch IV, a king of the Commogene kingdom; he ruled in the days of the Emperor Vespasian and was also deposed by him in the year 72 of the present era.

---

[1] Bossert: »Wie lange wurden hethitische Hieroglyphen geschrieben«, *Die Welt des Orients*, (1952), pp. 480-84. See also C. Küthman: *Schweizer Münzblätter*, I(1950), pp. 62f.

[2] Private communication.

Bossert assumed that the "Hittite" pictograph was selected to adorn the Commogene coin of the first century without any knowledge of what the sign signified, because the "Hittite" culture and language were things of a remote past; it does not sound convincing. Why exactly had the word "ruler" or "king" been selected from a very great number of "Hittite" pictographs found on ancient monuments? It is a translation of the Greek term "Basileus Megas" minted on the same coins. "Hittites" were of an era long past but the Chaldeans were known to the Romans and also admired for their secret knowledge. The world was eager to learn the secrets of the past, and the Persian magi, the Chaldeans, the Egyptian priests were thought to be carriers of such traditions. The Chaldeans as an ethnic group lived through Persian and Hellenistic times in the area adjacent to Commogene, close to Malatya and other sites where the monuments tell of the days when the Chaldeans ruled the region and, actually, most of the ancient East. In the days of Strabo, in the last decades of the pre-Christian and the first two decades of the Christian Era, the Chaldeans, as an ethnic group, still occupied the area and it is not necessarily only as a tribute to things archaic that the Commogene kings, descendants of the Macedonian generals, adorned their coins with Chaldean signs next to Greek letters.

In the style of its monuments the kingdom of Commogene preserved traits that seemed to go back to the time of the "Hittite Empire," supposedly twelve centuries before.

Theresa Goell, excavator of Nemrud-Dag, the capital of the Hellenistic kings of Commogene, reported: "Of particular interest for cultural and art history is the archaic survival of Hittite attributes and details comparable with features known from Yazilikaya, Tell Halaf, Karkemis. ... The colossal statues, guardian lions ... are details exhibiting unmistakable Hittite influence."[1]

But if the "Hittite" influence is in fact Chaldean, it is readily explained by the presence of Chaldean tribes in this region as late as the first century before this era.

---

[1] »Summary of Archaeological Work in Turkey in 1954«, *Anatolian Studies* (1955), p. 14

Mitanni

Still another kingdom will be dissolved when the centuries are placed
in their proper position.

A people of the Indo-European race lived within the "Hittite" region
– the people of Mitanni. The kings of Mitanni were among the active
correspondents of the el-Amarna period. Tushratta (Dushratta) wrote
a letter partly in Babylonian and partly in Mitannian. After much court-
ship on the part of the Egyptian royal house the kings of Mitanni
consented to give their daughters as wives to the pharaohs.[1] This fact
hints at the important position which the kings of Mitanni and their
country occupied.

It was not an easy task to find a geographical area in northern Syria
or in Mesopotamia not occupied by other peoples, and therefore – in
addition to other considerations – the region of Carchemish, already
allotted to the "Hittites" and to the Assyrians, was assigned to the
Mitanni people too; on historical charts the names of these three peoples
are written in different directions across the same area.

Mitra, Varuna, and Indra, of Indo-Iranian origin, comprise the pantheon of the people of Mitanni. The Mitanni had "Indo-Iranian techni-
cal terms in their vocabulary." If one assumes that this people lived on
the upper Euphrates one has to admit their migration from Iran in
some remote age. Who were the people of Mitanni?

It is asserted that the kingdom of Mitanni and its people disappeared
in the thirteenth or twelfth century, since nothing is known of them in
the following centuries. However, the Libyan pharaoh Sosenk referred
once more to Mitanni, and it was thought to be an anachronism.[3]

In the fifteenth to the thirteenth centuries the Indo-Iranian Medes
had not yet been heard of, but in the ninth to the eighth centuries, a
short while before their activity became prominent, their presence in
the circle of nations should be expected.

The role of the Medes in the alliance against Assyria, as pictured
in the annals of Nabopolassar, and the role of the Mitanni, also in
the alliance against Assyria, as described by Mursilis and by his father,
seem to coincide.

---

[1] See *Ages in Chaos*, Vol. I, p. 313.
[2] Albright: *From the Stone Age to Christianity*, p. 153.
[3] J. A. Wilson: »Egyptian Historical Texts« in *Ancient Near Eastern Texts*, ed. Pritchard, pp.
263-64; "Mitanni as a nation had ceased to exist at least four centuries earlier."

A patricide prince of Mitanni fled almost naked from his country, came to the father of Mursilis, and became Mursilis' brother-in-law, the marriage being concluded to secure an alliance for the impending war with Assyria.[1] From the brief description of the fall of Assyria in the annals of Nabonidus it can be concluded that the prince of the Medes, the ally of the Chaldeans, was a patricide. The political purpose of the alliance through marriage with the prince of Mitanni in the approaching war against Assyria is told at length in the Boghazkoi texts.[2] In Greek authors this fact took the form of a legend about Nabopolassar, who accepted a Median princess as a bride for his son Nebuchadnezzar.[3] But it has been observed that nothing is known from cuneiform texts about a Median consort of Nebuchadnezzar.[4]

Herodotus (v, 49) names the northwest part of Media under the Persian kings as the land of Matiene. This Persian satrapy was near Mount Ararat.[5] We connect the name Matiene with the name Mitanni of el-Amarna and Boghazkoi. We assume that Mitanni was the original name of the Medes and that their area was not on the central Euphrates but south of the Caspian Sea. The invasion of Media by the Scythians (Umman-Manda)[6] brought with it an influx of new blood, and after that the name Manada was also applied to the Mitanni.[7] The hybrid nation was called by the hybrid name of Media. But the original name of Mitanni was retained in the name of a separate satrapy in northwest Media.

Quite different from what is generally pictured were the true movements of racial groups from east to west, from north to south, from south to east and north, when Indo-Iranian groups went through the filter of Semitic peoples, and a combined culture reached Asia Minor.

---

[1] E. Weidner, ed.: »Die Staatsverträge in akkadischer Sprache aus dem Archiv von Boghazköi«, *Boghazköi Studien*, VIII-IX (1923).
[2] Luckenbill: *American Journal of Semitic Languages*, XXXVII (April 1921), Treaty between Shubbiluliuma of Hatti and Mattiuaza of Mitanni, 161-211.
[3] Alexander Polyhistor in Eusebius: *Chronicles*, I, 29.
[4] Dougherty: *Nabonidus and Belshazzar*, p. 55.
[5] Kiepert: »Vortrag über die geographische Stellung der nördlichen Länder in der phönikisch hebräischen Erdkunde«, *Monatsberichte der Akademie der Wissenschaften zu Berlin*, 1859 (1860), pp. 191-219.
[6] Gadd: *The Fall of Nineveh*; E. Meyer (*Geschichte des Altertums*, Vol. III, p. 94) regards Umman-Manda as a designation for Cimmerians who simultaneously with the Scythians invaded western Asia (Asia Minor).
[7] "In the royal inscriptions of the Neo-Babylonian Empire, the Umman-Manda are certainly identical with the Madai, Medes," Langdon: *The Venus Tablets of Ammizaduga*, p. 9, note.

Exodus or Exile

Nebuchadnezzar Visits Ramses II

When in Exile in Egypt, Jeremiah (43:7ff), in a symbolic act, took stones, hid them "in the clay in the brickkiln, which is at the entry of Pharaoh's house in Tahpanhes," and prophesied in the name of the Lord: "I will send and take Nebuchadrezzar the king of Babylon ... and will set his throne upon these stones that I have hid; and he shall spread his royal pavilion over them. And when he cometh, he shall smite the land of Egypt."

Also Ezekiel, in exile in Babylon, prophesied that Nebuchadnezzar would conquer Egypt (29:19). Were these prophecies fulfilled?

"Whether Nebuchadnezzar ever invaded Egypt as Ezekiel prophesied we do not yet know."[1] These words written at the beginning of the century are still valid among students of history. Thousands of clay bricks inscribed with the prayers of Nebuchadnezzar have been found, but only a single inscription of historical content is attributed to Nebuchadnezzar by modern scholars: it is a small mutilated fragment which records an expedition of his to Egypt. This tablet left much room for conjecture.

> The kings, the allies of his power and – his general and his hired soldiers
> – he spoke unto. To his soldiers – who were before – at the way of –
> In the 37th year of Nebuchadnezzar, king of Babylon – the king of Egypt
> came up to do battle (?) and -es, the king of Egypt – and – of the city
> Putu-Jaman – far away regions which are in the sea – numerous which
> were in Egypt – arms and horses – he called to – he trusted-[2]

Ever since this fragment was published[3] it has been often interpreted as an allusion to an invasion of Egypt by Nebuchadnezzar in his thirty-seventh year. A few guesses added to the mutilated text some allusions to military action. Of the name of the pharaoh there remained

---

[1] H. Winckler: *The History of Babylonia and Assyria* (New York, 1907), p. 318.
[2] Cf. Langdon: *Building Inscriptions of the Neo-Babylonian Empire*, p. 82.
[3] T. G. Pinches: »A New Fragment of the History of Nebuchadnezzar«, *Transactions of the Society of Biblical Archaeology*, Vol. 7, 188D (1882), pp. 210–25.

only the last part, -es or -as, and the reconstruction was made thus: "The only name of a king of Egypt of this period which ends with -as [-es] is Ahmes or Amasis."[1] Amasis ruled Egypt from about -568 to -526.

"This tablet is remarkable for the fact that it is the only historical tablet which we have from this epoch. That the king chose a small clay tablet whereon to record his conquest of the Egyptian and Mediterranean alliance is most surprising and demands explanation."[2] The author of this last quotation thought that the document was a royal letter.

But no reference to the fact that Nebuchadnezzar actually invaded Egypt exists in Egyptian or Greek sources. Nor do the Hebrew sources speak of a conquest of Egypt by him or of the fulfillment of the prophecies of Ezekiel and Jeremiah, though they do mention the fact that Nebuchadnezzar was able to remove the Jewish refugees in Egypt to Babylon.

A more critical examination of the tablet suggests that "this inscription used to be misunderstood as a reference to an invasion of Egypt by Nebuchadnezzar."[3] The expedition appears to have been a peaceful one, though infantry and cavalry accompanied the king.

What is the meaning of the broken sentences of the tablet? The king went toward Egypt, after a consultation with his nobles and a speech delivered before his army. He was accompanied by mounted and foot soldiers. A pharaoh whose name ends in -es and the city of the Greek mercenaries in Egypt[4] are mentioned in connection with this expedition.

My revised historical scheme leads me to believe that the pharaoh host of Nebuchadnezzar was Ramses II.

In the thirty-fourth year of Ramses II, Hattusilis came to Egypt to visit the pharaoh and to give him a daughter to wife. He also wanted to see the wonders of that country. The so-called "Marriage stele" in Egypt[5] records that the king of Kheta gathered his army and his nobles, and

---

[1] *Ibid.,* p. 216.
[2] Langdon: *Building Inscriptions of the Neo-Babylonian Empire,* p. 183.
[3] Hall: *The Ancient History of the Near East,* p. 547.
[4] Putu Yaman ("Yaman" means "Greek" in Babylonian).
[5] Breasted: *Records,* Vol. III, Secs. 415ff. The steles at Karnak, Elephantine, and Abu Simbel contain the text. See Ch. Kuentz in *Annales du Service des Antiquités de l'Egypte,* XXV (1925), and J. Wilson's translation in Pritchard: *Ancient Near Eastern Texts,* pp. 256ff. A good summary of the texts from Boghazkoi referring to the journey of Hattusilis to Egypt is found in the article of Elmar Edel: »Der geplante Besuch Hattusilis III in Ägypten«, *Mitteilungen der Deutschen Orient-Gesellschaft,* 92 (1960), pp. 16-20.

"then spake the chief of the land of Hatti to his army and his nobles" and explained to them the advantages of giving a daughter to Ramses for a wife.

> His majesty [Ramses] received the word – in the palace, with joy of heart ... when he heard such strange and unexpected matters ...

At that time many princes and rulers of foreign countries were gathered in the residence of the pharaoh. But when they heard that the Great King of Hatti was coming, awe seized them. "The great chiefs of every land came; they were bowed down, turning back in fear, when they saw his majesty the chief of Kheta came among them, to seek the favor of King Ramses (II)."

It was Nebuchadnezzar of whom the *Talmud* said that the terror he inspired in all kings was so great that in his lifetime all the world was in a state of anxiety and nobody dared to smile.[1]

The Marriage stele, in slightly damaged hieroglyphic lines, narrates the arrival of the great retinue:

> His army came, their limbs being sound, and they were long in stride ... The daughter of the great chief of Kheta marched in front of the army ... of his majesty in following her. They were mingled with foot and horse of Kheta; they were warriors as well as regulars; they ate and they drank not fighting face to face – between them ...[2]

Comparing the Egyptian text of the Marriage stele with the cuneiform tablet of Nebuchadnezzar, we find a number of parallels, beginning with the speech of the king of Hatti or Nebuchadnezzar to his army and to his nobles, followed by the march of infantry and cavalry toward Egypt, and ending with meeting the pharaoh and his numerous troops and the description of the trust they displayed toward one another.

Besides the Marriage stele of the thirty-fourth year of Ramses II, there exists a stele found in Coptos containing a reference to royal princes of Hatti who accompanied "his [the king's] other daughter" and to a coming "to Egypt for the second time." Either the Marriage or the Coptos stele is a counterpart of the tablet of Nebuchadnezzar.

We know from the autobiography of Hattusilis that for seven years he subordinated himself to his brother and nephew. During this time he was king of the Upper Land (either Assyria or some part of Anatolia) and commander-in-chief of the western army (army of Hatti).

---

[1] Bernstein: *König Nebucadnezar von Babel in der jüdischen Tradition*, p. 32.
[2] Breasted: *Records*, Vol. III, Sec. 424.

Figure 25: Hattusilis-Nebuchadnezzar bringing his daughter to Ramses II. Note the headdress and hairdo of the king.

Figure 26: The only known representation of Nebuchadnezzar, from Wadi Brissa. Although the relief sculpture is badly damaged, the head-dress of the king is still distinguishable.
From *Inscriptions Babyloniennes* by H. Pognon (1905), plate IV

As we saw, Nebuchadnezzar could reckon the years of his rule in different ways. If he counted the years of his reign from the date when he became king of Babylonia, the thirty-fourth year of Ramses would be the twenty-ninth or thirtieth year of Nebuchadnezzar, and the tablet written in his thirty-seventh year would refer to his second visit to Egypt; but if Nebuchadnezzar, as he certainly did in his later years, counted his royal years from the day his father died, the thirty-fourth year of Ramses would be the thirty-seventh year of Nebuchadnezzar. In this case the tablet of Nebuchadnezzar written in his thirty-seventh year is contemporary with the Marriage stele of the thirty-fourth year of Ramses.

A relief in the rock temple at Abu-Simbel in Nubia shows the king of Hatti bringing his daughter to Ramses II. She stands before her father; he raises his arms with open hands in an expression of respectful greeting. His face is shaven and he has a large tuft of hair falling down his neck from under a tall cone-shaped headdress that looks like a bishop's miter and is a Phrygian cap.

At Wadi Brissa in Lebanon, Nebuchadnezzar twice had his picture cut in rock; these are supposedly the only known portraits of this king. The figures are weathered and worn away, but it can be discerned that on one bas-relief he holds an animal – he is probably killing a lion – and on the other cutting down a tree, probably a cedar of Lebanon. Long sacerdotal inscriptions dedicated to his pious deeds accompany the bas-reliefs.[1]

Of Nebuchadnezzar's apparel on these reliefs, the best preserved and most characteristic is his cap. From under this Phrygian cap his hair, in a heavy tuft, falls along his neck. "His headdress is like the miter of a bishop!"[2]

Although the picture in Lebanon is damaged, the parts that are preserved offer a striking similarity with the picture of the "king of Hatti" at Abu-Simbel, especially as both pictures show the king in the same profile; his hairdo, identical in both portraits, is unusual.

---

[1] The inscriptions are translated into English by Langdon: *Building Inscriptions of the Neo-Babylonian Empire*, pp. 153-75

[2] F. H. Weissbach: *Die Inschriften Nebukhadnezars II im Wadi Brissa und am Nahr el-Kelb* (Leipzig, 1906), p. 3.

We have compared the historical annals, we compared also the mental portraits, now we have the opportunity to compare the physical portraits of the Chaldean and the "Hittite" kings, who were but one.

The Brick Kiln of Tahpanheth

In connection with his visit to Egypt, Nebuchadnezzar mentions Putuyaman, the colony of the Greeks. In the days of Nebuchadnezzar, Tahpanheth was the Hebrew name for the city of Greek soldiers in Egypt. To follow him on his visit to Ramses II we must proceed to Tahpanheth.

Tahpanheth was a frontier town east of the Delta.[1] It had a royal palace (Jeremiah 43:9) and was a fortress. Its Greek name was Daphnae, Tell Defenneh of today.[2] Greek soldiers were stationed there during the seventh and sixth centuries; the place was chosen to protect the Palestinian border of Egypt (Herodotus). Excavations undertaken there disclosed large quantities of Greek armor, tools, and wares.[3] Foundations of a temple built by Ramses II were also discovered. Part of a statue of Ramses II bearing his cartouches was found in the ruins.[4] Daphnae was supposed to have been built in the time of the Twenty-sixth Dynasty in about -664 and have existed until -565, and remains of a temple built by Ramses II were not expected by the excavators.[5]

Flinders Petrie, the excavator of Tahpanheth-Daphnae, was impressed by reddish kiln-baked bricks found at Tell Defenneh and in the neighboring village of Nebesheh. The building materials of Egypt had always been stone and mud bricks. The mud bricks were dried in the sun, a practice employed even today in Egypt.

Therefore kiln-baked bricks used at these two sites were very unusual in Petrie's eyes. In the temple at Nebesheh, Petrie also found a statue bearing the cartouches of Ramses II. He opened a few tombs. Right away the first tomb revealed the time of its origin. "Some fragments of

---

[1] Sir W. M. Flinders Petrie, A. S. Murray and F. Ll. Griffith: *Tanis, Pt. II, Nebesheh (Am) and Defenneh (Tahpanhes)* (London, 1888).
[2] *Ibid.*, p. 52. Herodotus, II, 30, 107.
[3] Petrie: *Tanis, Pt. II, Nebesheh and Defenneh,* p. 30.
[4] *Ibid.*, p. 30.
[5] *Ibid.*

wrought granite found in the tomb again agree to a Ramesside period. The employment of red brick in this tomb, and in the next, which is also Ramesside, is of great importance. Hitherto I had never seen any red brick in Egypt of earlier times than the Constantine period; and it appeared to be a test of that age. Now we see from these cases ... that baked brick was introduced in the Ramesside times in the Delta."[1]

Also in Tahpanheth (Daphnae) the archaeologist unearthed the foundations of a structure built of kiln-baked bricks. "The earliest remains found here are a part of the foundation of a building of red bricks."[2] As these bricks were identical with those of the tombs, the conclusion was drawn that some buildings had been erected in the time of the Ramessides.

It is essential to note this fact: that baked bricks were not discovered in Egypt of an age earlier than the time of the Ramessides, or of an age following that of the Ramessides; they reappear only in the time of the Christian emperor Constantine.

From where did this short-lived innovation come to Egypt?

R. Koldewey, the excavator of the palace of Nebuchadnezzar in Babylon, wrote on the first page of his account: "Nebuchadnezzar rebuilt the palace of bis father, replacing the walls of mud brick by walls of baked brick."[3] Describing the characteristic feature of the buildings of Nebuchadnezzar, the excavator of Babylon repeatedly stressed the "well baked, reddish Nebuchadnezzar-bricks," and Nebuchadnezzar himself refers to them time and again in his building inscriptions.

The manufacturing of kiln-baked brick was apparently an innovation introduced into Egypt from Babylon under Nebuchadnezzar.

We also have the testimony of Jeremiah that in his time there was a brick kiln in Daphnae-Tahpanheth. He took stones and hid them "in the clay in the brickkiln, which is at the entry of Pharaoh's house in Tahpanhes" (Jeremiah 43:9).

Since no kiln-baked bricks have been discovered in pre-Christian Egypt, except those of the Ramesside period, those who adhere to the conventional chronology must assume that the kiln stood for seven centuries from sometime after Ramses II down to Jeremiah without being used in the meantime and that the bricks made in the kiln in the days of Jeremiah all vanished.

---

[1] *Ibid.*, p. 19
[2] *Ibid.*, p. 47
[3] R. Koldewey: *Die Königsburgen von Babylon* (Leipzig, 1931), I.

Ramses' Marriage

The visit of Nebuchadnezzar to Egypt is not only recorded in the pictures and tablet mentioned above but also is testified to by his royal seals found in Egypt. These are "three cylinders of terra-cotta bearing an inscription of Nebuchadrezzar, an ordinary text referring to his constructions in Babylon. ... These were said to come from the Isthmus of Suez, and they apparently belong to some place where Nebuchadrezzar had 'set up his throne' and 'spread his royal pavilion.' As he only passed along the Syrian road, and Daphnae would be the only stopping place on that road in the region of the isthmus, all the inferences point to these having come from Defenneh [Daphnae], and being the memorials of establishment there."[1] In other words, these seals are indications of Nebuchadnezzar's visit to Tahpanheth-Daphnae.

Ramses II - Necho, in his turn, paid his respects to Nebuchadnezzar by visiting him in Babylon. The Bentresh stele of Ramses II informs us: "Lo, his majesty was in Naharin [Naharaim or Mesopotamia] according to his yearly custom."

It is of interest to find traces of his visits to Babylon.

A building inscription of Nebuchadnezzar mentions Beth-Niki, or the House of Necho, outside the walls of Babylon.[2] It was probably the house in which the former enemy, now a son-in-law, stayed during his yearly visits to Babylon. The place awaits its excavators.

When the daughter of "the Great Chief of Hatti" gave birth to a girl he wrote a letter to Ramses demanding that the little one be sent to him and he would give her later "to queenship."[3] Nebuchadnezzar was concerned that his granddaughter should not live the life of a minor princess in Egypt. Ramses had married the daughter of Nebuchadnezzar when he was already a middle-aged man; although his new wife became the chief wife, he had had a chief wife before who had borne him children. This former chief wife had corresponded with "her sister, the wife of the Chief of Hatti," and copies of these letters were preserved in the archives of Boghazkoi.[4]

---

[1] Petrie: *Tanis, Pt. II, Nebesheh and Defenneh*, p. 51.
[2] Koldewey: *Die Königsburgen von Babylon*, I, 63-64. "Beth-Niki" is generally understood to signify "The House of Expenditure."
[3] Luckenbill: *American Journal of Semitic Languages and Literatures*, XXXVII (April 1921), 195.
[4] *Ibid.*

The prophecy of Jeremiah that the king of Babylon would spread his royal pavilion at the entrance to the pharaoh's house in Tahpanheth was fulfilled. If the prophecy was made in the days of Ramses II, and not of his successor, then Jeremiah accurately foretold the spot where Nebuchadnezzar would set his throne. But if he prophesied in the days of Merneptah, the successor of Ramses II, then Jeremiah already knew the place where Nebuchadnezzar twice before had spread his pavilion.

The second part of the same prophecy – "And when he cometh, he shall smite the land of Egypt" – never was fulfilled, as far as the Egyptians were concerned, and as far as we can learn from the historical documents. But it came true as far as the Jews in Egypt were concerned, and this in accordance with the treaty for the extradition of the refugees.

Now we shall follow a few of these remnants of the people who were crushed between Nebuchadnezzar and Ramses when the two rulers were at war and again when they became friends.

The Israel Stele of Merneptah and the Lamentations of Jeremiah

The eight centuries of the settled life of Judah in his land were at an end. A people who had come from the bondage of Egypt at the dawn of this period was dragged into exile to Babylon.

Jeremiah, who had been chained with others and driven from Jerusalem to Riblah, was freed there. However, he did not accept the invitation to go as a free man to Babylon but returned to Judea where a small number of destitute peasants had been left behind by the Babylonian host.[1]

Gedaliah, son of Ahikam, was appointed governor over the remnant of the people in Palestine. The Jews who had been driven to Moab, Ammon, and Edom began to return to Gedaliah, who was in Mizpah in Judea. He took no heed of the warnings of his friends; stirred by the Ammonite king Baalis, insurgents fell upon Mizpah and killed Gedaliah together with his attendants and the Chaldeans who were found there. Fearing a merciless vengeance at the hand of Nebuchadnezzar, the last Jews of Palestine resolved to depart for Egypt.

---

[1] Jeremiah 40:4-6

JEREMIAH 42:14 ... we will go into the land of Egypt, where we shall see no war, nor hear the sound of the trumpet, nor have hunger of bread; and there will we dwell.

The Jewish emigrants who "were in Moab, and among the Ammonites, and in Edom" and who "returned out of all places whether they were driven" (Jeremiah 40:11-12), and came to Mizpah only to escape again to Egypt, might have been looked upon by the Egyptians as refugees from Edom, Moab, and Ammon. Other refugees, who would not return any more to Mizpah, streamed from Edom and Moab to Egypt, following the impoverished people fleeing from Judea.

A fragmentary letter of a frontier official has been found which reads:

> We have finished letting the Shosu tribes of Edom pass the fortress of Meneptah-hotephima'e, which are in the Tjeku-nome, in order to sustain them and sustain their flocks through the good pasture of Pharaoh life prosperity, health!, the good sun of every land.[1]

JEREMIAH 43:7 So they came into the land of Egypt: for they obeyed not the voice of the Lord: thus came they even to Tahpanhes.

In Tahpanheth there was a "Pharaoh's house" (Jeremiah 43:9)˙ The city was a frontier fortress east of the Delta and a royal palace was found there by Petrie.[2] Tjeku (T-k'), the frontier town east of the Delta, on the main road from Syria-Palestine has been identified as Tahpanheth of the Scriptures and Daphnae of the Greek authors.

The pharaoh, whose name is read "Binerē'-meramūn Merenptah-hotphi (r) mā'e" and who followed Ramses II, is the pharaoh Hophra of Jeremiah. The reading "hotphi (r) mā'e" should be repaired to "hophrāma'e". The letter "t" in "hotep" ("beloved") was apparently not sounded ("Amen-hotep", likewise, is "Amenophis" in Greek) and thus "Hotphir" was transliterated "Hophra" in Hebrew and "Apries" in Greek.

Jeremiah, while in exile in Egypt, said of this pharaoh (44:30).

> Thus saith the Lord; Behold, I will give Pharaoh-hophra king of Egypt into the hand of his enemies ... as I gave Zedekiah king of Judah into the hand of ... his enemy.

---

[1] R. Caminos: *Late-Egyptian Miscellanies* (Oxford, 1954), p. 293.
[2] Petrie: *Tanis, Pt. II, Nebesheh and Defenneh*.

The Greek form of the name "Hophra" is "Apries". According to both Jeremiah and Herodotus, Hophra-Apries followed Necho-Nekos closely.[1]

One scholar[2] conjectured that the above letter of the official in the fortress at Takh concerning the entry of migrants into Egypt was a description of the coming of Jacob and his sons to the land of the pharaoh; this, of course, if Merneptah was not the Pharaoh of the Exodus, as is accepted by most scholars of today.

But how wide of the mark! Merneptah was not the Pharaoh of Joseph, or of the Exodus, but the Pharaoh of the Exile. The long history of Israel – the stay in Egypt, the wandering in the desert, and the periods of the Judges and the Kings – lay between.

Why was the role of the Pharaoh of the Exodus ascribed to Merneptah? Chiefly it was because of the so-called Israel stele. It was found in 1886 by Petrie. This monument should be called "the Libyan stele," as it contains a description of the Libyan campaign, but it has twelve concluding lines from which its name has been derived: the Israel stele.[3]

For a better understanding of the final verses it is necessary to determine the spirit in which the stele was written. The king is called in this inscription

> the Sun, driving away the storm which was over Egypt, allowing Egypt to see the rays of the sun, removing the mountain of copper from the neck of the people. ...

The lines preceding the mention of Israel are:

> One comes and goes with singing, and there is no lamentation of mourning people. The towns are settled again anew; as for the one that ploweth his harvest, he shall eat it. Re has turned himself to Egypt; he was born, destined to be her protector, the King Merneptah.

The concluding lines follow here:

> The kings are overthrown, saying: "Salam!" Not one holds up his head among the Nine Bows. Wasted is Tehenu, Kheta is pacified, plundered is Pekanan, with every evil, carried off is Askalon, seized upon is Gezer, Yenoam is made as a thing not existing. Israel ('-s-r-'-r) is desolated, his

---

[1] Herodotus (II, 161) interposed the six-year reign of Psammis between Necos (Necho) II and Apries.
[2] B. D. Eerdmans: *Alttestamentliche Studien,* II (Giessen, 1908), 67.
[3] J. Wilson in Pritchard: *Ancient Near Eastern Texts,* pp. 376-78. See *Ages in Chaos,* Chapter I, Section, »What Is the Historical Time of the Exodus?«

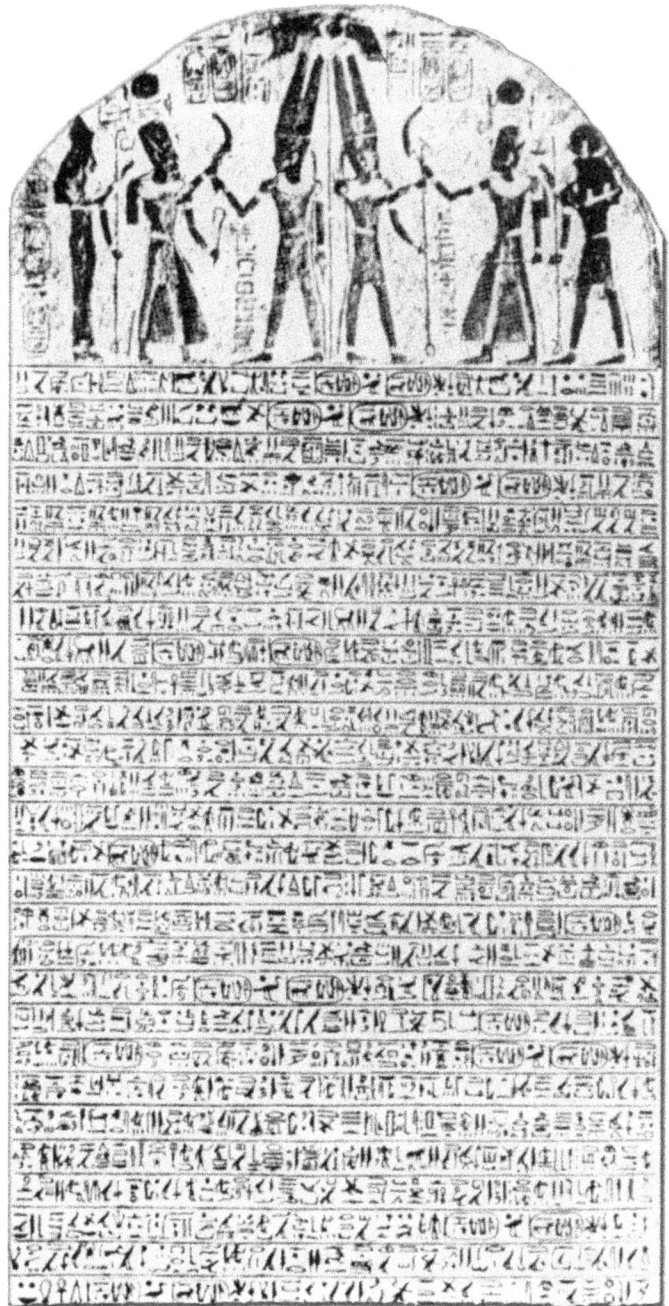

Figure 27: The "Israel Stele" of Merneptah

seed is not; Palestine (H'-rw) has become a widow for Egypt. All lands are united, they are pacified; everyone that is turbulent is bound by King Merneptah, given life like Re, every day.

The line, "Israel is desolated, his seed is not," in the concluding passage of the stele inspired a vast literature; it is agreed that here Israel's name is mentioned for the first time in writing, even before the oldest passages of Hebrew traditions were put down in written characters.[1] We are assured that it is not only the earliest but also the sole mention of Israel in the extant records of Egypt.

"His seed is not" was more than once interpreted as a reference to the slaying of the male children of the Israelites by the Egyptians, but this interpretation is regarded as strained by the majority of scholars, who hold to the view that this line on Merneptah's stele describes a defeat dealt by the hand of Pharaoh to Israel escaping from Egypt to Palestine. It was stressed that "Israel" was written without an accompanying sign of settled people or place. Volumes of controversy and debate are stacked high to shed light on this single line.[2] Its few words begin the written history of the "eternal people"; they are also, for many scholars, the "alpha" of computation of the time of the Exodus.

What was the reason for the assertion that the stele of Merneptah is a document concerning the Exodus of the Israelites from Palestine? Because he was a pharaoh who despoiled Palestine? The history of the Exodus does not know of the despoiling of Palestine by the Pharaoh of the Exodus. Because he defeated the Israelites? The history of the Exodus does not know of a defeat of the Israelites by the pharaoh; it only knows of a disaster which overtook the Egyptian host. If the vague line means that the Israelites were vanquished by Merneptah, then it would be proof against and not for the identification of Merneptah with the Pharaoh of the Exodus.[1]

The history of the Exodus knows neither that Egypt was threatened by the Hittites nor that it pacified the Hittites; the city of Pekanon, evidently important in Palestine, is not included in the detailed list of the Book of Joshua, which enumerates the Palestinian cities found in

---

[1] "The monument has attracted wide attention, because of the reference to Israel in the last section. This is the earliest mention of Israel known to us in literature, not excluding the Hebrew Scriptures themselves." Breasted: *Records*, Vol. III, Sec. 603.

[2] Some of the controversial material previous to 1925 is found in J. W. Jack: *The Date of Exodus in the Light of External Evidence* (Edinburgh, 1925).

[3] S. A. B. Mercer: *Tutankhamen and Egyptology* (Milwaukee, 1923), pp. 48f.

Canaan by the Israelites after they left Egypt.[1] Also the fact disclosed by the Egyptian documents written by the frontier officials of Merneptah, to the effect that Semites were admitted from Palestine to Egypt in his day, does not harmonize with the fact of the Exodus. "The name of the people of Israel here is very surprising in every way: it is the only instance of the name Israel on any monument, and it is four centuries before any mention of the race in cuneiform; it is clearly outside of our literary information, which has led to the belief that there were no Israelites in Palestine between the going into Egypt and the entry at Jericho; whereas here are Israelites mentioned in the Ynuamu (Yenoam) in North Palestine, at a time which must be while the historic Israel was outside of Palestine. ... But the question of the Exodus is made more difficult by the obvious quietude of the frontier shown by the frontier diary. ... It would seem, then, that the Egyptians were welcoming more Semitic tribes ... only a few years before the Exodus."[2]

The Israel stele contains nothing to identify Merneptah with the Pharaoh of the Exodus. What, then, is the real meaning of the concluding lines of the Israel (Libyan) stele?

The secure position of Egypt, as compared with the desolation of Palestine, is emphasized in the sequence of the lines. It is the same idea that is expressed in the Book of Jeremiah (42:14) by those who decided to escape into Egypt: "[In Egypt] we shall see no war ... nor have hunger of bread."

Jeremiah, in exile in Egypt, spoke to his people about the land of Judah and Israel in expressions similar to those of Merneptah:

> JEREMIAH 44:2 ... Ye have seen all the evil that I have brought upon Jerusalem, and upon all the cities of Judah; and, behold, this day they are a desolation, and no man dwelleth therein,
>
> 6 ... the cities of Judah and ... the streets of Jerusalem ... are wasted and desolate. ...
>
> 22 ... your land [is] a desolation, and an astonishment, and a curse, without an inhabitant, as at this day.

---

[1] In the volume covering the period of the Assyrian domination I show that Pekanon was a name for Samaria enlarged by one of the last kings of Israel, Peka. Since the days of Sargon II and Sennacherib settlers from the northern provinces of Assyria lived there.
The city Yenoam mentioned on the stele was probably the name of Dan and of Jerusalem alike, because of the templar oracles speaking in the name of Yahweh ("Yenoam" means "Yahweh speaks"); in the passage from the stele Jerusalem is meant.

[2] Petrie: *A History of Egypt,* III, 114-15.

Jeremiah said that the streets of Jerusalem were "desolate"; Merneptah used the same expression on his stele in reference to Israel. Jeremiah even used the same metaphor as Merneptah, who spoke of Palestine as "a widow." The Lamentations of Jeremiah open with these words: "How doth the city sit solitary, that was full of people! how is she become as a widow!"

Jeremiah (47) in his burden "against the Philistines, before that Pharaoh smote Gaza," spoke about the fate of the Philistine shore: "Baldness is come upon Gaza; Ashkelon is cut off with the remnant of their valley."

These words remind us of "carried off is Askalon" of the stele. Jeremiah does not say whether his words concerning Ashkelon refer to the destruction resulting from the march of Necho (Ramses II), as we understand them with the help of the bas-relief of Ramses II, or to the exploits of some troops of Hophra (Merneptah).

The question of whether the concluding lines of the Libyan stele refer to a campaign by Merneptah into Syria-Palestine was argued and answered positively by some scholars, negatively by others.[1] The latter maintained that a march into Syria and a victory there would not be mentioned in a few vague words but would be memorialized in a manner peculiar to Merneptah, as illustrated by the memorials to his initial victories in the Libyan campaign.

Into this controversy might be introduced what Herodotus wrote about a victorious campaign by Apries against the coast of Palestine-Syria before his Libyan campaign.[2] Diodorus of Sicily also referred to Apries, who terrorized the Phoenician coast, saying that Apries "took Sidon ... and so terrified the other cities of Phoenicia that he secured their submission."[3]

If this was a regular campaign it needed the consent of Nebuchadnezzar. Nebuchadnezzar did not care much for the country that had been ruined and emptied of its people. The only time Merneptah-Apries would have been able to act on his own discretion in Palestine was during the period of Nebuchadnezzar's mental derangement. Some troops of Apries (Merneptah), taking advantage of the anarchical state of the desolate land, raided Gezer and Ashkelon and other cities in the Philis-

---

[1] See E. Naville: »Did Mernephtah Invade Syria?« *Journal of Egyptian Archaeology*, II (1915), pp. 195-201.

[2] Herodotus, II, 161.

[3] *The Historical Library*, I, 68.

tine lowlands. Ammonites[1] and Edomites,[2] ravenous and greedy, came to the unwalled villages, to cities stripped of gate and bar, and preyed upon their ashes. Perhaps Egyptian bands also were among them.

The Chaldeo-Babylonian Empire (Kheta) was pacified by the treaty and by bonds of kinship; this was why Egypt felt that brass mountains had been removed from her shoulders. Jeremiah prophesied in vain that the king of Babylonia would come and smite the land of Egypt. The doom of Egypt was not yet sealed. But neither was the doom in the prophecy of Merneptah concerning Israel – "Israel is desolated, his seed is not" – sealed.

> JEREMIAH 46:27 But fear not thou ... O Israel: for, behold, I will save thee from afar off, and thy seed from the land of their captivity. ...

More than this, said Jeremiah when all the evil he foretold came to pass and he turned to bless the remnants of the people: not until the ordinances of the sun, the moon, and the stars depart from before the Lord shall "the seed of Israel ... cease from being a nation before me for ever" (31:36).

The same period, the same events, moved Merneptah and Jeremiah to similar expressions about "desolated land," cities that are made "as a thing not existing," towns on the Palestinian shore that were "carried off," a land that "became a widow," and the "seed of Israel."

The scrolls of Jeremiah and the stele of Merneptah alike shed light on the political situation in the seventies of the sixth century in the countries on the eastern shore of the Mediterranean.

The Libyan Campaign

After having compared the concluding passage of the stele of Merneptah-Hophrama'e with Jeremiah's reference to the pharaoh Hophra, it is of interest to compare Merneptah's monumental inscriptions on his Libyan war with what Herodotus said about Apries, the pharaoh Hophra.

---

[1] Jeremiah 41:10; 49:1.
[2] Ezekiel 25:12.

The Egyptian sources enable us to see Merneptah "facing the evil conditions on his Libyan frontier. ... The Libyans have for years past been pushing into and occupying the western Delta. They pressed in almost to the gates at Memphis. ... They had made a coalition with the maritime peoples of the Mediterranean, who now poured into the Delta from Sardinia on the west to Asia Minor on the east. The mention of these peoples in these documents is the earliest appearance of Europeans in literature, and has always been the center of much study and interest."[1]

A newly discovered inscription of Merneptah from Heliopolis reads:

> Regnal year 5, second month of summer, one came to say to His Majesty: "The vile chief of the Libyans ... and every foreign land which is with him are penetrating to transgress the boundaries of Egypt." Then His Majesty ordered [his] army to rise up against them.[2]

The great Karnak inscription enumerates Merneptah's enemies:

> Ekwesh, Teresh, Luka, Sherden, Shekelesh, Northerners coming from all lands.

The European peoples, from Sardinia in the western part of the Mediterranean to Asia Minor in the east, were recognized in these names: Etruscans (Teresh[3]), Sardinians (Sherden, Sardan), later explained as people of Sardis, Lycians (Luka), Sicilians (Shekelesh). They poured into Cyrenaica (eastern Libya) and participated in the invasion across the western frontier of Egypt.

It was the sensation of the 1860's when the inscriptions of Merneptah were translated and interpreted in the above manner; the influx was called the invasion of Egypt by the Aryan peoples in the thirteenth century.

This participation of the north Mediterranean peoples in the wars in Libya and Egypt in the thirteenth century before this era, before the siege of Troy, and half a millennium or so before the time of Homer, was regarded as a most strange and remarkable fact. It became a matter of major importance for the entire field of Hellenic studies. Greek sources know nothing of an invasion of Egypt by the Hellenic or any

---

[1] Breasted: *Records*, Vol. III, Sec. 570.
[2] H. Bakry: »The Discovery of a Temple of Merneptah at On«, *Aegyptus*, LIII (1973), p. 7.
[3] Another identification makes Teresh signify the people of Tarsus in eastern Asia Minor. But E. Schorr suggests that Teresh signifies the people of the Aegean island of Thera who established a colony in Cyrenaica (Herodotus, IV, 159).

other people in the thirteenth century. Now it was postulated that what had been concealed from the sight of the Greek historians and poets was preserved in the Egyptian inscriptions and modern students of the Aegean past have to draw from the well of Egyptology.

But how can the presence of European armies in Egypt in the thirteenth century be explained, or how can we understand Herodotus, who wrote that Apries (in the sixth century) was the first Egyptian to battle against the Greeks, that Psammetich two or three generations earlier (in the seventh century) had been the first to admit Greek freebooters to Egyptian soil, taking them into his service, and that before Psammetich the Egyptians had not known the Greeks?

The reference to the invaders coming from the northern littoral of the Mediterranean sea and its islands in the inscriptions of Merneptah and references to the Sardan warriors in still earlier documents – of Seti and Ramses II – frustrated every attempt at explanation and confused Hellenic studies. Scholars in these studies at first refused to believe that such an interpretation of the Egyptian texts could be correct;[1] but little by little they came to see the necessity of revising their accepted notions. The earlier skepticism was forgotten and out of repetition grew conviction, and thus the books dealing with the Helladic ages contain records of "the first appearance of European peoples" in the documents of world history.

It was now considered that the history of early Greece was illuminated by written material of contemporaneous Egyptians; and that what Herodotus and Thucydides did not know had become an open book.

Libya was a thorn in Merneptah's side. He went with his army "to overthrow the land of Libya." "The Libyans plotted evil things, to do them in Egypt" (Karnak inscription). The chief of Libya came to invade the Walls-of-the-Sovereign-Memphis (Israel stele). The Karnak inscription, the Cairo column, the Athribis stele, the inscription from Heliopolis, and the Israel stele describe this war with the Libyans but apparently only its opening stage.

Merneptah wrote: "The boasts which he [the chief of Libya] uttered, have come to naught," but the war was not over when these memoirs were cut in stone. Every inscription that contains any historical material from the time of Merneptah is concerned with the Libyan campaign. In his fifth year he was able to block the route of the Libyans

---

[1] See Hall: *The Oldest Civilization of Greece* (London and Philadelphia, 1901), pp. xxvii, 96, 173, 220.

who had crossed the border, and even to put the Libyan advance guard to rout; still this victory was achieved in a defensive war.

The Cairo column says in the name of a god: "I cause that thou cut down the chiefs of Libya whose invasion thou hast turned back."[1]

In the usual bombastic style the Athribis stele[2] records that "the families of Libya are scattered upon the dykes like mice," and the pharaoh is "seizing among them like a hawk." Before this battle the Libyans had already succeeded in occupying Egyptian territory and capturing booty, and this is what is meant by the figurative expression, "Deliver him [the Libyan chief] into the hand of Merneptah, that he may make him disgorge what he has swallowed, like a crocodile." At that moment the prospects for a decisive Egyptian victory were good. The pharaoh counted the uncircumcised phalli of the invaders, which were loaded upon asses and brought from the field of battle to his capital. "Every old man says to his son: Alas for Libya." Yet the Libyan chief succeeded in retreating unharmed. "The wretched fallen chief of Libya fled by favor of night alone."

The conflict was not over; the invasion of the Libyans and the attempts to repulse them grew into a prolonged war with fluctuating success. In later years Merneptah had less reason to commemorate his military triumphs. He did not reveal what the outcome of those protracted campaigns was. The pharaoh wrote of himself that he was appointed to be the doom of the Libyans; but in matters of fate only the outcome counts. Nor did he disclose what eventually happened to the north Mediterranean troops, the mention of which threw the established historical schemes into confusion.

I shall compare the content of the quoted inscriptions of Merneptah with the historical treatment of Apries by Herodotus. In the Second Book of his *History*, the Greek historian gave a short account: "Apries sent a great host against Cyrene and suffered a great defeat." In the Fourth Book Herodotus gave a full description of the war. It took place in the sixth century and it was the migration of Greeks to Cyrene (eastern Libya) that precipitated hostilities.

> The Pythian priestess admonished all Greeks by an oracle to cross the sea and dwell in Libya with the Cyrenaeans; for the Cyrenaeans invited them, promising a new division of lands; and this was the oracle:

---

[1] Breasted: *Records*, Vol. III, Sec. 594.
[2] *Ibid.*, Secs. 598ff.

"Whoso delayeth to go till the fields be fully divided Upon the Libyan land, the man shall surely repent it."
So a great multitude gathered together at Cyrene, and cut off great tracts of land from the territory of the neighboring Libyans.[1]

Soon the new settlers came into conflict with the neighboring population and Egypt became involved in the conflict.

Apries mustered a great host of Egyptians and sent it against Cyrene; the Cyrenaeans marched out to the place Irasa and the spring Thestes, and there battled with the Egyptians and overcame them; for the Egyptians had as yet no knowledge of Greeks, and despised their enemy; whereby they were so utterly destroyed that few of them returned to Egypt.[2]

After this defeat the army of Apries revolted.

Merneptah-Apries memorialized his victories in the early stage of the Libyan campaign in a number of inscriptions, of which five are extant. But of his wretched end he would not and could not write anything. Herodotus, however, described it. The Egyptian army on the Libyan front mutinied. Apries sent Amasis (Ahmose), the general, to win over the rebels. Instead, Amasis himself was persuaded by the army to become king. Apries sent his vizier to arrest Amasis, and through him Amasis replied that he would come with his men. Apries cut off the nose and ears of his vizier for bringing this message. Because of this deed the people of the capital became hostile to the king. Apries had to fight his own army, and he could not depend on his bodyguard of Carians and Ionians, descendants of the mercenaries settled in Egypt by Seti (Psammetich) and Ramses II (Necho).

He [Apries] armed his guard and marched against the Egyptians; he had a bodyguard of Carians and Ionians, thirty thousand of them.[3]

The battle took place at Momemphis (Memphis)[4] and Apries was defeated. This was the end of the long war. The Libyan campaign was ill fated for Merneptah-Apries.

Amasis captured Apries and kept him in his palace; but the people clamored for his life and he was strangled by the mob.[5]

---

[1] Herodotus (transl. Godley), IV, 159.
[2] *Ibid*.
[3] *Ibid,*, II, 163.
[4] Petrie interprets Momemphis as a place called Menouf west of Benha.
[5] Herodotus, II, 169, and Diodorus, I, 68.

Figure 28: Merneptah: Pharaoh of the Exile.
From *Ancient Near East in Pictures Relating to the
Old Testament*, Princeton University Press, 1950

Jeremiah's prophecy (44:30) that Pharoah Hophra would be given into the hands of his enemies, as Zedekiah, king of Judah, was given into the hands of his enemy, was fulfilled.

Amasis, who had not deprived his captive of royal clothes and crown, paid him royal honor after his death; the body was embalmed and placed in a burial vault.

In the skull of the mummy of Merneptah is a hole made by a sharp instrument.[1] To explain this injury it is conjectured that a surgical operation had been performed on Merneptah's head during his life-

---

[1] G. Elliot Smith: »The Royal Mummies«, *Catalogue général des Antiquités Egyptiennes du Musée de Caire* (Cairo, 1912), p. 68; James Harris and Kent Weeks: *X-raying the Pharaohs* (New York, 1973), p. 157.

time, or that it was made after his death. But this hole is apparently the result of the mortal wound at the hands of the assassins.

The imbroglio over the presence of the north Mediterranean immigrants in Cyrene is clarified. They were the new settlers of Cyrene, who came from all parts of the Greek world. "All Greeks" admonished by the Pythian oracle to migrate and settle in Cyrene, and the "great multitude of them" that crossed the sea, were the "Ekwesh, Teresh, Luka, Sherden, Shekelesh, Northerners coming from all lands."

The notion that Aryans were present in Libya and Egypt in the thirteenth century before the present era is a fallacy. It was the sixth century.

The Persian Conquest of Chaldea and Egypt

From the battle of Carchemish, with the description of which we started this volume, to the deposition of Merneptah-Hophrama'e (biblical Hophra, Greek Apries), less than fifty years passed. True, we flashed back to the reign of the father of Hattusilis, thus surveying two generations of the Chaldean kingdom, and went back also to relate in short the role of Seti-Ptah-Maat (the Psammetich of the Greek authors) in the protracted conflict in which the Assyrians, helped by the Egyptians, fought and lost to the alliance of the Chaldeans, Medes, and, toward the end, Scythians. To carry this volume to the end of the Neo-Babylonian (Chaldean) Empire, and to the end of what is an amalgam of the Manethonian Nineteenth and Twenty-sixth Dynasties, and thus to add a few more decades to the narrative, we will not use much ink.

The westward pressure of the Chaldeans, culminating in the temporary occupation of the Phrygian capital of Gordion, a pressure still sustained in the days of Nergil (Nergilissar), who fought on the border of Lydia, was crippled in the later years of Nebuchadnezzar – in the days of his feeble successors it met decisive counterpressure. Croesus, son of Gyges, king of Lydia, with his capital at Sardis, ruined Boghazkoi in -546. Boghazkoi was not ruined by the mythical Peoples of the Sea in ca. -1200: it was burned by Croesus six and a half centuries later.

> Croesus ... began the war. When he reached the Halys, he crossed it by the existing bridges. ... When the army was over the river and had reached

the district called Pteria in Cappadocia (Pteria is the strongest place here-abouts and lies more or less in line with Sinope on the Black Sea), Croesus encamped and began to devastate the crops of the Syrians'[1] land. He captured the town, enslaved the inhabitants, and took all of the neighboring settlements. ...[2]

Thus Herodotus tells of Croesus devastating Pteria, and it is the consensus of modern scholars that Herodotus' Pteria occupied the place of the old capital Boghazkoi-Hattusha:[3] it was the very capital from where Mursilis, son of Suppiluliumas, less than eighty years earlier planned and then executed the conquest of Babylon and established the Neo-Babylonian Empire.

The destruction of Boghazkoi by Croesus can be read about in the archaeological report:

> Clear signs of disaster have been found everywhere in the royal citadel. Not a single building was spared and the surface of the streets and open squares was found covered with thick layers of charred wood and mudbrick reddened by fire.[4]

After this conquest Croesus reigned supreme in Anatolia only a few months longer. Cyrus, emerging from Anshan in Media, invaded Asia Minor and in the same year, -546, took Sardis and carried Croesus away to accompany him on his further war exploits as a prisoner. In -539 Babylon fell, after a night of visions and feasting, in the palace built by Nebuchadnezzar for his descendants for eternity.

In Egypt, Amasis ruled; his prisoner, the former pharaoh Merneptah, son of Ramses II, had been delivered to the mob, who killed him – the story preserved in Herodotus about the end of Apries found confirmation when the mummy of Merneptah was examined recently by a team of experts in Cairo.[5] A hole in the skull made by a sharp instrument and other damage detected by X rays of the mummy all testify to a violent and cruel death.[6]

---

[1] The so-called White Syrians of Cappadocia. The Egyptian name for them, "Hatti", also means "Syrians," the land of Hatti being Syria.

[2] Herodotus: I, 76.

[3] W. M. Ramsey: *Historical Geography of Asia Minor* (1890), pp. 33f; J. Garstang: *The Land of the Hittites* (1910), pp. 32f and 197. Cf. Kurt Bittel: *Hattusha, Capital of the Hittites* (1970), pp. 155-56. The identification had already been made by Texier in 1834.

[4] Bittel: *Hattusha*, p. 90.

[5] The examination of the mummies in the Cairo Museum was undertaken by a team of experts between the years 1966 and 1971.

[6] Harris and Weeks: *X-raying the Pharaohs*, p. 157.

To what is known of Amasis' supposedly forty-three years of reign we have little to add. He was an admirer of the Greeks: he opened for them the Mediterranean seacoast for colonization – through the millennia of Egyptian history this swampy coast was a neglected region – and merchants, sailors, Greek priests, and just settlers built on the coast many Greek votive chapels representing various city-states of Hellas. The coast got the name of Hellenic (Helou) coast.

The Greeks had no less admiration for the Egyptians. The trickle of statesmen and philosophers started their pilgrimage to the temples of Egypt and its priests, in search of ancient wisdom and knowledge of what had happened to the world in ages past.

But only fourteen years after the fall of Babylon, and but a few months after Amasis' death, the land of Egypt with its many capitals and temples fell before Cambyses, son of Cyrus. Cambyses caused much havoc in the country along its full length, and in *Peoples of the Sea* the story is told more fully. Only recently it was reported that the armor and the remains of the large expeditionary force sent by Cambyses across the desert to attack Carthage was found not far from the Siwa oasis. All the 50,000 men, Herodotus told us, perished in a sandstorm.[1]

Of the long reign of Amasis only very few objects attributable to him were found, and no monumental remains whatsoever – though from Herodotus we know of great buildings erected by him.[2] But the reason for this is known from Cambyses himself. Cambyses claimed that his mother had been a daughter of Merneptah (Apries) whom Cyrus had married. Thus he considered himself a legitimate pharaoh by birth and inheritance, and saw in Amasis a lawless occupant of the throne of Egypt, or a criminal usurper. He ordered destroyed all that carried the name of Amasis, and if not all was destroyed, all cartouches of Amasis on monuments were erased. More attentive researchers could attribute much of surviving art to Amasis, who died leaving the misery of occupation and degradation to his son and heir.

---

[1] Report from Cairo by the Agence France-Presse news agency, February 1977
[2] Herodotus, II, 177.

Questions and Answers

The story has been brought to a point where it is linked with the narrative contained in *Peoples of the Sea* – the Persian domination of the ancient East.

Reassessing the evidence and its validity, the arguments and their strength, I ask myself what kind of counterarguments I may expect from exacting critics. There are several, and each of them receives mention here; certain single subjects either have been or will be discussed by me at greater length in other places.

And here are the questions I expect:

1. The identification of Psammetich, Necho, and Apries in the Greek writings with Seti, Ramses, and Merneptah, known from the monuments, raises the question: If the first are known as pharaohs with Tanis on the eastern side of the Delta as their capital, while the later kings are known as Saitic pharaohs with their capital at Saïs, on the other side of the Delta, how can this difference be harmonized?

2. The art – architecture, sculpture, painting; the language – literary works, orthography and epigraphy (writing); and also religion: do not all of them in the Nineteenth Dynasty (of Seti and Ramses II) show closeness and affinity to the art, language, and religion of the end of the Eighteenth Dynasty? What is the true situation? I reserve a detailed discussion of a large number of examples from all of the above fields for the volume of this reconstruction that deals with the period following the end of the house of Akhnaton. Suffice it to say here that the Eighteenth and Nineteenth Dynasties are notable for the dissimilarity of their style of art, language, and religion, while many features of Libyan and Ethiopian style mimic closely the uses of the Eighteenth and Nineteenth Dynasties respectively, reviving them, supposedly but inexplicably, after a hiatus of many hundreds of years.

3. It has been known since antiquity that Ramses II reigned for sixty-six years – but Pharaoh Necho definitely less; further, to Ramses' father Seti modern scholars ascribe a comparatively short reign of about

eleven years, but the present reconstruction ascribes to him a long reign of over fifty years. What is the true evidence?

4. The "Hittite" king Suppiluliumas was one of the correspondents of the el-Amarna letter exchange found in the state archive of this short-lived capital of the heretical king Akhnaton. How could he be so long-lived as to be a contemporary of Assurbanipal the Assyrian or Tirhaka the Ethiopian? In the revised – or synchronized – history, between the time the el-Amarna letters were written and Suppiluliumas, a contemporary of Assurbanipal and Tirhaka, over one hundred and fifty years passed. What is the answer?

5. The age of Seti and Ramses is the Bronze Age; Psammetich and Necho, however, lived in the Iron Age. This question requires a closer examination. The section »Bronze and Iron«, which I wrote over a quarter of a century ago, when I thought to handle the entire reconstruction in two volumes, I allow to stand. I find no incentive to rewrite »Bronze and Iron«, since subsequently published works have not changed the problem as it stood in 1952, and as it is, it already exceeds in length the other questions discussed here.

6. Stratigraphy dominates all judgments of professional archaeologists. Literary monuments are considered of definitely secondary value and, when found in wrong stratigraphical positions, are considered to be intrusions. Pottery, however, especially Mycenaean and post-Mycenaean (Geometric in various stages, and Orientalizing), defines by its presence the chronological placement of the strata. Scarabs, often carrying royal Egyptian names, are second only to pottery (usually sherds) as arbiters of age. What is then the verdict coming from pottery and scarabs in the court where conventional chronology and the revised scheme of it stand before the bar?

7. And what is the verdict coming from radiocarbon laboratories? I gave the story in short in the Introduction to my *Peoples of the Sea*. In *Pensée* VI, Winter 1973-74, pp. 5ff, I published a collection of letters spanning two decades, detailing my efforts to obtain radiocarbon tests of materials dating from the Egyptian New Kingdom. The single test which I succeeded in having performed in 1964 brought a result that vindicated the reconstructed version of history. In *Pensée* IV, Spring-Summer 1973, pp. 12ff, which was devoted to the bearing of radiocarbon dating on the revised chronology, I published also a paper of mine on »The Pitfalls of Radiocarbon Dating«[1] in which I discussed the

---

[1] {This paper is published in the supplement to this book. Note by the publisher}

problem of the applicability of this dating method to a past environment that experienced cosmic cataclysms with intrusions of carbonaceous materials of extraneous origin and worldwide conflagrations that must have imbalanced the $^{14}C : {}^{12}C$ ratio in the hydrosphere and biosphere.

8. Finally, there is the argument of "astronomical dating." Until recently it was regarded as a formidable one. With the help of Sothic calculation, or the movement of the day of the heliacal (simultaneous with the sun) rising of the star Sothis around the calendar of 365 days, a chronology was erected, and the words "astronomically established" had a baleful preeminence over any and every chronological dating – and a reverential status also among scholars in all disciplines. By this dating, a new Sothic period, called "era of Menophres," started in -1321 before the present era; and it was also canonized in the recent edition of the *Cambridge Ancient History,* as the date of the one-year-long reign of Ramses I (Menpehtire), father of Seti the Great, though a few Egyptologists, M. B. Rowton and D. B. Redford among them, tended, like myself, to regard Menophres as the name for Memphis (Men-Nofre) and not of a person.

Since I have discussed extensively the problem of the Sothic calendar and astronomical chronology in general in the Supplement to *Peoples of the Sea,* there is nothing to add, unless to state that not even the harshest critic of *Peoples of the Sea* dared to claim any validity for the "astronomical chronology," a field in which the efforts of the so-called "giants" in the field, among them Eduard Meyer and Ludwig Borchardt, efforts so highly acclaimed, turned out to be nothing but a great exercise in futility.

This subject will not be discussed again.

It remains to deal with questions 1, 3, 4, 5, and 6.

1. Tanis and Saïs

The present reconstruction offers ample evidence that the Nineteenth Dynasty is the same as the Twenty-sixth, and that Seti I, Ramses I, Seti II, Ramses II, and Merneptah are the same as Psammetich (Sethos), Necho I, Psammetich II, Necho II, and Apries (Hophra) of the Greek historians. Now we have to find an explanation of why the Twenty-sixth Dynasty is known as the Saitic dynasty, or of the city of Saïs , whereas the dynasty of Seti and Ramses had its capital at Tanis.

The ruins of Tanis are spread on a vast field in the eastern part of the Delta. Petrie in the last century and Montet in this explored the ancient metropolis and found numerous and rich relics of the residence, with palaces and temples and a necropolis. Today a village of fishermen, San el Hagar, occupies a part of the ancient Tanis. Not far away is Tell Nebesheh where, too, Ramesside structures and tombs were unearthed.

Saïs was placed by Lepsius, over a hundred years ago, at the western part of the Delta, on the Rosetta branch of the Nile, at a place called Sa el Hagar, similar to the name of the village that occupies the place of Tanis. His identification was not questioned. However, no ancient ruins of the residence were found. From Herodotus (II, 169; 175-76), as also from other sources, we know that Saïs had great and luxurious buildings and royal sepulchers erected above the ground. The city suffered damage at the hands of Cambyses, who ruined the tomb of Amasis. But again, in the age of the Ptolemies, Saïs was an important center. Where are the ruins? Saïs was one of the oldest and most important cities in Egypt, and ruins of all ages, and certainly of the Middle Kingdom, the New Kingdom, and, of course, of the Twenty-sixth, the Saitic, Dynasty, and of the Hellenistic period, must have survived. Then where are the ruins?

Our main source about Saïs is Herodotus. But Herodotus (II, 17), enumerating the arms of the Delta, omits to mention the Tanitic branch and, instead, names the Saitic branch of the Nile where the Tanitic branch should have been named. Furthermore, Herodotus describes the Saitic as a branch splitting off from the Sebennytic. This fits the Tanitic branch but does not fit the Rosetta branch, where Saïs is usually thought to be. The geographer Strabo (XVII, i, 20) differentiates between Saïs and Tanis but writes that the Saitic branch of the Nile is the same as the Tanitic. This identification by an early historian and an early geographer of the Saitic branch of the Nile with the Tanitic makes the modern view that separates these two branches of the Nile, placing one in the east and the other in the west of the Delta, very questionable.

According to the Scriptures (Numbers 13:22), Tanis was founded seven years after Hebron. Its Hebrew name is "Zoan". Strangely, its

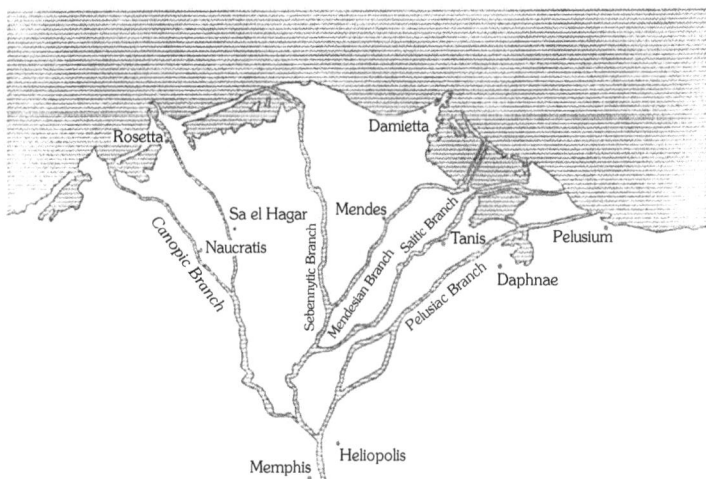

Figure 29: The Nile Delta as Described by Herodotus.
After Omar Toussoun: »Anciennes Branches du Nil«,
Mémoires de l'Institut d'Egypte, IV (Cairo, 1922-23).

Egyptian name in the days of the Ramessides, whose capital it was, is unknown,[1] and as "Zane" appears first in the *Papyrus Wenamon*, the date of which is definitely later.[2] Isaiah (19:11, 13; 30:4), about the year -700, and Ezekiel (30:14), a hundred years later, speak of Zoan as of the metropolis of Egypt. Assurbanipal called it "Saanu".

Tanis is mentioned in the Scriptures as the capital of Egypt when, according to both the conventional plan and this reconstruction, Saïs was the capital.

The question is asked here: Is not Saïs another name for Tanis? However, if the two cities were not identical, Saïs must have been close to Tanis, on the same branch of the Delta: possibly it could have been situated at Tell Nebesheh, only a few miles away, where numerous ruins of the same age as in Tanis are found.[3]

From Strabo we know that Saïs, the capital of Lower Egypt, was the place of the cult of the Libyan Isis-Athene, Neith, which was also called "Saïs". Apparently because of this Libyan cult of Saïs, the city was thought to have been located on the Libyan side of the Delta; however,

---

[1] Cf. A. H. Gardiner: *Journal of Egyptian Archaeology*, V (1818), 248.
[2] The time of Wenamon's travels is discussed in the volume *Peoples of the Sea*.
[3] The ruins of this plain are so numerous that Ch. Hayes suggested that Tanis should be looked for some distance to the south from Sa el Hagar.

the city was of much greater antiquity than the Libyan Dynasty in Egypt. Saïs also claimed to contain within its borders the tomb of Osiris (Herodotus, II, 17; Strabo, XVII, i, 20), and the Osiris mysteries were performed on a holy lake. It was the center of Egyptian culture when Solon, in the sixth century, visited Egypt.

Tanis was the cultus state of Isis-Athene, and its name is derived from "Tanit", the name of the Carthaginian Athene:[1] Tanit and Saïs are two names for the same Libyan or Carthaginian goddess. Tanis was also sacred to Osiris: Plutarch says that the cask of Osiris floated through the Tanitic mouth of the Nile into the sea.[2]

We have every ground to revise the modern view originating with Lepsius, who placed Saïs on the Libyan side of the Delta, and to locate it on the Tanitic branch of the Delta, following Herodotus and Strabo. This would explain why no ancient ruins are found on the putative site of Saïs in the west of the Delta. The abundant ruins in "the fields of Zoan" on the Tanitic-Saitic branch of the river are the relics of the royal residences of the Nineteenth, the same as the Twenty-sixth, Dynasty. This explains why in the seventh to sixth centuries, in the days of the "Saitic Dynasty," the Hebrew prophets Isaiah and Ezekiel regarded Tanis as the capital of Egypt.

3. How Long Did Seti and Ramses II Reign?

The present reconstruction of ancient history elucidates the length of the reigns of Seti, Ramses II, and Merneptah if not to a year, then in close approximation. Seti-Ptah-Maat (Psammetich of Herodotus) reigned from -663 (the year he returned with the retinue of Assurbanipal to Egypt) to -609 (three years after the fall of Nineveh in -612), altogether for fifty-four years.

Ramses II was made co-ruler while he was still an infant. In his own words:

> When my father made his state appearance before the people, I being a child in his lap, he said referring to me: "Crown him as King that I may see his qualities while I am still living" And he ordered the chamberlains

---

[1] Even today Tunis, near the rains of Carthage, carries the name of the goddess Tanit as Athens the name of Athene.

[2] Plutarch: *De Iside*, 13.

to place the Double Crown upon my brow. "Let him administer this land: let him show himself to the people" – so spake he through his great love of me.[1]

Ramses II is also shown on a bas-relief as a youth being taught the use of bow and arrow by his father, King Seti.[2] Ramses' first campaign toward Carchemish took place in his second year, obviously counted from the beginning of his reign as a sole ruler; on his second campaign he proceeded in his fifth year; Gaza and Ashkelon he took in his ninth year; he concluded the peace treaty with Nebuchadnezzar in his (Ramses') twenty-first year; he married a daughter of Nebuchadnezzar in his thirty-fourth year, always counted from the death of his father, Seti.

Jeremiah, when in exile in Egypt and before he was removed to Babylon,[3] refers to Pharaoh Hophra, whom we identified as Merneptah-Hophrama'e. Merneptah's reign, judged by the dates on his inscriptions, endured for ten or eleven years. *If* the figure of forty-three years for Amasis' reign[4] is true, then he must have begun his rule in -568, or nineteen years after the destruction of Jerusalem: in -525 Egypt was conquered by Cambyses, the Persian, only a few months after Amasis' death. Of these nineteen years the longer part belongs to Ramses; Merneptah, however, might have been a co-ruler in the last years of Ramses. That Amasis, after he seized the throne, allowed Merneptah to wear a crown and be a co-ruler with himself, we learn from Herodotus (II, 169).

It follows that Ramses II reigned over thirty years; should, however, the years of his co-regency with Seti be added, his entire reign endured for most of his life and might have exceeded sixty years.

In modern textbooks on history, Ramses II is invariably invested with a sixty-six-year reign. The issue on which certain authorities disagree and are engaged in a protracted debate is whether Ramses II reigned from -1304 to -1238 or from -1290 to -1224. As the reader is aware by now, a problem of very different dimensions faces historiography. Yet the question, How long did Ramses II reign? is pertinent and should

---

[1] Transl. by C. Aldred in *Akhenaten* (1968), p. 102. Cf. K. A. Kitchen: *Ramesside Inscriptions* (1969), Vol. II, pp. 323-26. For a discussion of the question of a coregency between Ramses II and Seti see Schmidt: *Ramses II,* Ch. V, »The Coregency«, pp. 154-64.
[2] North wall of the great Hypostyle Hall at Karnak.
[3] Jeremiah 44:30.
[4] Herodotus: III, 103, and Africanus' version of Manetho give forty-four years as the length of Amasis' reign; but Eusebius and the Armenian version of Eusebius allot only forty-two years to Amasis.

be dealt with in the light of the historical events of the seventh and sixth centuries.

The figure of sixty-six years is found in Eusebius' version of the Manethonian dynasties. According to this version, in the Nineteenth Dynasty, Sethos reigned for fifty-five years and after him his son Ramses for sixty-six: thus the ruling years of the father and the son combined comprise one hundred and twenty-one years.

Africanus, the other compiler of Manetho's lists, gives these figures: Sethos' reign – fifty-one years, Rapsaces' (who followed him) – sixty-one years, together one hundred twelve years – still very long for a father-son succession on the throne, *unless there was a co-regency.*

Josephus, the third compiler of Manetho, has in the Nineteenth Dynasty a King Sethos who, "after expelling Hermaeus, reigned fifty-nine years and his eldest son Rampses, sixty-six years."

To compound the issue, Eusebius has in the preceding, the Eighteenth Dynasty, a King Ramesses ruling sixty-eight years. Josephus has in the Eighteenth Dynasty a King Miamun (the royal nomen of Ramses II) reigning for sixty-six years and two months. Africanus, however, omits this king (Ramesses of Eusebius, Miamun of Josephus) from the register of the kings of the Eighteenth Dynasty.

At what solution did the modern historians arrive? Ramses in the Eighteenth Dynasty is, of course, an error or an invention.

To Ramses II of the Nineteenth Dynasty is allotted a reign of sixty-six years, as Eusebius has it, but to his father Seti only eleven years are assigned, and not fifty-five, the figure Eusebius has for him.

Despite the vivid description by Ramses II of how he was made a co-ruler while still an infant, the fact that his first campaign toward Syria was recorded by him in his "second year" and the second campaign in his "fifth year" made modern historians believe that his royal years began to be counted when he became sole ruler – as an infant he could not lead the army.

With the Eighteenth Dynasty ending, presumably, in the latter part of the fourteenth century, the Nineteenth Dynasty, it was figured out, could not have started long before -1300. The calculations were made with the help of astronomical computations the validity of which were negated in our discussion of the Sothic period chronology in *Peoples of the Sea*. Assigning a long reign to Ramses, not too many years were left for Seti.

Figure 30: The colossi of Ramses II at Abu Simbel.

For assigning to Ramses II the very long reign, several arguments carried weight. There are a great many monuments dating from the reign of Ramses II, some of them of colossal proportions. There exists a document dated in the sixty-seventh year of Ramses; and there exists a written supplication by one of the later Ramessides to be granted by the divine powers a life double in years that of Ramses II – which implies that in later generations Ramses' life or reign was regarded as having been of a prodigious length.

This evidence does not stand unchallenged. Of the multitude of Ramses' antiquities, most refer to the first three or four decades of his reign and, strangely, hardly any document is dated in the last two or three decades of his reign. In the beginning of his reign – as on the monuments commemorating his campaign toward the Euphrates (year 2, year 5), Ramses II marked the years from his accession. But late in his reign he may have reverted to dating from the beginning of the co-regency. Whether this is so or not, the fact is that Ramses II was not a very old man when he died and therefore did not reign sixty-six years – all that is necessary to establish.

If he had reigned for sixty-six years as sole ruler after the death of his father, Ramses II must have reached his late eighties or nineties at his death.

Rudolph Virchow, the renowned anatomist of the second part of the nineteenth century, was known for his interest in archaeology. He investigated the skull of Ramses' mummy and wondered at the form of the jawbone; it could not be that of a very old man.

G. Elliot Smith, the anatomist at the University of Cairo, who examined all available royal mummies of Egypt, wrote of Ramses II's mummy: "The teeth are clean and in an excellent state of preservation; they were only slightly worn. It is a curious problem to determine why this exceedingly old man should have healthy and only slightly worn teeth."[1]

This investigator of the royal mummies was puzzled to find that the teeth of Ramses II were not of a man of ninety or eighty or seventy: even for the age of sixty the teeth of the king were unusually well preserved. His view on the dental condition of Ramses II was more recently challenged by J. E. Harris and K. E. Weeks,[2] who made an X-ray examination of Ramses' body, oral cavity included. They found "what must have been painful alveolar abscesses," yet they did not dispute Smith's evaluation of Ramses' age at his death. Dr. Wilton Krogman, working with the University of Michigan team that performed the X rays, interprets the results as indicating that Ramses II was in all likelihood "between 50 and 55" years old at the time of his death. This figure was obtained from a careful study of demineralization of the pelvis.[3]

The sternum (the breastbone) is a good indicator of the age of a person. Smith examined the sternum and wrote: "Part of the sternum had been broken off the upper part of the thorax. On raising this I was very much surprised to find that, in spite of the great age to which Ramses had attained, the manubrium sterni was not ankylosed to the gladiolus, and the ossified second costal cartilages still articulated by joints with the sternum."[4]

This points to a definitely younger age of Ramses II at his death than had been assumed. Between a figure on a document and anatomical expertise, it is always the latter that carries the greater weight. Would

---

[1] G. E. Smith: *The Royal Mummies* (Cairo, 1912), p. 63.
[2] *X-raying the Pharaohs*, p. 155.
[3] *Philadelphia Inquirer*: June 15, 1975, p. 14.
[4] Smith, op. cit., p. 64

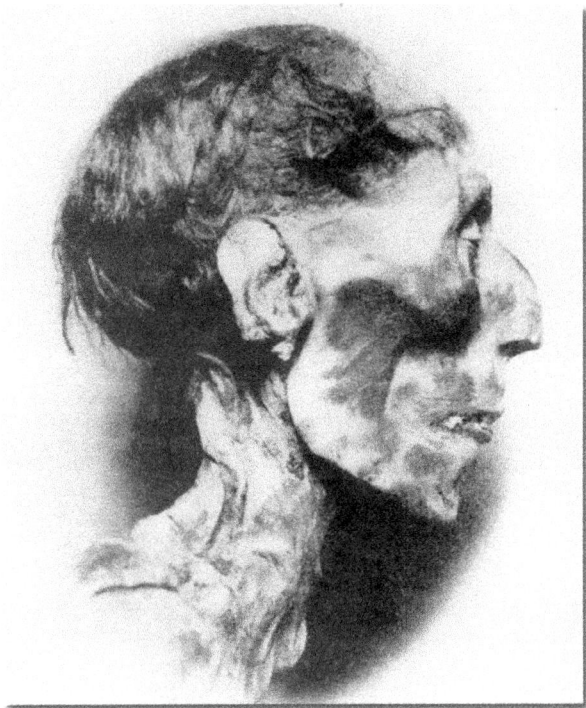

Figure 31: The mummy of Ramses II

a Scotland Yard anatomist certify the age of a dead man – or of a living one for that matter – on the basis of the state of ossification or on the basis of a date on a wedding certificate?

At his death, Ramses II was no more than in his sixties, and the data as we know them from the Scriptures agree with the findings of two great anatomists, R. Virchow and G. E. Smith.

Unless the famous mummy of Ramses II is not of this king, his reign as sole ruler for sixty-six years is impossible. If the document of the sixty-sixth year refers to Ramses II and not another king, then it was reckoned by the regnal years since the investiture in his infancy. The supplication by a later king (actually the last king before the reconquest of Egypt by Artaxerxes III) could have had reference to the entire length of Ramses' co-rule and rule, unless not Ramses but Seti ("Sethos called Ramesses" of Josephus) was meant.

Manetho allots to Psammetich of the Twenty-sixth Dynasty fifty-three years, the length of the reign of Seti, as shown above; but to Necos (Necho), Manetho gives only six years; Herodotus, however, says sixteen. The last figures are far from the historical values – after Seti's reign of fifty-three years, Ramses reigned as sole ruler not six or sixteen and not sixty-six, but some thirty years.

4. Two Suppiluliumas

It has already been argued that Suppiluliumas, the author of two letters of the el-Amarna collection, could hardly be the king by the same name who was the father of Mursilis. In the conventional chronology, between the death of Amenhotep III (-1375) and the twenty-first year of Ramses II (-1279), when the treaty with Hattusilis was signed, one hundred and five years passed, which appears to be too long for the ruling years of three successive generations, especially when one takes into account that only part of the reigns of Suppiluliumas and Hattusilis are included in this span.[1]

According to my reconstruction of history, between the period of the el-Amarna letters and the time of Suppiluliumas, the grandfather of Hattusilis, over one hundred and sixty years must have elapsed (from the time of Jehoshaphat to the time of Manasseh), and it is impossible that an author of an el-Amarna letter could have been a grandfather of Hattusilis.

The el-Amarna letters, as I have endeavored to demonstrate (*Ages in Chaos*, »The El-Amarna Letters«), were written in the middle of the ninth century in the days of the Assyrian king Shalmaneser III (-859 to -824). Actually, Shalmaneser refers to his warlike relations with Suppiluliumas ("Sapalulme") of Hatti ("Hattina").[2]

On the proper page of this volume some of the political and military activities of Suppiluliumas II have been briefly discussed, leaving the subject for more detailed treatment in the volume on *The Assyrian*

---

[1] Breasted: *Records,* Vol. III, note; "As [Max] Müller has suggested [*Vorderasiatisch-ägyptische Gesellschaft, Mitteilungen,* VII] the Amarna letter may be from an earlier Seplel [Suppiluliumas]."

[2] *Reallexikon der Assyriologie,* IV, s.v. Hattina. Cf. J. D. Hawkins: »Assyrians and Hittites«, *Iraq* 36 (1974), pp. 81-83. The name of the country is sometimes read "Pattina".

Conquest. In the biography of Suppiluliumas written by his son Mursilis,[1] one item deserves mention here. An Egyptian queen named Dakhamun, upon the death of her royal husband, having no male child, sent messengers to Suppiluliumas with a letter requesting that the addressee should send her one of his sons for her to marry and to put on the throne of Egypt, since she was loath to marry any of her subjects.

It is usually assumed, and is so stated in many textbooks, that the queen who wrote this letter to the "Hittite" king Suppiluliumas was the widow of Tutankhamen, Ankhesenpaaten, daughter of Akhnaton.[2] But this surmise is built on very poor reasoning, aside from the fact that Ankhesenpaaten (ca. -830) and Suppiluliumas II (seventh century) were not contemporaries but were separated by over a hundred and sixty years.

The historical scene at the Egyptian Thebes lends no credence to the idea of Ankhesenpaaten assuming the role of a widowed queen requesting from a foreign king a son to remarry. Upon the death of Tutankhamen at the age of eighteen, or possibly seventeen, Ankhesenpaaten was most probably sixteen years of age, if not younger. The realm was under the heavy hand of Ay, who proclaimed himself king (pharaoh) and without delay, even before donning the crown and mounting the throne, married Ankhesenpaaten, now renamed Ankhesenpaamen, only by marrying a princess of royal blood could he inherit the regalia.[3] The child queen was probably not even asked whether she would tolerate her maternal granduncle (Ay was a brother of Queen Tiy, mother of Akhnaton) as husband; and after the nuptials nothing further was heard of her – she was a plaything in the political game of the crafty Ay. The scene at Thebes and the roles of the various members of the royal house and of the palace entourage are illuminated in detail in my *Oedipus and Akhnaton.*

Suppiluliumas II was contemporary with Tirhaka, the Ethiopian king who also ruled Egypt. Tirhaka died in -663, leaving no heir. It must

---

[1] H. G. Güterbock:»The Deeds of Suppiluliuma as Told by His Son Mursili II«, *Journal of Cuneiform Studies,* Vol. X (1956), pp. 41-50, 59-68, 75-130.

[2] For instance, A. Götze: »The Struggle for the Domination of Syria«, *Cambridge Ancient History* (3rd ed.; 1975), Vol. II, Pt. 2, pp. 17-18; Güterbock: »The Deeds of Suppiluliuma«, p. 94; Alan Gardiner: *Egypt of the Pharaohs,* p. 241.

[3] In the absence of a legitimate heir – the eldest son of the chief queen (W. Stevenson Smith: »The Old Kingdom in Egypt«, *Cambridge Ancient History* (3rd ed., 1975), Vol. I, Pt. 2, p. 166) – the pretender sought to legitimize himself by marrying a member of the royal house; either the chief queen herself, or a princess in the direct line of the last legitimate pharaoh.

have been his widow who wrote the much-quoted letter to Suppiluliumas. Now the .check on this conclusion is at hand. The story as reported by Mursilis, son of Suppiluliumas, gives the name of the pharaoh as "Bib-khururia" (or "Nib-khururia"[1]). The royal name of Tirhaka ends with "khu-ra."[2] The name of his queen was Duk-hat-amun.[3] The name is unique among all the queens of Egypt.

In the frame of conventional chronology the name "Dakkamun" in the text from Boghazkoi cannot be explained. "What appears to have been her name has through some error received a distorted form."[4] As an alternative, a hypothesis was offered that Dakhamun is not a name at all, but a status;[5] this strained view only points up the difficulty of the conventional chronology in which Suppiluliumas, father of Mursilis, is placed at the close of the Amarna period.

The prince sent by Suppiluliumas after repeated requests of Dakhamun (Duk-hat-amun in Egyptian) was assassinated in Syria while on his way to Egypt. It was unwise to send the prince by a land route, especially in view of the fact that Assurbanipal was in control of Syria. In -667 Assurbanipal, after a protracted war with Tirhaka, had penetrated deep into Egypt, and the Ethiopian, retreating into the Sudan, died there soon after from wounds. It is at this juncture that the appeals of Dakhamun reached Suppiluliumas as he was engaged in a war in northern Syria in the vicinity of Carchemish.

The last short-lived thrust by the Ethiopians into Egypt came four years later, in -663 under Tanutamen, a nephew of Tirhaka. The Assyrian reaction was swift. Assurbanipal drove Tanutamen out of Egypt, occupied and ruined Thebes, and thus put an end to the Ethiopian period of Egyptian history.

---

[1] Güterbock: »Deeds of Suppiluliumas«, p. 94, note.
[2] R. Gauthier: Le Livre des rois (Mémoires, l'Institut français d'archéologie orientale du Caire, t. 20, 1916), pp. 31-42. One of Tirhaka's names, engraved on a scarab found at Tanis (Louvre N. 632) begins with "neb-khu". See J. Leclant and J. Yoyotte: »Scarabée Commémoratif de la crue du Nil«, Kêmi 10 (1949), p. 39.
[3] Petrie's reading. Maspero reads "Dikahitamanou."
[4] Gardiner: Egypt of the Pharaohs, p. 241; H. R. Hall, »The Hittites and Egypt«, Anatolian Studies, presented to Sir W. M. Ramsey (London, 1923), p. 179: "We do not know this queen from Egyptian sources. She can hardly be the same person as Tutankhamen's consort, the well-known Ankhsenamen."
[5] Walter Federn: »Dahamunzu (KBo V 6 iii 8)«, Journal of Cuneiform Studies, Vol. XIV, No. 1 (April 1960), p. 33.

5. Bronze and Iron

In the thirties of the nineteenth century a scholar,[1] following in the footsteps of Hesiod and Lucretius, proposed that the past of mankind be divided according to the material from which, in successive ages, historical man manufactured his tools and utensils, differentiating the ages of stone and bone, of bronze, and of iron. This proposal was successful, and the introduction of further divisions dotted modern books on history and archaeology with letters denoting the "Early," "Middle," and "Late" periods of each age, with subsequent subdivisions of I, II, and sometimes III. The Early Bronze Age is more accurately called the "Copper Age".

Archaeology generally construes its ages either according to the character of pottery or according to the metals used for tools; the latter division is more definite, so that pottery of different kinds is labeled in terms of metal periods, e.g., ceramics of Late Bronze Ia or Early Iron IIb, and so on. We shall see in the following section the confusion that underlies the division of ceramic ages. Here we intend to examine briefly the metal ages and their bearing on chronology.

By bringing Egyptian history six or seven centuries closer to our time, do we not cause a displacement of the metal ages? A sailing vessel takes only two or three days to bring cargo from Egypt to Palestine; the desert road was traversed by Thutmose III with his army in nine days. One would expect that conventional chronology took into consideration the closeness of countries like Egypt and Palestine; thus, if the beginning of the Iron Age in Palestine is commonly thought to have taken place in -1200, in the time of the Judges, then in the conventional scheme the Iron Age in Egypt must also have started about -1200.

This is not the case. "There are few subjects that are more disputed than that of the date when iron first came into general use in Egypt."[2] Consequently there is no ground for fear that the revised chronology will bring confusion to the Bronze-Iron scheme; the confusion is already there. When the Iron Age began in Egypt cannot be established by relying on conventional chronology. It is also clear why this is so.

---

[1] Christian Thomsen. Cf. Hesiod: *Works and Days.*
[2] A. Lucas: *Ancient Egyptian Materials and Industries*, p. 193.

The time of the Nineteenth Dynasty is not antecedent to the Twenty-sixth Dynasty by seven hundred years; they are one and the same. And the Twentieth Dynasty of Ramses III does not precede the time of Necho II by six centuries but follows it by two centuries. With such erroneous premises, it is, of course, hopeless to try to establish the time when the Iron Age in Egypt had its beginning.

Keeping this in mind, and in order to reconstruct the succession of ages, we must ask: When did iron come into use for the first time? When did the process of the extraction of iron from the ore become known? When did iron replace bronze for most of the purposes for which iron is preferred to bronze in our time?

Iron ore is more widely distributed on the earth than copper or tin, and the metallurgy of iron is simpler than that of bronze.[1] Iron is found in native form in meteorites, making the process of extraction unnecessary. It is extracted from ore (smelted) by heating at about 500° C; when it is red-hot it is malleable into the desired form. The addition of carbon (smelting on charcoal) followed by quick cooling produces steel. In order to make iron fluid (to melt it) so that it can be poured into molds, a temperature of over 1500° C is required.

Copper is less generously bestowed by nature; it is found in its native state and is also extracted from malachite and other ore by heating. Its extraction requires a temperature of about 1085° C, at which temperature it also melts and can be poured into molds. Unlike iron, copper possesses the quality of being malleable in a cold state. But this is a defect as well as an advantage; it means that the metal is soft. Hammering strengthens it; too much beating makes it brittle. Bronze, an alloy of copper and tin, is much harder than copper. The manufacture of alloys marks a definite progress in the metallurgic art; it is an advanced stage by comparison with that when only extraction from ore and hammering into shape were known.

Copper in alloy with zinc is called brass. This alloy is known from comparatively late times; "brass," the translation of the scriptural "nechoshet", really means "copper" and "bronze", without discriminating between them.

---

[1] Lucretius differed on this point. He wrote: "The use of bronze was known before iron, because it is more easily worked and there is greater store. With bronze men tilled the soil of the earth, with bronze they stirred up the waves of war. ... Then by small degrees the sword of iron gained ground ... then with iron they began to break the soil of the earth." *De Rerum Natura* (transl. W. H. D. Rouse; London, 1924), 1281ff.

Iron ores are found in Egypt in fairly large deposits but of poor quality.[1] Copper was brought from over the border of Egypt proper. Malachite mines belonging to the Egyptians have been discovered in the southwest Sinai massif. They were exploited, the inscriptions inform us, as early as during the Old Kingdom; heaps of slag near the mines indicate that extraction was performed on the spot. Before the end of the Old Kingdom the copper mines of Cyprus were delivering metal to Egypt. The island either gave its name to the metal or received its name from it.[2]

The high temperature necessary for the extraction and melting of copper (1085° C) was attained by using bellows, as can be seen in ancient Egyptian drawings, and also by constructing furnaces with a flue for draft. By these means iron could easily be extracted from its ore (smelted) at a lower temperature and hammered into shape.

Tin has not yet been found in the centers of the bronze civilization: Cyprus, Egypt, or Greece. It was imported from afar for making bronze.[3] Ezekiel (27:12) says that the maritime people of Tyre traded in tin which they brought from Tarshish. Tin is mentioned earlier by Isaiah[4] and is repeatedly referred to by Homer.[5] Herodotus told of its being imported into Greece, and the "tin islands" probably signify the British Isles.[6] Posidonius in the second century before this era referred to the Iberian Peninsula as the mining source of imported tin;[7] so did Pliny, and Diodorus told of its being mined in Cornwall.[8] In the first century of the present era tin was transported by way of Egypt to India.[9]

As it is generally supposed that Stone Age man crossed the sea only by chance and not in regular voyages, the copper period of the Bronze Age must have seen the conquest of the sea, and Bronze Age man must have already developed a sea trade in tin.

---

[1] W. F. Hume: *The Distribution of Iron Ores in Egypt* (Cairo, 1909). See also his *Geology of Egypt* (1925-37), 2 vols.
[2] Hill: *A history of Cyprus,* I, 82.
[3] In recent years it has been conjectured that alluvial fragments of tin were brought down by winter streams from the Syrian hills to the neighborhood of Byblos and were gathered in the dry beds during the summer.
[4] Isaiah 1:25. Compare Numbers 31:22.
[5] *Iliad:* XI, 25, 34; XVIII, 474, 565; XX, 271, etc.
[6] Herodotus, III, 115.
[7] Quoted by Strabo.
[8] Pliny: III, 2, 9; Diodorus, V, 2.
[9] Lucas: op. cit., p. 211.

In Egypt the copper period began in pre-dynastic times, and the Old Kingdom is also regarded as belonging to the age of copper. There are only a few bronze objects left from the end of the Old Kingdom (Sixth Dynasty). The Bronze Age embraces the Middle Kingdom and lasts until some indefinite date. The divergence of opinions regarding the beginning of the Iron Age in Egypt is extremely great. "The date of the commencement of the Iron Age in Egypt is perennially discussed, and unfortunately but little fresh evidence comes along as time progresses.[1]

The Iron Age in Egypt "may yet be proved to have even preceded the Bronze Age,"[2] is the opinion of one group of authors.[3] The Iron Age began about -1800 with the end of the Middle Kingdom, is the opinion of another group, or in the time of Ramses II, according to a third group. The developed Iron Age in Egypt began about -1200, or in the days of Ramses III, a few scholars maintain. Many favor the date -1000 under the Libyan Dynasty.[4] "The early Iron Age of Egypt did not begin until -800 (between the XXII and XXV Dynasties)."[5] The year -700 "may be considered as the beginning of the Iron Age in Egypt,[6] is a statement often made. It is also asserted that the earliest smelting in Egypt (at Naucratis) dates from the sixth century. All shades of opinion covering the entire length of Egyptian history have their advocates. "Iron has had more contradictory statements made about it than any other metal."[7]

A criterion from the beginning of the Iron Age must be defined, and the problem must be divided into two parts: When did man become able to manufacture iron, and when did iron come into general use, cutting down considerably the use of copper and bronze?

The precedence of iron was postulated, not only because of the simpler technological process involved in manufacturing the metal, as compared with bronze, and the widespread presence of iron ore, but also because of the evidence provided by the work executed. The stones

---

[1] H. Garland and C. O. Bannister: *Ancient Egyptian Metallurgy* (London, 1927), pp. 85-86.
[2] *Ibid.*, p. 5.
[3] This view already had its proponents in the last century. Cf. St. John V. Day: *The Prehistoric Use of Iron and Steel* (London, 1877).
[4] Cf. H. C. Richardson: »Iron, Prehistoric and Ancient«, *American Journal of Archaeology*, XXXVIII (1934), 555.
[5] R. A. Smith: »Archaeology, Iron Age«, *Encyclopaedia Britannica* (14th ed.), II, 252.
[6] Lucas: *Ancient Egyptian Materials*, p. 406.
[7] Sir W. M. Flinders Petrie: »The Metals in Egypt«, *Ancient Egypt* (1915), II, 18.

for pyramids were cut in square blocks during the Old Kingdom – copper or bronze tools would not have cut the limestone rock. Sarcophagi of granite with carved sharp corners of perfect angles and knife-like edges and plumb-straight lines, sculptures with finely cut lines of eyelids and lips dating from the Fourth Dynasty, and the sharp lines of hieroglyphics cut into granite and basalt, both very hard stones, and into diorite, the steely stone, hardest of them all, indicate that a medium as hard as steel was employed. A modern sculptor would scoff at the idea that anything less than hard steel could even scratch these stones which blunt the steel chisel after a few strokes.

Actually various objects wrought of iron were discovered in the Egypt of the Old Kingdom, and even in pre-dynastic Egypt. At Gerzah, some fifty miles south of Cairo, iron beads were found and identified as belonging to pre-dynastic times[1] An iron chisel was found between the stones of the Great Pyramid of the Fourth Dynasty.[2] A number of chisels and other tools dating from the Fifth Dynasty were found in Saqqara not far from Cairo.[3] Several pieces of a pickax from the Sixth Dynasty were unearthed at Abusir,[4] and a heap of broken tools from the same period at Dahsbur;[5] a lump of iron dust, probably a wedge, was discovered at Abydos.[6]

Most of these objects showed a nickel content, suggesting that they were made of meteoric iron. The Great Pyramid and Abydos pieces contained "traces of nickel," but the analyses were not conclusive. Meteoric iron does not require extraction from the ore (smelting). If only meteoric iron was used, and no extraction from the ore was undertaken, the process of manufacturing cannot be regarded as complete and the Iron Age had not yet begun. On the other hand, meteoric iron is more difficult to hammer into shape than iron from ore. Some scholars stress that geologists have collected only a few hundred tons of meteoric iron, largely in the Western Hemisphere, and hence, as long as the source was scarce, the real Iron Age could not begin. Others think that man, who has used metals for only five or six thou-

---

[1] G. A. Wainwright: »The Coming of Iron«, *Antiquity*, X (1936), 7.
[2] R. W. H. Vyse: *Operations Carried on at the Pyramids of Gizeh in 1837* (London, 1840-42), I, 275-76.
[3] Olshausen: *Zeitschrift für Ethnologie*, 1907, p. 373
[4] Found by G. Maspero in 1882.
[5] *See* Olshausen, op. cit., p. 374
[6] Sir W. M. Flinders Petrie: *Abydos*, II (*Egyptian Exploration Fund, Memoirs*, Vol. 24; London, 1903), 33

sand years, had at his disposal at the time he learned to use metal the meteorites that had fallen during hundreds of millions of years.

However, one or two iron objects of the Sixth Dynasty are declared to contain no nickel and therefore to be not of meteoric origin. This means that already in the Old Kingdom the process of smelting iron ore was known. If the first successful attempt to smelt iron from the ore is to be regarded as the beginning of the Iron Age, then the Iron Age had already started at that early date. But the question remains, Why did iron extracted from ore not come into general use, if the smelting process was known? And generally, why did the Bronze Age come first and the Iron Age second? Here we have learned that at least it was not because of lack of skill that iron was not utilized to a greater extent during the Old and Middle Kingdoms.

Bronze and Iron after the Fall of the Middle Kingdom. The historical parts of the Scriptures, covering the period from the Exodus to the return from Exile, present Palestine in a simultaneous iron and bronze civilization. Copper and bronze were used for many purposes for which they are not used today, but iron was a familiar metal and its manufacture was a familiar process. "Barzel" ("iron") and "nechoshet" ("copper, bronze") are mentioned equally often in the Scriptures.

The Israelites, on arriving in Palestine after their wandering in the desert, found iron being used by the inhabitants of the land (the iron bed of Og, king of Bashan; the iron vessels of Jericho). But as soon as the process of conquest was interrupted by the Philistine-Amalekite bloc, the Israelites were barred from the production of tools and had no access to the mining regions.[1] When in need of the work of a smith, the Israelites had to go down to the valley of the Philistines. The Philistines used bronze for armor but iron for spearheads.[2] The Canaanites had iron chariots, the Israelites had none.[3]

Because of these conditions objects of metal were scarce in the hills occupied by Israelite tribes, and not many of them have been left for archaeologists to find. In the Shefela (the coast) of the Philistines iron, left unprotected, rusts away in a few years, and only under especially favorable conditions would it be preserved for thousands of years. Such favorable conditions prevailed in Gezer.

---

[1] I Samuel 13:19.
[2] I Samuel 17:5–7.
[3] Joshua 17:16-18; Judges 1:19.

A curious exception to the total absence of iron in the earlier Semitic periods must however be mentioned. At the very bottom of the sloping part of the Water-passage were found two wedge-shaped lumps of iron, apparently parts of axe-blades or hoes. How these had got down to their resting-place, which was sealed up some four or five hundred years before the use of iron became general, is not easily explained.[1]

As has been said before, the excavator of Gezer changed the ages of the Semitic periods of his former excavations by some five hundred years. The iron blades of Gezer date most probably from the time of the Judges when Gezer was a Philistine-Amalekite city.

In the days when the Amu-Hyksos ruled Egypt from Auaris their policy with respect to metal manufacturing must have been similar to that employed in Palestine. An example of an iron tool from Egypt corresponding to the iron blades of Gezer is a chisel found together with a ferrule of a hoe handle near Esnah; these pieces date from the Seventeenth Dynasty, at the end of the Hyksos domination.[2]

In the last part of the eleventh century, when the Israelites under Saul and David achieved independence, they re-entered the Iron and Bronze Ages. David took in Damascus "exceeding much brass."[3] Chariots and bows (II Samuel 1:18) became the new war equipment of the Israelites, when "the people of the bow,"[4] i.e., the Amu or the Amalekites, lost their imperial position. Swords and shields were made of bronze ("brass"), but agricultural implements, "harrows of iron" and "axes of iron," were made of the gray metal.[5]

For the building of the house of worship David prepared "iron in abundance for the nails for the doors of the gates, and for the joinings; and brass in abundance without weight." Each of the metals had its proper use ("the brass for things of brass, the iron for things of iron"). The princes of Israel gave their share for the erection of the house: eighteen thousand talents of copper and bronze and one hundred thousand talents of iron, which proves that iron was of more common use than copper and bronze.[6]

Changes on the political scene were accompanied by the acquisition of metal manufacture by the Israelites; with the end of the Amalekite

---

[1] Macalister: *The Excavation of Gezer* (1902-09), II, 269.
[2] Wainwright: *Antiquity*, X (1936), 8.
[3] I Samuel 8:8.
[4] Gardiner: *Admonitions*, 2:2.
[5] II Samuel 12:31.
[6] I Chronicles 22:3; 22:14; 29:7.

domination the Israelites came into possession of sources of copper and iron in the Edomite region of the Araba and other places, and they learned artistic metal working from the Phoenicians and from their compatriots living in the vicinity of the Phoenician cities.[1]

The Araba mining district, between the Dead Sea and the Aqaba Gulf, with Sela, or Petra, at its center, was under active exploitation in the days of David and Solomon. It bore the name of the "Valley of the Smiths", and the Kenites or Kenizzites living there were the smiths who supplied the arsenal of the allied Amalekites with weapons, before the latter's downfall and the conquest of the valley by David. The district is rich in cupriferous minerals and iron ore (oxides). In recent years it has been explored by N. Glueck.[2] Ruins of smelting furnaces are found scattered along the valley; copper and iron were processed in them in the days of Solomon. Large iron nails actually have been unearthed and ascribed to the time of Solomon.

Solomon's harbor of Ezion-Geber on the Aqaba Gulf was an industrial community where furnaces equipped with the forced-draft system were employed in the "smelting and refining of copper and iron and the manufacturing of metal articles for home and foreign markets."[3]

In the days of Solomon silver was brought in large quantities in ships from afar, setting off another metal revolution, as we may read in the Scriptures and in the inscriptions of the viziers of Hatshepsut. In Palestine and in Egypt alike new luxurious buildings were erected, and in some instances silver was used for floors.[4]

The rapid acquisition of metallurgical skill by the Israelites was followed by a similarly rapid process in Egypt. Thutmose III (Shishak) had twelve hundred chariots, which played an important part in the conquest of Palestine and Syria. Prisoners from Rezenu (Palestine) were employed in metal workshops in Egypt, and the Egyptians learned the craft from them, as the pictures in the tomb of Rekhmire, the vizier of Thutmose III, show.[5] Copper was brought as tribute from Syria and Cyprus; and mining activity in the district of Sinai was resumed. In the list of tribute from one of Thutmose III's campaigns in Syria vessels of iron ("bia") are mentioned.[6]

---

[1] II Chronicles 2:7.
[2] N. Glueck: *The Other Side of the Jordan* (New Haven 1940), pp. 51ff.
[3] *Ibid.*, p. 94.
[4] See *Ages in Chaos* I, »The Desire of the Queen of Sheba«
[5] N. de Garis Davies: *The Tomb* of *Rekh-mi-re at Thebes* (New York, 1943), Vols. I and II.
[6] Breasted: *Records*, Vol. II, Sec. 537.

A list of the temple treasures of Qatna, drawn up some time before the conquest by Thutmose III, includes seven objects of iron, six of which were set in gold.[1] This does not mean that iron was particularly scarce. Iron kept in temples was of meteoric origin. The word "bia" means "metal" in general but more specifically "iron" or "the metal of heaven." Meteorites were held in veneration in many sanctuaries: in the temple of Astarte at Tyre, in the temple of Amon in Thebes, in Delphi, in Mexican temples, and to the present day in Mecca.[2] Because of its origin the meteorite iron was set in gold and kept in the temple of Qatna, as it was in other places.

The various peoples in the lands around the Mediterranean had their preferences for one or the other metal. In most cases the natural distribution of ore dictated whether the preference would be copper or for iron.

In the ninth-century palace of Assurnasirpal and Shalmaneser III at Nimrud, in which Tiglath-Pileser also dwelt in the second half of the eighth century, spearheads, arrowheads, axes, and sickles of iron were found: "hoards of iron" were unearthed in Khorsabad and Nineveh. The ore for this iron was mined in the Tiyari hills northeast of Nineveh and in the Chalybes region southeast of the Black Sea; in about -881 a rich load of iron was sent from the latter place to Assurnasirpal in Nineveh. This region was within the dominion of the Chaldeans; we would therefore expect to find mention of iron already in the earlier portions of the Boghazkoi archives. And in fact there is "a long list of mentions of iron in these documents, which reach down to the end of the Hittite Empire about -1200. ... Here iron is the common metal, not the bronze to which one is accustomed in other lands of the Near East."[3]

The Phoenicians of the Syrian shore, because of their closeness to Cyprus with its rich copper mines, were not fond of ironwork, though iron, too, was occasionally worked there in small quantities. It is no wonder that most of the metal found in Ras Shamra across the strait from Cyprus was bronze; yet rusted iron objects were found in Ras Shamra too.[4]

---

[1] C. Virolleaud: *Syria, Revue d'art oriental et d'archéologie*, IX (1928), 92. Qatna (el-Mishrife) was excavated by Du Mesnil du Buisson.
[2] Wainwright: *Antiquity*, X (1936), 6.
[3] *Ibid.*, 14.
[4] Schaeffer: *Syria, Revue d'art oriental et d'archéologie*, X (1929), 292.

One of the main arguments in support of the theory that the Mycenaean Age antedated that of the Homeric epics is based on the assumption that the Mycenaean tombs belong to the Bronze Age while the *Iliad* and *Odyssey* reflect an Iron Age. The weapons of the Homeric heroes are of bronze, but iron is mentioned forty-four times in the epics, and although, from some references, it had been concluded that iron was rare in those times,[1] the Iron Age had already superseded the Bronze Age, and steel manufacture was already known.

In the Mycenaean tombs bronze is abundant, but iron is not absent.[2]

As in the days of Solomon, so in the time of Homer (presumably the eighth century), Sidon was "abounding with bronze," and if the Mycenaean graves belonged to the Carians who migrated from Ugarit or to Argive princes who were supplied with armor by the Phoenician traders, it would not be surprising to find that bronze is abundant in the tombs and iron rare.

The copper-mining region of Cyprus, Temessa, was exporting copper not only to Egypt but to the Aegaean region too, and ships sailing to Cyprus to take on copper sometimes brought iron there.[3]

Because of this distribution of deposits, with large centers of copper in Cyprus and in Sinai and the poor iron ore of Egypt, bronze was the chief metal of Phoenicia and Egypt, but iron was more in use in and around Assyria and Chaldea.

A correspondent of the el-Amarna period, Tushratta of Mitanni, wrote to his son-in-law Amenhotep III that he was sending him a sacred knife ("mittu") of iron and iron rings covered with gold. To Akhnaton he also sent iron rings covered with gold and a dagger, the blade of which was of iron and the handle of gold set with precious stones.[4] The fact that an iron dagger has a handle of gold or bronze does not necessarily mean that iron was rarer than gold or bronze. Following such reasoning, a future archaeologist, finding a set of table knives with silver handles, might think that silver was less precious in our day than steel.

Iron rings were sometimes covered with gold for the purpose of saving the gold, as is also done in our day when gold is laid over a less

---

[1] *Iliad,* XXIII, 826ff.
[2] Also iron of Late Minoan I was found in Greece: Forsdyke in *Annual of the British School at Athens,* XXVIII (1926-27), 296.
[3] *Odyssey:* I, 182ff. The copper mines of Cyprus, worked since the days of the Old Kingdom in Egypt and in the time of Homer, are still in operation.
[4] Letters 22 and 25.

precious metal. In Megiddo iron tools were found beside an iron foundry; iron rings covered with gold were uncovered there too.[1]

In the tomb of Tutankhamen copper is more abundant than bronze, though the Copper Age ended before the Middle Kingdom. A steel dagger set in a gold handle was found there together with a few small objects of iron.[2] At this time the process of controlling the carbon content of iron was perfected, at least in the north, so that a dagger blade of tempered steel was sharper than one of bronze, and could also compare favorably in flexibility and durability. In all ages the secret of tempering steel brought fame first to one place, then to another – in later times Damascus and Castilian blades were superior to the products of other localities.

When the Ethiopians superseded the Libyans in Egypt a new source of iron was opened up to this country in the south.[3] Slag from iron ore, found in heaps in Meroe in Nubia, is ascribed to this period, which is often regarded as the beginning of the real Iron Age in Egypt. Tools and small iron foundries were discovered in Egypt of the Ethiopian Dynasty. The Assyrian conquest of Egypt was carried on with iron arms, and Assyrian tools made of iron were found in Egypt.[4] Iron is not among the booty that Assurbanipal took in Egypt in about -663, but the same king enumerated spoils of iron taken in Syria.[5] The general impression is that nations which used iron, especially for armor, were able to subdue nations that employed bronze. The Assyrian conquest of Phoenician cities, the Ethiopian conquest of Egypt, the long contest between Assyria and Ethiopia over Egypt are examples.

With the beginning of the Nineteenth, i.e., the Twenty-sixth, Dynasty, the Ethiopian source of iron in Egypt was eliminated. Greeks of Daphnae, and later of Naucratis in Egypt, reduced iron ore to ingots, from which they manufactured tools. Iron tools were confined mainly

---

[1] "One iron object, a ring, has been attributed to the Late Bronze II period. It is not later in any event. Four iron objects came from Early Iron I burial, a dagger blade, a ring overlaid with gold, a fragment of a knife blade, and a bracelet." Guy: *Megiddo Tombs,* p. 162. On the iron foundry of Megiddo and iron implements, see Schumacher: *Tell el-Mutesellim,* I, 130-32, and Watzinger, ed.: *Tell el-Mutesellim,* II, 80-81. The date of this foundry is "uncertain, but in any case is probably before 926 B.C." Wainwright: *Antiquity,* X (1936), 20.

[2] Carter: *The Tomb of Tut-ankh-Amen,* Vol. II, Plates 77B, 82A, 87B; *ibid.,* Vol. III, Plate 27.

[3] Petrie: Ancient *Egypt,* II (1915), 22.

[4] *Ibid.,* p. 22; also Petrie: *Six Temples at Thebes,* 1896 (London, 1897), p. 18f.

[5] "The absence of iron from the list is in noticeable contrast to the harvests that had been garnered by the Assyrians for two hundred years from the cities of Syria and Palestine." Wainwright: *Antiquity,* X (1936), 22.

to Greek settlements, a situation very characteristic of Egypt.[1] Not even from later times – of the Persians, Ptolemies, or Romans – has there remained so much iron in Egypt as from these Greek settlements of the Saitic period.[2] But as the hematite of Egypt is of poor quality, domestic iron could best be employed for objects that did not require fine material: fences, buckles, chains, and the like. Ramses II imported iron of a better grade from the north.

A letter in the Boghazkoi archives, probably written by Hattusilis (Nebuchadnezzar) to Ramses II, reads:

> What concerns the pure iron, about which thou hast written to me, there is no pure iron in Kiswadna in my storehouse which is closed. The time was unfavorable to make iron. But I ordered in writing to prepare iron.[3]

Thus Hattusilis and Ramses II lived in a fully developed Iron Age. The reason an order was placed for iron from the north at a time when iron was smelted by the Greek mercenaries in Egypt was because of the differences in the qualities of the metal smelted in Egypt and in the north.

Jeremiah at the same time asked (15:12): "Shall iron break the northern iron and the steel?"

In that epoch iron was brought even from the western Mediterranean: Tarshish traded with Tyre in silver, iron, tin, and lead (Ezekiel 27:12). "Bright iron" was also brought from Javan (Ionia).[4]

Iron and bronze enriched the language with metaphors: "I have made thee … an iron pillar, and brasen walls" (Jeremiah 1:18); and Ezekiel (4:3) symbolically built "a wall of iron." "I am your wall of iron," Ramses II said of himself.[5]

It is also acknowledged that "by the time of the XIX Dynasty (c. 1300 – 1200 B.C.) iron had become the regular metal at Gerar in south Palestine, of which were manufactured knives, dagger-knives, spearheads, lance-heads, chisels, borers, hooks and sickles."[6] Actually the Nineteenth Dynasty ruled in the seventh-sixth centuries.

---

[1] "Rather later iron tools are common in the Greek settlement of Naukratis, but they do not appear in purely Egyptian sites." Petrie: *Ancient Egypt*, II (1915), 22.

[2] Garland and Bannister: *Ancient Egyptian Metallurgy*, p. 17.

[3] B. Meissner: *Zeitschrift der Deutschen Morgenländischen Gesellschaft*, LXXII (1918), 61.

[4] Ezekiel 27:19.

[5] A. Erman and A. M. Blackman: *The Literature of the Ancient Egyptians* (London, 1927), p. 268. Cf. A. Alt: *Zeitschrift der Deutschen Morgenländischen Gesellschaft*, LXXXVI (1933), 40.

[6] Wainwright: *Antiquity*, X (1936), 19.

Because the Egyptians had at their disposal the deposits of Sinai, and the Phoenicians the deposits of Cyprus, they were skilled in the manufacture of copper and bronze articles.[1] This remained true for Egypt until the days of the Moslem conquest,[2] and although the mines of Sinai have long since ceased operation, fondness for copper utensils is apparent in Egypt even today.

Gold, silver, and electrum (a mixture of gold and silver) are noble metals, not corrodible, and Egyptians who knew the corrodible quality of iron would not have included objects made of it among the funeral furniture and utensils of the dead, especially a noble person, still less a pharaoh: the purpose of mummification was to prolong the sepulchral life of the deceased. As the tombs built for the nobles are among the main sources of archaeological finds of metals in Egypt, the rare occurrence of iron smelted from ore can be explained to some extent by its deliberate omission in the choice of objects for the funeral chambers.

Besides a natural fondness for shiny copper and bronze in preference to iron, a religious tabu may have played a role in the slow progress of iron. A tabu against using iron for certain purposes is known to have existed in Palestine – the stones of the Israelite altar must have been shaped without the use of iron;[3] a similar tabu was observed in Greek and Roman cults;[4] it was and still is widespread.[5] In Egypt iron was called "bones of Seth," and played a role in religious beliefs and superstitions. Tiny symbolic instruments, which served for "opening the mouth" of the deceased and which were made of "bia", the heavenly metal, the iron that fell from the sky, were placed in tombs. They are mentioned in the Egyptian Psalms for the Dead but are not often found.[6]

Religious beliefs, the natural distribution of iron and copper, the quality of iron ore, the nature of the soil under cultivation – muddy (in Egypt) or stony (in Assyria and Palestine) – were the chief factors in the competition between iron and copper.

---

[1] T. A. Rickard: *Man and Metals* (New York, 1932), I, 240.
[2] "Copper and bronze were used in Egypt for arrow tips up to Arab times." Garland and Bannister: *Ancient Egyptian Metallurgy*, p. 104.
[3] Deuteronomy 27:5.
[4] See literature in H. B. Walters: *Catalogue of the Bronzes, Greek, Roman and Etruscan, in the British Museum* (London, 1899), p. xviii.
[5] J. G. Frazer: *The Golden Bough* (1911-35), I, 172.
[6] Wainwright: *Antiquity*, X (1936), 11.

It would be wrong to date medieval Cairo earlier than Nimrud, Nineveh, or Khorsabad of the ninth-seventh centuries before this era merely because in these places iron was found in greater quantities than in Egypt in any age.

When the Ethiopians or Assyrians invaded Egypt they brought iron with them; so did the Greek mercenaries. The Greek settlements in Egypt show that the Greeks favored iron while the Egyptians favored bronze. To fix chronology by weighing the iron and bronze found is an erroneous procedure. What matters is that during the entire period under discussion in this book Egypt, like other countries, knew and used iron; it is referred to in the sources and it is found in the excavations. Equally important is the fact that, in its relations with foreign countries, be it tribute from Syria to Thutmose III or a load of iron ordered by Ramses II, the New Kingdom of Egypt was in the middle of the Iron Age of the Near and Middle East. On the other hand, the Scriptures and the classic authors from Homer on down demonstrate by scores of references that iron did not displace bronze in many uses, especially in armor, until near the close of the period we call the Hellenic Age of ancient history. In Egypt the "progress was much the same though rather slower," and "the change was not accomplished till Roman times."[1]

It can be said in conclusion that the partition of historical periods into ages of bronze and iron, with divisions of each of these ages into Early, Middle, and Late, with subdivisions of each of them into I, II, and III, and with a further differentiation of each of them into a and b may be defended as a method of describing the succession of ages for a particular country, but it cannot bring clarity to comparative archaeology since iron did not progress at the same pace in all countries of the Mediterranean basin. Conventional history did not claim such simultaneity, but conventional chronology enmeshed itself in many conflicting statements by employing metal ages and their subdivisions for synchronizing historical periods in the countries of the ancient world.

---

[1] *Ibid.*, X (1936), 21.

6. Scarabs and Stratigraphy

Scarabs or beetles of ceramics, of glass, semiprecious stones, or metal often have names engraved on them: the cartouches of the kings and sometimes the names of private persons. Apparently these were used as seals. It is doubted that scarabs were used as money: there is no known literary reference to their use as such, nor does any picture show scarabs being given in payment. Some scarabs were used to commemorate an important occasion, like the large ones memorializing the wedding of Amenhotep III and Tiy. A few served to convey good wishes, such as "a happy New Year," like the cards that are sent today. Those of the last category could be regarded as amulets, but not the others. Those bearing cartouches of the royal names must serve as datable objects.

"Not all Egyptian scarabs were used as seals. Some, but a very small number compared to the seal class, were used as amulets."[1] "Their [scarab-shaped seals] value as corroborative evidence to other historical data must not be overlooked, nor can certain classes of them be lightly cast aside as bric-a-brac by the archaeologist who sets himself the task of solving, or of inquiring into, the many problems that have lately arisen concerning the early people of the Mediterranean region."[2] These problems resulted from the fact that on innumerable occasions scarabs were found in surroundings supposedly several centuries younger. All kinds of explanations were devised.

Some scarabs may not be genuine; for instance, they may be the product of modern forgers of antiquities. But if found in situ, as for instance in an undisturbed tomb, they should be regarded with more confidence. Money and seals have been counterfeited in all ages, but when Greek or Roman coins are found in the process of excavation their genuineness is rarely looked upon with suspicion. Moreover, forgers of ancient times must have imitated current coins and seals.

In other cases when the genuineness of the scarabs cannot be doubted, they are pronounced heirlooms handed down from one generation to another over the centuries, at last to be deposited in surroundings not of their own age. This is the second method of depreciating their value as witnesses to the age of the deposit in which they are found.

---

[1] P. E. Newberry: *Scarabs* (London, 1906), p. 1, note (1).
[2] *Ibid.*, p. 3.

Sometimes a large collection of scarabs, all pointing to one and the same period, is found in a tomb which, for some reason, is ascribed to another age six hundred years later.[1] It is then conjectured that the collection was transferred from some old grave to the new one, the builders of which must have been grave robbers. In view of the fact that the Palestinian and the Egyptian histories are disrupted as to their contemporaneity, we would expect that the scarabs found in Palestine would be consistently of much older dates than the surroundings in which they were discovered.

In the closing years of the last century Macalister participated with Bliss in archaeological work in Palestine and followed the chronological evaluation of the strata by the latter. On digging in Gezer, he changed the evaluations of their previous archaeological work by a number of centuries. He "tried to arrange his chronology so as to cover a hiatus of several centuries (circa 9th-6th centuries) in the history of the city and consequently reduced most of his dates between 1200 and 300 B.C. by several centuries. This erroneous telescoping of chronology was carried much farther by the Germans, misled by similar gaps at Jericho and by premature historical interpretation of their finds; in their case the error amounted at one point to about eight hundred years."[2]

> As a matter of fact, Macalister's shift to lower dating for this (Early Iron II, or 'Middle Iron') pottery is easy to explain. At Gezer there is an almost complete lacuna after the tenth century.[3]

The real cause of these changes is in the conflicting evidences of Palestinian archaeology, which relies on Egyptian chronology. In some cases this adherence to the Egyptian timetable is untenable because of other evidence in a layer under investigation; in such cases the Egyptian objects are pronounced heirlooms. Later, on reconsideration, the heirlooms are often made contemporaneous with the level in which they were found. (This is particularly the case with the scarabs of Egyptian signets.)

Wherever the archaeologists excavated in Palestine they found scarabs with Egyptian signs, and often with the names of Egyptian kings, but these names regularly pointed to centuries long past. How could these finds be explained?

---

[1] For instance, cf. Petrie: *Illahun, Kahun and Gurob* (London, 1891), p. 24.
[2] Albright: *From the Stone Age to Christianity*, p. 26.
[3] W. F. Albright: *The Excavation of Tell Beit Mirsim* (New Haven, 1932), Vol. I, 76

When Bliss and Macalister, digging in Tel es-Safi and other places in Palestine, found thirty scarabs with the names of Thutmose III, Amenhotep III, and other pharaohs in a level they recognized as belonging to the Israelite settlements, they wrote:

> Evidently some of them, if not all, are mere Palestinian imitations of imported specimens, and are therefore of no value in fixing the date of associated objects. It is an elementary archaeological canon that under the most favourable circumstances scarabs alone can give a major limit of date only; when the element of copying, perhaps long subsequent to the engraving of the original exemplar, is introduced, their chronological importance practically disappears.[1]

Scarabs were the presents of the pharaohs; they were also the official seals of the reigning monarch used in Egypt and the dependent countries; their impressions have been found in Palestine on the handles of jars that had contained oil or wine, and also on stones used as weights. Why should the impressions for legal and other official purposes have been imitations of seals of ancient pharaohs?

Many scarabs found in Palestine in subsequent years show all the marks of genuineness: they do not differ in any respect from scarabs found in Egypt in graves of the officials of the kings whose names are on the scarabs. Another explanation, therefore, had to be given for their presence and use in Palestine six hundred years after identical scarabs had been made and used in Egypt. The explorers of Jericho, Sellin and Watzinger, wrote:

> It is beyond doubt that all scarabs found are of genuine Egyptian workmanship of their time, not one a foreign or late imitation.[2]

And again:

> It has already been frequently established in the Palestinian excavations that the old scarabs were worn centuries later as unintelligible amulets, and therefore, when we find them, we obtain but a terminus a quo. Furthermore, handles stamped with scarabs exactly like those from Jericho were never found in the same level of the excavations as the handmade Canaanitic ceramics.[3]

---

[1] F. J. Bliss and R. A. S. Macalister: *Excavations in Palestine* (1898-1900) (London, 1902), p. 152.
[2] Sellin and Watzinger: *Jericho*, p. 157.
[3] *Ibid.*

According to the last observation, then, genuine scarabs were used in Palestine after centuries of disuse, and also they were not found in the Canaanite level contemporaneous with the time of the pharaohs who made these scarabs. This is, to say the least, strange; and no less strange is the fact that the Israelites did not use as amulets the scarabs of their own time, but only old scarabs.

> We are compelled therefore to assume that it was a custom in Palestine to use old scarabs ... at a time when there was no longer any understanding of their original meaning"[1]

The Israelites employed these seals not primarily as amulets but for making impressions on jars and stone weights. There is no more reason for using genuine seals of ancient pharaohs for that purpose than imitations of old seals. Hebrew seals on jar handles are regarded as contemporaneous with the level in which these jars are found; only in the case of handles with Egyptian signs (sometimes found in the same lot[2]) are the Israelites supposed to have preferred ancient seals, But the Israelites did not use the ancient objects of the Canaanite period together with their own utensils or pottery.

Is, then, the theory that "the scarab had passed as an heirloom, or had been discovered and adapted as a seal in a century later than its own" tenable?[3]

We go a little way from Gezer and come to Beth-Shemesh, Ain-Shems of today. This city was in existence during the period of the Judges and it prospered in the time of the Kings.[4] Since the time of the Kings comprises roughly the period from -1000 to -600, it can be anticipated that in a timetable based upon Egyptian chronology the zenith of Beth-Shemesh will appear half a millennium earlier.

> The most prosperous and dignified centuries at Beth-Shemesh ... were those between 1500 and 1100. During these 400 years Beth-Shemesh was a place of considerable importance and culture.[5]

But other evidence, not connected with Egypt, must have intervened, and we have, for instance, the following:

---

[1] *Ibid.*

[2] Bliss and Macalister: *Excavations in Palestine,* Plate 56, No. 31s.

[3] Macalister: *The Excavation of Gezer,* vol. 2, p. 329. See also pp. 314 and 323. "... found in Third Semitic debris, but no doubt properly of Second," is a recurrent phrase referring to the scarabs discovered.

[4] I Samuel 6:9-20; I Kings 4:9; II Kings 14:11-13; II Chronicles 28:18.

[5] E. Grant: *Ain Shems Excavations* (1298:31), Pt. III (Haverford, 1934), p. 19.

"Room 380, In its southern wall ... are reinforcing stone posts and at the base of one of them was the wedding scarab of Amenophis (Amenhotep) III, already 300 to 400 years old when put to its latest use in the wall-foundations. It may have been placed there as late as 1000 B.C., a potent charm for the security of the house, or to defend the northern side of the town."[1] This "limestone scarab with its ten lines of writing" is no different from such scarabs in the Aegean tombs and in Enkomi on Cyprus, where they are regarded as the chief evidence of the age of the levels and of Mycenaean culture in general. "It dates from 1400 B.C., and was a treasured antiquity when it was deposited for its magical value."

It was actually deposited about -870, during the first part of the reign of Jehoshaphat, shortly before the el-Amarna correspondence; it was not "a treasured antiquity" at that time, and its deposition in the wall foundations as a document destined to testify to the age of the foundation in days to come would preclude its being already old at the time of deposition. Such a deposition has many parallels in the architectural archaeology of the Orient; this usage has survived down to the present day all over the civilized world.

Megiddo of the Bible is identified with present-day Tell el-Mutesellim overlooking the Jezreel Valley, at the northern entrance of the pass that leads through Carmel into the Sharon plain. Schumacher's excavations there early in this century turned up material that seemed on examination to belong to widely separated chronological periods. When, more than two decades later, the finds of Megiddo were published, the editor of the report, Watzinger, assumed the following: "It becomes clear that in the process of digging too freely the deeper strata were invaded and finds from these more ancient layers were marked as belonging to the same layer as finds made on the floor."[2]

The later American excavation at Megiddo, carried out on a large scale, also produced equivocal material. Remains of buildings and graves

---

[1] *Ibid.*, p. 66. It is worth noting that room 380, where the scarab was found, belongs, according to the excavator's report, to the level labeled by him "Early Iron II" (*ibid.*, map 1). The Early Iron II level is dated (p. 4) to between -900 and -600. Also A. Rowe: *A Catalogue of Egyptian Scarabs ... Palestine Archaeological Museum* (Cairo, 1936), p. 129, No. 538, agrees that the scarab was found in the Early Iron II level.

[2] "Es stellt sich dabei freilich vielfach heraus, dass bei der Grabung gern in die Tiefe gegangen wurde und dann Funde aus grösserer Tiefe, also aus älteren Schichten zusammen mit den über dem Fussboden gemachten Funden unter derselben Schichtnummer verzeichnet werden." *Tell el-Mutesellim*, ed. C. Watzinger (Leipzig, 1929), Vol. 2, p. v.

were found in Megiddo. At some time point a new race came into the country and settled there. "A new people with a strong artistic feeling for its religion was invading the country at the end of the Middle Bronze Period. From the evidence of scarabs we must conclude that it was closely related to the earlier Hyksos. ..."[1] But the Hyksos are known to have been devoid of "artistic feeling" for their religion or anything else; they did not manifest any artistic activity in Egypt. Then who could have been the invaders who carried a new culture into Palestine in the early days of the Hyksos Empire and their hegemony on the Mediterranean coast?

According to the revised scheme presented in this work, the Philistines and the Israelites arrived in Palestine practically at the beginning of the Hyksos-Amalekite period. The new culture in Palestine, from the fifteenth century on, is explainable by the presence there of these two peoples.

In the middle of the tenth century Solomon fortified Megiddo. In the fifth year after Solomon's death Thutmose III invaded Palestine and, as we now know, laid siege to Megiddo and took it. In the stratum of the Megiddo palace, ascribed to Early Iron I, seals with the name of Thutmose III were found. "Occurrences of the prenomen of Thutmose III ... [are] not surprising in view of the known predilection of the later Egyptians for scarabs bearing that king's name."[2] With this casual explanation the testimony of the seals was brushed aside.

Since these lines were written by the excavators of Megiddo, again and again, all over Palestine, scarabs with the name of Thutmose III were found and always in formations five to six hundred years younger, leaving the finders in a constant state of surprise bordering on astonishment.

Yet where the remotest possibility seemed to exist of sustaining the accepted chronological table by a reference to a scarab, its genuineness or its stratigraphical position was never questioned; usually, however, such finds, on closer examination, prove to be of almost no stratigraphical, and therefore of any chronological, value for the purpose selected.

In the conventional chronology King Sosenk of the Libyan Dynasty was the pharaoh Shishak of the Scriptures who conquered Palestine in the fifth year of Rehoboam, son of Solomon. A fragment with the name of Sosenk on it was found at Megiddo. "A fragment of his stela

---

[1] H. G. May: *Material Remains of the Megiddo Cult* (Chicago, 1935), p. 35
[2] P. L. O. Guy: *Megiddo Tombs* (Chicago, 1938), p. 185.

found here proved that he occupied the town for a time at least."[1] However, as I have shown, Thutmose III was the biblical Shishak, and Pharaoh So of the Scriptures, to whom Hoshea of Israel sent tribute, was the pharaoh Sosenk;[2] a stele of Sosenk at Megiddo would therefore not be out of place. Damaging to its evidential value is the fact that "the fragment of the [Sosenk] stela came from one of the old surface dump heaps, or the refuse of earlier excavations:"[3]

An object found on a dump heap does not warrant drawing a conclusion like this: "From the evidence of our Sheshonk [Sosenk] stela fragment ... it follows naturally that Stratum IV (1000-800) was built before the period of Omri and Ahab"[4]

Megiddo was the fortress to which Ahaziah, king of Judah, tried to escape during the revolt of Jehu, shortly after the end of Ahab's reign. It was an important garrison city. Having been fortified by Solomon,[5] restored after the siege of Thutmose III, and garrisoned by Amenhotep III, it is no wonder that the superstructure of the palace of Megiddo "parallels exactly the masonry from the Omri and Ahab palaces found at Samaria."[6]

Another such case, regularly called upon to verify the accepted synchronism between the House of Omri and the Libyan Dynasty in Egypt, will be discussed by us in greater detail at another place, but we shall not omit it in review here because, on the provenance of a Libyan seal impression *found in Samaria, a* chronological edifice was built.

On the floor of the palace of Omri and Ahab a number of small Egyptian objects were found. The carvings on the scarabs are mostly decorative designs, but on one of the scarabs a cartouche, or king's name, is engraved. The cartouche is that of Thutmose III. Since there was no plausible explanation for the presence of the cartouche of Thutmose III in the palace at Samaria, presumably built about six centuries after this pharaoh had died, the excavator suggested: "This may be a local imitation of an Egyptian scarab."[7] But in accord with the present reconstruction of history, Thutmose III reigned only a few decades before Omri; the cartouche apparently is genuine.

---

[1] Fisher: *The Excavation of Armageddon,* p. 16.
[2] *Ages in Chaos,* Vol. 1, »The Temple in Jerusalem«
[3] *Ibid.,* »The Israelites Meet the Hyksos«
[4] R. S. Lamon and G. M. Shipton: *Megiddo I (Strata I-V)* (Chicago, 1939), p. 61.
[5] I Kings 9:15.
[6] Fisher: *The Excavation of Armageddon,* p. 73.
[7] Reisner, Fisher, and Lyon: *Harvard Excavations at Samaria,* Vol. 1, p. 377

According to conventional history, Ahab was a contemporary of Pharaoh Osorkon II of the Libyan Dynasty. And a jar with the cartouches of Pharaoh Osorkon II was actually found near the palace of Samaria.[1] This pharaoh of the Libyan Dynasty was selected by the historians as the biblical Pharaoh Zerah, adversary of Asa, in the days of Omri and Ahab.[2] But we have already identified Pharaoh Zerah as one of the kings of the Eighteenth Dynasty, Amenhotep II - Okheperure, successor of Thutmose III.[3] How can we, from our standpoint, explain the presence of Osorkon's jar in Samaria?

It happened that beneath the layer of Osorkon's jar were discovered written documents that shattered its significance as chronological evidence: Ostraca, or inscribed potsherds, were found near the palace. They were first thought to date from Ahab's reign; but, upon re-examination, they were attributed to Jeroboam II's reign.[4] Now, according to the excavators, the foundations of the Ostraca House (containing the inscribed sherds) "must have been destroyed previous to the construction of the Osorkon House"[5] (so called because of the jar found in its ruins). It follows that the potsherds were of an earlier date than the Osorkon jar, or the time of its deposition; and that, if anything, the jar can prove only that Osorkon lived after Jeroboam II, not in the days of Ahab. Nevertheless we read again and again that the jar with the seal impression of Osorkon II proves that Ahab and Osorkon were contemporaries.[6]

Thus we see that scarabs found in Palestine – and elsewhere, too – are regularly denied their chronological value on a variety of pretexts – but a few, definitely unacceptable cases are elevated to the representa-

---

[1] *Ibid.*, p. 247.
[2] Doubts as to this identification were expressed, for the Bible refers to Zerah as an Ethiopian and Osorkon was a Libyan. G. Maspero (*The Struggle of the Nations,* p. 774, note) remarks: "Champollion identified Osorkon I with Zerah, who according to 2 Chronicles 14:9-15; 16:8, invaded Judah. But this has no historical value, for it is clear that Osorkon never crossed the Isthmus [of Suez]."
[3] *Ages in Chaos*: Vol. 1, Chap. V.
[4] Albright: *Archaeology and the Religion of Israel,* p. 41; idem, in *Ancient Near Eastern Texts,* ed. Pritchard, p. 321.
[5] Reisner, Fisher, and Lyon: *Harvard Excavations at Samaria,* p. 131.
[6] "La date des ostraca de Samarie est fixée par les circonstances de la trouvaille et cette date est confirmée par la présence dans les mêmes débris de fragments d'une vase au nom d'Osorkon II (874-853), contemporain d'Achab." R. Dussaud: »Samarie au temps d'Achab«, *Syria,* 6 (1925). This statement, compared with the record of the excavators, is not precise. Jack: *Samaria in Ahab's Time,* p. 41, also says that Osorkon's jar was found "in the same debris" as the ostraca.

tive role of verifiers of the conventional order of things. Yet the value of scarabs for chronological purposes is almost unique; it is not different from the chronological value of coins with the name of the kings under whom they were stamped, when, after being hoarded and hidden, they are found centuries later by excavators.

Retrospect

At the beginning of this volume the curtain rose over the land of a small and ancient people who, guided by its prophet and led by its king, mustered its defenses and brought up an army to block the advance of one of the most powerful and certainly most pompous of the Egyptian pharaohs, whose goal was to participate in the division of the Assyrian Empire. Only shortly before, Nineveh, the capital of Assyria, had fallen under the onslaught of the allied troops of the Chaldeans, Medes, and Scythians. In the painted scene from the palace of Ramses II we recognized the Judean king Josiah, pierced by a thrown lance and dying.

Three years later a battle on the shore of the Euphrates took place between the Egyptian and the Chaldean armies. The description of this battle in hieroglyphics and its depiction on murals was compared with the narrative in the books of Jeremiah, II Kings, and II Chronicles. The composition of the Egyptian army, the course of the battle and the outcome of it, the impression it made on the peoples of the Middle East – all are equally reflected in the Egyptian and the Hebrew sources. In the process of reconstructing the events we were able to locate Kadesh of the Egyptian sources at Carchemish, north of Arima and Bab where two divisions tarried and then hurriedly retreated toward Egypt. Tell Nebi-Mend does not play the role of a spurious Kadesh and recognized as Riblah, the fortress built by Seti the Great, father of Ramses II, and the scene of some tragic events in the life of Jewish kings as described in the Scriptures.

No wonder that the misalignment of Egyptian history with that of Judea and that of the Chaldean kingdom wrought incalculable damage to the writing of history and created perplexities without end. Whether the tomb of Ahiram was built in the thirteenth century, the assumed time of Ramses II, or at the end of the seventh century, depends on whether Egyptian objects or objects from other countries serve as indices of the time the tomb was built. For scores of years protracted debate did not settle the problem.

Does not the gold tomb of Carchemish present the same problem, this time because of competing evidence from the strata and from the jewelry with miniature copies of the rock reliefs of Yazilikaya on the outskirts of the capital of "Hittite Empire"? However, the reliefs of Yazilikaya, first adjudged to have originated in the seventh century, were assigned to the thirteenth century, owing to the finding of archives at Boghazkoi with the Babylonian version of a treaty signed with Ramses II.

The existence of the "Hittite Empire," first devised on the strength of monuments with pictographic script found in Asia Minor and northern Syria, mainly in the area known from Greek authors to have been occupied by the Chaldeans, appeared to have been wonderfully confirmed by the archive discovered at Boghazkoi. But archaeological difficulties grew with every passing year until it was admitted, almost with self-castigation, that the Hittite question is unsolvable; and no repairs, ingenious or not, have been of avail. The "Hittite" remains in Syria were dated five to seven centuries younger than the remains in Anatolia, and Syro-Hittite kingdoms were postulated – this because their monuments were found above monuments of the late Assyrian kings (Marash), or their pictographic inscriptions have parallel texts dating, again, from the time of the late Assyrian kings (Karatepe) .

In Anatolia, too, the strangest stratigraphy came to light. The explorers of Boghazkoi resolved not to pay attention to stratigraphy or the sequence of layers in which the finds were made. But the excavator of Alisar found that the relics of the "Hittite Empire" are found *only* in Phrygian or post-Phrygian, never in pre-Phrygian, levels, and the excavator of Gordion, the short-lived capital of the Phrygians, resolved his difficulties by devising a remarkable arrangement by which the Persians who occupied the country in -546 carried from the long-since non-existent "Hittite Empire" earth and clay with the relics of that empire, all the way across the site of modern Ankara, across rivers and mountains, and spread it evenly over the Phrygian capital, so that the Phrygian relics rightfully appear *under* the multitudinous relics of the Hittite Empire, instead of being in a stratum over them; antiquities, supposedly of the fifteenth to thirteenth century, came to rest over antiquities of the kingdom that saw its end in -687 with the passage of the Cimmerians. But then from -687 to -546 nothing attests to any occupation, a further complexity recognized by the excavator, who did not dare to offer a theory that the Persians carried this hundred-forty-year-old stratum to some other place to cover it with a foreign layer.

It is an unheeded warning of Ekrem Akurgal, a Turkish archaeologist, who vainly searched the expanse of Asia Minor for any remains of habitation between -1200, the putative date of the end of the Hittite Empire, and -750 and proclaimed that he had found none. Should not such a warning, stated and repeated, be heeded? And Greek authors from Homer to Herodotus to Strabo, all of them natives of Asia Minor, all of them describers of the many races of Asia Minor, never heard of the Hittites; and Xenophon, who traversed the region, like Herodotus before him, never met Hittites but described the land where their monuments are found as that of the Chaldeans. And how it is that the habit of writing on lead strips preserved in rolls was practiced by the "Hittite" and Greek merchants alike, by the latter in the third and second centuries before the present era? And why do the Greek sculptures with Persian motifs found in Arslan Tash have Hittite signs? Or, better, why would coins of the Commogene kings on the western shore of the Euphrates be minted with "Hittite" royal titles, and this in the days of the Roman emperor Vespasian, when the "Hittite Empire" was supposed to have been dead for thirteen centuries, and no Greek or Roman ever heard of their race? But the Chaldeans, as Roman and Greek authors testify, were still present in Commogene and in Asia Minor till at least the first century of the present era.

These and many other equally striking facts prepare us to read the annals of the Hittite Empire with great caution and with some anticipation as to the identity of their authors. The question, Where are the war records of the Chaldean kings of the Neo-Babylonian Empire, and first of all of Nebuchadnezzar? a question asked since the war annals written by the Assyrian kings were read, is nearing a solution. I have offered a comparison of the annals of several consecutive "Hittite" kings with what we know of the life and wars of three consecutive Chaldean emperors, and the warlike and honest record of the king I identify as the alter ego of Nabopolassar was scrutinized against what is known of him from Greek sources as well as from cuneiform chronicles composed under the Persians; I also compared the autobiography of the adversary of Ramses II with what we know of Nebuchadnezzar from his building inscriptions, from the Scriptures, and from Greek-writing authors. The similarities, actually identities, of persons, facts, and events are so pronounced that I permitted myself the audacity of dealing with these documents from the royal archives of the Forgotten Empire ere I spread before the reader the panorama of the numerous archaeological impasses, of some of which I have just reminded the reader in this concluding section.

In the last chapter of this volume I resumed the narration of the events on the stage of the Middle East following the conclusion of the peace treaty between the Egyptian and Chaldean monarchs. The visit of the "Hittite" king to Egypt, where he brought his elder daughter to be the queen of his former adversary, gave us a chance to compare the likeness of the "Hittite" king made by the Egyptian artist at the behest of Ramses II with the portrait of Nebuchadnezzar, as carved on a rock in northern Syria.

In Daphnae-Tahpanheth Nebuchadnezzar put his pavilion, as Jeremiah prophesied; but the prophet erred – the Chaldean came this time not to conquer but to marry his daughter to Ramses II. The kiln-baked bricks of Daphnae, spoken of by Jeremiah, were excavated by archaeologists and dated to the time of Ramses II. Similar, almost identical bricks were found in Babylon, where they had been used for building Nebuchadnezzar's palace.

Merneptah, whose throne name reads Hophrama'e, was Pharaoh Hophra of the Scriptures, and the Israel stele, supposedly the first mention of Israel in history, is not a reference to the Exodus from Egypt but an echo of the lamentations of Jeremiah with identical expressions and even sentences. It was the time of the Exile.

The Libyan campaign of Merneptah which resulted from an involvement in the affairs of Cyrenaica, to which Greeks and other northerners flocked, summoned to do so by the Pythian oracle, ended tragically for the pharaoh, and retribution, if there is such a thing in history, came to the house of Ramses, not from the Chaldeans but from the Libyans. Amasis, who next mounted the throne, was not separated from the king he deposed by seven hundred years – he kept him as a prisoner in his palace until the day he delivered him to the mob.

It is a little surprising that Solon visited Egypt when Ramses II sat on the throne. But history is surprising and this is one of its charms.

The Pitfalls of Radiocarbon Dating

Offering in 1952 his new radiocarbon method for calculating the age of organic material (the time interval since the plant or the animal died), W. F. Libby clearly saw the limitations of the method and the conditions under which his theoretical figures would be valid:

A. Of the three reservoirs of radiocarbon on earth – the atmosphere, the biosphere, and the hydrosphere, the richest is the last – the oceans with the seas. The correctness of the method depends greatly on the condition that in the last 40 or 50 thousand years the quantity of water in the hydrosphere (and carbon diluted in it) has not substantially changed.

B. The method depends also on the condition that during the same period of time the influx of cosmic rays or energy particles coming from the stars and the sun has not suffered substantial variations.

To check on the method before applying it on various historical and paleontological material, Libby chose material of Egyptian archaeology, under the assumption that no other historical material from over 2000 years ago is so secure as to its absolute dating. When objects of the Old Kingdom and Middle Kingdom of Egypt yielded carbon dates that appeared roughly comparable with the historical dates, Libby made his method known.

With initial large margin of error and anything that did not square with expectation, judged as "contaminated," the method appeared to work and was hailed as completely reliable – just as the atomic clock is reliable – and this nobody doubted.

But as the method was refined, it started to show rather regular anomalies. First, it was noticed that, when radiocarbon dated, wood grown in the 20th century appears more ancient than wood grown in the 19th century. Suess explained the phenomenon by the fact that the increased industrial use of fossil carbon in coal and in oil changed the ratio between the dead carbon ^{12}C and the ^{14}C (radiocarbon) in the atmosphere and therefore also in the biosphere. In centuries to come a body of a man or animal who lived and died in the 20th century would appear paradoxically of greater age since death than the body of a man or animal of the 19th century, and if the process of industrial use of fossil, therefore dead, carbon continues to increase, as it is expected will be the case, the paradox will continue into the forthcoming centuries.

As years passed and more tests were made (soon by laboratories counted in scores), a rather consistent deviation between radiocarbon age and historical age started to receive the attention of researchers. The radiocarbon dates diverge from the historical dates by several hundred years (often 500 to 700), and, interestingly, in the Egyptian samples more so than in samples from most other ancient civilizations. This led Libby to write in 1963: "The data [in the Table] are separated into two groups – Egyptian and non-Egyptian. This separation was made because the whole Egyptian chronology is interlocking and subject to possible systematic errors ..." Also, "Egyptian historical dates beyond 4000 years ago may be somewhat too old, perhaps 5 centuries too old at 5000 years ago..."[1]

The combined efforts of several researchers led them to believe that one of the conditions stipulated by Libby for a flawless functioning of his method was not historically sustained; it is claimed that the influx of cosmic rays varied with time. Yet, since this influx comes from many sources, the sun being only one of them, sunspot activity could be related to the variation only in a very limited degree. Therefore the claim was made that the magnetosphere around the earth, discovered in 1958, suffered occasional weakening, thus allowing more cosmic rays to pass it and to hit the nitrogen atoms in the upper atmosphere, changing them to radiocarbon. It was further claimed that the magnetic field of the earth might have reversed its polarity in the last 40 thousand years, a phenomenon known to have happened in geological epochs. If such reversals were not instantaneous but required thousands of years, the atmosphere during that time would not be shielded from cosmic rays and substantially more of them would reach it. However, the scientific literature of the last few decades did not contain any reference to a reversal observed on human artifacts like pottery – though a paper by Manley in 1949 [2] told of the work of G. Folghereiter done

---

[1] *Science*, 140, 278
[2] *Science News*, Penguin Publication

at the turn of the century on Attic and Etruscan pottery: he found that the polarity was reversed in the eighth century before the present era.

To determine the extent of correction necessary to render the radiocarbon method reliable, dendrochronologists devised a plan to control the radiocarbon dates by building a chronology of tree rings of the white bristlecone pine, the longest living tree. The method caught the fancy of the radiocarbon researchers. However, three or four rings formed in one year is not uncommon, especially if the tree grows on a slope, with the ground several times in a year turning wet and dry because of rapid outflow of water[1] And certainly the building of tree "ladders," or carrying on the count from one tree to another may cause erroneous conclusions. One and the same year may be dry in South California and wet in the northern part of the state.

Now let us review in the light of research in cosmic catastrophism the correctives that, in our view, need to be introduced into the method. We must also evaluate the basic reliance on Egyptian chronology that, as we shall see, needs to be discontinued.

Speaking of my research as far as it affects the radiocarbon dating method, I would like to separate the finds concerning natural events (*Worlds in Collision, Earth in Upheaval*) from finds concerning the true chronology of Egypt and of the ancient world in general (*Ages in Chaos*).

Libby's discoveries, published in 1952, gave immediate support and even vindication to three independent conclusions of my research into natural events of the past. In *Worlds in Collision* I claimed that the time since the last glaciation needs to be drastically shortened: the figure considered valid in 1950, the year *Worlds in Collision* was published, was still Lyell's of 100 years earlier, namely 35 thousand years. Libby found (and I quote Frederick Johnson, who participated in his volume, *Radiocarbon Dating*) that "the advance of the ice occurred about 11,000 years ago ... previously this maximum advance had been assumed to date from about 25,000 years ago," actually 35,000 if one looks up the literature of the time. A few years later Rubin and Suess of the Geological Survey of the U. S. A. found that, as I also claimed, another advance of ice took place only 3500 years ago.

---

[1] Glueck et al.: *Botanical Review*, 7, 649-713; and 21, 245-365

The second confirmation came concerning the age of the petroleum. In 1950 in the *American Journal of Science* (the present publisher of *Radiocarbon*) a review was published by its editor, Yale geologist Longwell, with a rejection of my entire theory on the basis that oil is never found in Recent formations, being itself many millions of years old. A similar criticism appeared in the article by astronomer Edmondson, who cited the Indiana University geologist, J. B. Patton. One of the early radiocarbon datings of petroleum and petroleum-bearing formation on and off-shore in the Gulf area was by P. V. Smith of Esso Research Laboratory. The "surprising" fact was that oil was found there in Recent sediment and must have been deposited *during* the last 9200 years." (Emphasis added)

Actually I asked Libby whether he would see to it that petroleum should be subjected to tests and it was he who drew my attention to the work done by Smith.

A third confirmation also concerned one of the important conclusions of *Worlds in Collision*. To the above-mentioned article by Longwell a Mexicologist also contributed. The Mexicologist, Professor George Kubler of Yale, stressed that certain traditions contained in Mesoamerican heritage were referred by me to events of the pre-Christian era. Kubler insisted that this heritage could not date from the 8th to 4th pre-Christian centuries, but rather was generated in the 4th to 8th century of the Christian era. But in December, 1956, the National Geographical Society in conjunction with the Smithsonian Institution made it known that excavations at LaVenta proved by radiocarbon that the classical period of the Meso-American civilizations (Olmec, Toltec, Maya, etc.) needs to be pushed back by a full thousand years and ascribed not to the 4th to 8th centuries of the Christian era but to the 8th to 4th centuries before that era.

With these three confirmations (time the Ice Age ended, time petroleum was deposited, time of the classical period of the Meso-American civilizations), my *Worlds in Collision* received very substantial confirmations.

But I could not and should not satisfy myself with this support without repaying by demonstrating where the difficulties and pitfalls of the method are hidden.

In the cataclysmic events reconstructed in *Worlds in Collision* and also those that preceded the fall of the Middle Kingdom in Egypt, various effects could not but vitiate the radiocarbon performance, some of these effects tending to make organic life appear older than its actual age, and others making it appear more recent.

Bursts of cosmic rays and of electrical discharges on an interplanetary scale would make organic life surviving the catastrophes much richer in radiocarbon and therefore, when carbon dated, that organic matter would appear much closer to our time than actually true. But if the invasion of the terrestrial atmosphere by "dead" (non-radioactive) carbon from volcanic eruptions, from meteoric dust, from burning oil and coal and centuries-old forests, predominated the picture, then the changed balance of radioactive and of radio-inert carbon would make everything in the decades following the event appear much older. Thus, it is the competition of these factors that would decide the issue in each separate case. My own impression is that in the catastrophes of the eighth century and beginning of the seventh, the second phenomenon was by far more dominant. For the events of the middle of the fifteenth century before the present era, both phenomena were very expressed, but the burning petroleum added to the exhaust of all volcanoes burning simultaneously, added also to the ash of the proto-planet in near-collision must have outweighed the greatly increased advent of cosmic rays (which resulted also from interplanetary discharges). But in the catastrophe of the Deluge, which I ascribe to Saturn exploding as a nova, the cosmic rays must have been very abundant to cause massive mutations among all species of life, and correspondingly, these cosmic rays must have also changed the radiocarbon clock and certainly made ensuing life, subjected today to radiocarbon tests, appear much more recent than historically true. I am not in a position to point to the century or even millennium when the Universal Deluge took place, but it must have happened between five and ten thousand years ago, probably closer to the second figure.

The Deluge also increased the water basin or hydrosphere on earth, and if we can believe some indications, the Atlantic Ocean (called the "Sea of Cronus" by the ancients) originated in part during the Deluge. It is quite possible that the volume of water was more than doubled on earth in this one cataclysm.

Thus both conditions stipulated by Libby (that is, constant rate of influx of cosmic rays, and constant quantity of water in the hydrosphere) have been violated, but following the uniformitarian doctrine these violations have been discarded from consideration. We are left with a method in which the researchers have failed to take heed of the warnings expressed by its inventor.

The sustained effort of radiocarbon researchers to find support in Egyptian chronology, and their reliance on that chronology, is fundamentally a mistake. As I tried to show in *Ages in Chaos*, the Egyptian chronology is basically wrong. I drew the attention of Libby to this fact in my letter of October 7, 1953, and I sent him a copy of *Ages in Chaos*; his answer was that he is not at all learned in ancient history; thus he continued to rely on what is unreliable. He cannot be blamed for it because in historical circles the conventional chronology is still the accepted dating in absolute and in comparative sense – the latter meaning that Mycenaean or Minoan civilizations that have no absolute chronology of their own, by relations with the Egyptian past can be dated accordingly; but this means that if the Egyptian datings are wrong, the Minoan and Mycenaean are wrong, too.

Here I shall give a few figures to visualize the extent of the errors in the Egyptian chronology: The end of the Middle Kingdom of Egypt, -1780 in accepted chronology, actually took place ca. -1450 – a difference of over 200 years. The following Hyksos period endured, not 100 years, but over 400 years in close agreement with the old Egyptian (Manetho) and Hebrew (*Ages in Chaos*, I, Ch. 2) sources. The beginning of the 18th Dynasty (New Kingdom) falls not in -1580 but in ca. -1050 – over 500 years difference. Thutmose III belongs to the second part of the tenth century, not to the first part of the fifteenth. Akhnaton belongs not in the first half of the fourteenth but in the middle of the ninth century. Thus, as I showed in detail in vol. I of *Ages in Chaos*, there exists an error of ca. 540 years through the entire period covered by the 18th Dynasty.

Even more important is that the dynasty of Seti the Great and Ramses II, termed the Nineteenth Dynasty, did not follow the Eighteenth; the Libyan (Dynasties 22nd to 23rd) and the Ethiopian (Dynasties 24th to 25th) periods intervened. The Libyan Dynasty of Sosenks and Osorkons reigned for 100 years only, instead of over 200; the

Ethiopian Dynasty, however, is the only one that in the conventionally written history of Egypt maintains its proper place. During the Nineteenth Dynasty the error of the accepted Egyptian chronology reached the high figure of over 700 years; and together with it the time of the contemporaneous rulers of the so-called Hittite Empire is equally misplaced by over 700 years.[1] Finally the Twentieth Dynasty – that of Ramses III and his adversaries – Peoples of the Sea – needs to be brought closer to our time by a full 800 years and placed just a few decades before Alexander of Macedon. The Twenty-first Dynasty began under the Persian kings, continued contemporaneous with the Twentieth – its rulers reigned in the Libyan Desert oases – and lasted until the second Ptolemy.

Now if the historical basis of radiocarbon studies fails so completely, many conclusions drawn and much data left unpublished require reconsideration. From some correspondence that originated at the Metropolitan Museum of Art, I have concluded that when Libby first asked for specimens, he received not only those dating from the Old and Middle Kingdoms, but also from the New Kingdom – but nothing ever was published of those early tries on New Kingdom specimens. A similar situation concerns more recently tested short-living organic material from the tomb of Tutankhamen.

After many efforts (from 1952 to 1963) to have the New Kingdom of Egypt tested in a systematic way I succeeded in having three little pieces of wood from the tomb of Tutankhamen handed over by the Laboratory Director of the Cairo Museum to Mrs. Ilse Fuhr of Munich, who was directed by me to send them to Dr. Elizabeth Ralph of the University of Pennsylvania Laboratory. Two of the pieces were from the comparatively short-lived thorn plant, Spina Christi, and one from the long-living Cedar of Lebanon. The three small pieces were processed together, since a test requires ca. 30 grams (1 ounce) of material. The result was -1120 ± 52 (or following Libby's half life of ^{14}C, -1030 ± 50). Now the accepted chronology has Tutankhamen dying in -1350; my reconstruction has him entombed in ca. -830. According to Dr. Iskander Hanna of the Cairo Museum, the wood was from 30 to 50 years dried before being used for funerary equipment. The Lebanon Cedar would not have been cut as sapling - the tree reaches thousands of years of age. The sample could have been from inner rings of

---

[1] In this connection, the figure for the "Hittite" fortress, Alisar III, 800 years later than the conventional chronology has it (Radiocarbon Dating, 1952), is very nearly true.

a trunk. Dr. E. Ralph confirmed to me on March 5, 1964, that tree rings, when carbon dated, show the date of their formation, not of the year the tree was felled. I wrote to her on March 2, 1964, suggesting that if short-living material (like seeds, papyrus, linen or cotton) should be subjected to tests from the tomb of Tutankhamen, most probably the result will show "ca. -840."

In spring, 1971, or seven years later, the British Museum processed palm kernels and mat reed from the tomb of Tutankhamen. The result, according to Dr. Edwards, Curator of the Egyptian Department of the British Museum, was -899 and -846 respectively. These results were *never* published.[1]

These cases make me appeal that *all* tests, irrespective of how much the results disagree with the accepted chronological data, should be made public. I believe also that the curiosity of the British Museum Laboratory officials should have induced them to ask for additional material from the Tutankhamen tomb instead of discontinuing the quest on the assumption that tested material was contaminated. The tomb of Tutankhamen had not been opened since soon after the entombment. It is dry – water did not percolate through its roof or walls.

Another way of dulling the sharp disagreements between the accepted chronology and the results of the tests is described by my librarian assistant, Eddi Schorr.[2] In the case described nothing was purposely hidden but two different approaches were applied.

In one and the same year the University of Pennsylvania Laboratory tested wood from a royal tomb in Gordion, capital of the short-lived Phrygian Kingdom in Asia Minor, and from the palace of Nestor in Pylos, in S.W. Greece. In Gordion the result was -1100; in Pylos -1200. However, according to the accepted chronology, the difference should have been nearly 500 years – -1200 for Pylos of the end of Mycenaean age was well acceptable, but -1100 for Gordion was not – the date should have been closer to -700. Dr. Ralph came up with the solution for Gordion. The beams from the tomb were squared and the inner rings could easily be four to five hundred years old when the tree was

---

[1] {In the May 1972 issue of *Pensée* (»A Record of Success«) these data were mentioned (samples BM-658 und BM-659). The result of the ensuing exchange of letters was that the British Museum suddenly denied having tested material from Tutankhamen's tomb at all. This correspondence is published in *Pensée* IV.1, 19}

[2] {»Carbon 14 Dates and Velikovsky's Revision of Ancient History: Samples from Pylos and Gordion« in *Pensée, Immanuel Velikovsky Reconsidered* IV (Spring-Summer 1973), pp. 26-32.}

felled. But in Pylos, the description of the tested wood indicates that these were also squared beams – yet the corrective was not applied – this "because -1200 was the anticipated figure. However, as I try to show in detail in the planned *The Dark Age of Greece*, a separate volume of *Ages in Chaos* series, there were never five centuries of Dark Age between the Mycenaean Age and the historical (Ionic) Age of Greece. The Pylos beams are -800, the Gordion beams date from -700.

Now the question arises, how can the radiocarbon method be used for deciding between the conventional and the revised chronologies. Many a reader of Volume I of *Ages in Chaos*, and a few readers to whom I made available the sequel volumes in typescript would agree that the reconstruction is built with such profusion of contemporaneities and linked episodes that the credence given to the conventional history to serve as a control over carbon datings should be now transferred to the reconstruction and let it control, not be controlled by, carbon tests. Yet, for less convinced audiences, the method can serve in two manners. For the period before -500, only comparative tests can serve profitably for the solution of the chronological problems: King Saul was a contemporary of kings Kamose and Amose – and lived not 540 years after them; similarly, King Solomon was a contemporary of Queen Hatshepsut, and Thutmose III of Rehoboam of Judea and Jeroboam of the Ten Tribes; and Amenhotep II of King Asa; Amenhotep III of Omri and Ahab; Akhnaton also of Ahab of Samaria and Jehoshaphat of Jerusalem, and of Shalmaneser III of Assyria. Therefore if we can compare material from two areas contemporaneous in my reconstruction but separated by 540 years in the conventionally written history, we may receive the carbon answer as to which of the two time tables is correct and which is wrong. The ivory of the Shalmaneser III fort near Nimrud and the ivory of Tutankhamen's tomb must yield very close dates.

For the period separated by 200 years from the last cosmic upheaval involving our planet (-687), say for after -500, we may apply the tests without any need to compare contemporaneous samples. Thus the 20th and 21st Dynasties, which in conventional histories occupy the 12th to the middle of the 10th century but in my reconstruction from -400 to -340 (20th) and ca. -450 to -280 (21st), are perfect choices for carbon tests.

Now we see that not only were the warning signals that Libby offered with his method disregarded, but also an unearned reliance on the accepted version of ancient history has caused much stumbling in the dark, more and more tests of diminished value, and a maze of findings, with many undisclosed results of tests, wrong deductions and much exasperation that mark the first decades of application of Libby's most imaginative method.

Synchronical Tables

Year	Egypt	Judah	Chaldea
-615			
-610	Ramses II sole ruler (-609)	Josiah mortally wounded in battle (-608)	Death of Nabopolassar-Mursilis (-607)
-605	Battle of Carchemish	Jehoiakim becomes king (-608 to -598)	Reign of Nergil (Nergilissar I)
-600			Lamash-Marduk Nebuchadnezzar-Hattusilis usurps the throne
-595			(ca. -600)
-590	Treaty with Nebuchadnezzar-Hattusilis (ca. -588)	Zedekiah blinded, Fall of Jerusalem (-587)	Treaty with Ramses II - Necho (Necos) (ca. -588)
-585		Exile to Babylon	
-580		Gedaliah killed	
-575	Ramses II marries a daughter of Nebuchadnezzar (-577)	Jeremiah in Egypt	Nebuchadnezzar-Hattusilis visits Ramses II
-570	Accession of Merneptah-Apries (Hophra) (ca. -569)		
-565		Ezekiel	
-560	Libyan War of Merneptah-Apries Amasis Pharaoh Merneptah killed		Death of Nebuchadnezzar Reign of Evil-Marduk
-555			Reign of Nergilissar II
-550			Reign of Labash-Marduk II (?)
-545			Croesus sacks Boghazkoi (-546)
-540			Nabonidus and Belshazzar (-556 to -538)
-535		Edict of Cyrus First exiles return	Cyrus conquers Babylon (-538)
-530			
-525	Cambyses conquers Egypt		

Lydia - Phrygia	Media - Persia	Greece	Year
	Reign of Cyaxares (-634 to -597)		-615
Alyattes becomes king of Lydia (-617), wages war against Miletus	Cyaxares fights at Nineveh (-612)	Solon (Athens)	-610
		Thales (Miletus)	-605
			-600
	Astyages becomes king of Media (-594)		-595
			-590
			-585
			-580
			-575
			-570
		Pisistratus	-565
Death of Alyattes, Croesus becomes king (-560)	Cyrus becomes king of Persia		-560
			-555
			-550
Croesus sacks Hattusas (Boghazkoi) End of the kingdom of Lydia (-546)	Cyrus conquers Lydia (-546)		-545
			-540
	Cyrus conquers Babylon (-538)		-535
		Polycrates of Samos	-530
	Cyrus killed (-529) Cambyses becomes king		-525

Index

(**Hint for the user**: Page numbers followed by 'f' or 'ff' refer to the following page(s) as well, usually indicating a more detailed reference to the topic.)

Bibliography

(**Hint for the user**: The page numbers in italics following the "•" refer to the pages in this book, where the respective source is quoted. Because of their great number, quotations from the Bible are not listed here.)

Abulfeda: *Tabulae Syriae* (Leipzig 1786) • *22*

Akurgal, Ekrem: *Die Kunst Anatoliens* (Berlin 1961).• *156*

Akurgal, Ekrem: *Die Kunst der Hethiter* (1967).• *146, 159*

Akurgal, Ekrem: *Phrygische Kunst* (Ankara 1955) • *153*

Albright, W. F. in *Ancient Near Eastern Texts*, ed. Pritchard • *240*

Albright, W. F.: *Archaeology and the Religion of Israel* (Baltimore 1942) • *240*

Albright, W. F.: *Bulletin of the American Schools of Oriental Research*, LXXIV (1939) • *56*

Albright, W. F.: »Comment on Recently Reviewed Publications«, *Bulletin of the American Schools of Oriental Research,* 105 (1947).• *167*

Albright, W. F.: *From the Stone Age to Christianity* (Baltimore 1940) • *176, 234*

Albright, W. F.: *Journal of the American Oriental Society,* LXVII, 1947 • *72, 78*

Albright, W. F. in *The Aegean and the Near East*, studies presented to Hetty Goldmann, 1956 • *78*

Albright, W. F.: *The Excavation of Tell Beit Mirsim* (New Haven 1932) • *234*

Aldred, C.: *Akhenaten* (1968) • *209*

Alt, A.: *Zeitschrift der Deutschen Morgenländischen Gesellschaft,* LXXXVI (1933) • *230*

Aubert, L.: »Le Code hittite et l'Ancien Testament«, *Revue d'histoire et de philosophie religieuses,* IV (1924) • *98*

Babylonian Talmud • *22, 52, 105, 132*

Bakry, H.: »The Discovery of a Temple of Merneptah at On«, *Aegyptus,* LIII (1973) • *196*

Barth, H.: »Versuch einer eingehenden Erklärung der Felssculpturen von Boghaskoei im alten Kappadocien«, *Monatsberichte der Königlichen Preussischen Akademie der Wissenschaften* (Berlin 1859) • *142, 144*

Bauer, H.: *Der Ursprung des Alphabets* (Leipzig 1937) • *80*

Bengston, Hermann: *The Greeks and the Persians from the Sixth to the Fourth Centuries* (New York 1965) • *139*

Bernstein, S. G.: *König Nebucadnezar von Babel in der jüdischen Tradition* (Berlin 1907) • *125, 127, 139, 181*

Bissing, F. W. von: »Untersuchungen über Zeit und Stil der ›chetitischen‹ Reliefs«, *Archiv für Orientforschung,* VI (1930-1931) • *150*

Bittel, Kurt: *Die Felsbilder von Yazilikaya* (Bamberg 1934) • *150*

Bittel, K. and Güterbock, H.: »Bogazkoy«, *Abhandlungen der Preussischen Akademie der Wissenschaften, Philosophische-historische Klasse,* 1935 (Berlin 1936) • *149, 151*

Bittel, Kurt: *Hattusha, Capital of the Hittites* (1970) • *202*

Bliss, F. J. and Macalister, R. A. S.: *Excavations in Palestine* (1898-1900) (London 1902) • *235f*

Bossert, Helmuth Th.: *Altanatolien* (Berlin 1942) • *166*

Bossert, Helmuth Th.: »Das hethitische Pantheon«, *Archiv für Orientforschung,* VIII (1923-1933) • *150*

Bossert, Helmuth Th.: »Wie lange wurden hethitische Hieroglyphen geschrieben?«, *Die Welt des Orients* (1952) • *174*

Breasted, J. H.: *A History of Egypt* (New York 1905) • *15*

Breasted, J. H.: *Ancient Records of Egypt* (Chicago 1906) • *13, 17, 25, 32, 38f, 41, 59, 62, 180f, 192, 196, 198, 216, 226*

Breasted, J. H.: *The Battle of Kadesh* (Chicago 1903) • *22, 41*

Brugsch, H. K.: *Geographische Inschriften altägyptischer Denkmäler* (Leipzig 1857 – 1860) • *22*

Buckingham, J. S. in *Travels in Mesopotamia* (London 1827) • *45*

Budge, E. A. W.: *A History of Egypt* (London 1902 – 1904) • *15*

Burchardt, Max: *Die Altkanaanäischen Fremdworte und Eigennamen im Ägyptischen* (Leipzig 1909-1910) • *69*

Caminos, R.: *Late-Egyptian Miscellanies* (Oxford 1954) • *189*

Carpenter, R.: »The Antiquity of the Greek Alphabet«, *American Journal of Archaeology,* XXXVII (1933) • *81f*

Carter, H.: *The Tomb of Tut-ankh-Amen* (London 1923-1933) • *229*

Champollion, J. F.: *Lettres écrites d'Egypte* (Paris 1833) • *21*

Champollion, J. F.: *Monuments de l'Egypte et de la Nubie* (Paris 1835-45) • *28*

Christian, V.: *Archiv für Orientforschung,* IX (1933) • *150*

Conder, Claude R.: »Kadesh«, *Quarterly Statement of the Palestine Exploration Fund,* 1881 • *22, 38f*

Contenau, G.: »Ce que nous savons des Hittites«, *Revue historique,* CLXXXVI (1939) • *99*

Crowfoot, J. W. and G. M.: *Early Ivories from Samaria* (London 1938) • *83*

Day, St. John V.: *The Prehistoric Use of Iron and Steel* (London 1877) • *222*

de Garis Davies, N.: *The Tomb of Rehk-mi-re at Thebes* (New York 1943) • *226*

De Rougé: *Œuvres diverses,* Vol. V (Paris 1914) • *69, 91*

Delaporte, Louis: *Die Babylonier, Assyrer, Perser und Phöniker* (Freiburg im Breisgau 1933) • *123*

Delaporte, Louis: *Les Hittites* • *107*

Delaporte, Louis: *Malatya, Fouilles de la Mission Archéologique Française* (Paris 1940) • *164*

Diodorus of Sicily: *The Historical Library* (transl. Oldfather 1933) • *14, 20, 24, 107, 111, 172, 194, 199, 221*

Diringer, D.: »The Palestinian Inscriptions and the Origin of the Alphabet«, *Journal of the American Oriental Society*, LXIII (März 1943) • *80*

Dougherty, R. P.: *Nabonidus and Belshazzar* (London 1929) • *58, 103, 110f, 132, 171, 177*

Drummond, Alexander: *Travels ... as Far as the Banks of the Euphrates* (London 1754) • *39*

Dunand, M.: *Fouilles de Byblos*, I (1937) • *87*

Dussaud, R.: *Archiv für Orientforschung*, V (1929) • *76*

Dussaud, R.: »Les Inscriptions phéniciennes du tombeau d'Ahiram, roi de Byblos«, *Syria, Revue d'art oriental et d'archéologie*, V (1924) • *73, 75, 77*

Dussaud, R.: »Samarie au temps d'Achab«, *Syria, Revue d'art oriental et d'archéologie*, VI (1925) • *74, 240*

Dussaud, R.: *Syria, Revue d'art oriental et d'archéologie*, XI (1930) • *78*

Ebert's Reallexikon der Vorgeschichte • *83*

Edel, Elmar: »Der geplante Besuch Hattusilis III. in Ägypten«, *Mitteilungen der Deutschen Orient-Gesellschaft*, 92 (1960) • *180*

Eerdmans, B. D.: *Alttestamentliche Studien* (Giessen 1908) • *190*

Encyclopaedia Britannica (14th ed.) • *96, 172, 222*

Ephrem: *Commentaire sur l'Ecriture Sainte, Opera Omnia*, IV • *46*

Erman, Adolf: »Die Bentresh Stele«, *Zeitschrift für ägyptische Sprache und Altertumskunde*, XXI (1883) • *130*

Erman, Adolf: *Life in Ancient Egypt* (London 1894) • *40*

Erman, A. and Blackman, A. M.: *The Literature of the Ancient Egyptians* (London 1927) • *230*

Erman, A., Grapow, H.: *Wörterbuch der ägyptischen Sprache* • *41*

Eusebius: *Chronicles* • *177*

Faulkner, R. O. in *The Cambridge Ancient History*, II, 2 (1975) • *34, 47, 62*

Federn, Walter: »Dahamunzu (KBo V 6 iii 8)«, *Journal of Cuneiform Studies*, Vol. XIV, No. 1 (April 1960) • *218*

Fisher, C. S.: *The Excavation of Armageddon* (Chicago 1929) • *239*

Forrer, E.: »Die astronomische Festlegung« in *Forschungen*, II (Berlin 1926) • *144*

Forrer, E.: *Geschichtliche Texte aus Boghazkoi* II (Leipzig 1926) • *100*

Forrer, E.: »The Hittites in Palestine«, *Quarterly Statement of the Palestine Exploration Fund*, 1936 • *94*

Forsdyke in *Annual of the British School at Athens*, XXVIII (1926-1927) • *228*

Frankfort, H.: *Studies in Early Pottery in the Near East* (London 1927) • *149*

Frankfort, H.: *The Art and Architecture of the Ancient Orient* (Baltimore 1954) • *157, 166*

Frazer, J. G.: *The Golden Bough* (1911-1935) • *231*

Friedrich, J.: »Aus dem hethitischen Schrifttum«, II, *Der Alte Orient* (Leipzig 1922) • *130*

Friedrich, J. and Zimmern, H.: »Hethitische Gesetze«, *Der Alte Orient* (Leipzig 1922) • *105*

Friedrich, J.: »Staatsverträge des Hatti-Reiches in Hethitischer Sprache«, *Mitteilungen, Vorderasiatisch-ägyptische Gesellschaft*, XXXIV (1936) • *144*

Gadd, C. J.: *The Fall of Nineveh* (London 1923) • *13, 102f, 177*

Gardiner, A. H.: *Egyptian Grammar* (London 1927) • *40*

Gardiner, A. H.: *Egyptian Hieratic Texts*, I (Leipzig 1911) • *69f*

Gardiner, A. H.: *Egypt of the Pharaohs* • *217f*

Gardiner, A. H.: *Journal of Egyptian Archaeology*, V (1918) • *209*

Gardiner, A. H.: *Quarterly Statement of the Palestine Exploration Fund*, 1939 • *77, 82*

Gardiner, A. H.: *The Admonitions of an Egyptian Sage from a Hieratic Papyrus in Leiden* (Leipzig 1909) • *225*

Gardiner, A. H.: *The Kadesh Inscriptions of Ramesses II* (Oxford 1960) • *26f, 29, 33, 39ff*

Garland, H. and Bannister, C. O.: *Ancient Egyptian Metallurgy* (London 1927) • *222, 230f*

Garstang, J.: *The Land of the Hittites* (1910) • *202*

Gauthier, R.: *Le Livre des rois* (*Mémoires*, l'Institut français d'archéologie orientale du Caire, t. 20, 1916) • *106, 218*

Ginzberg, Louis: *Legends of the Jews* (Philadelphia 1925 - 1938) • *12, 60, 86, 105, 109, 119, 124f*

Ginzel, F. K.: *Specieller Kanon der Sonne und Mond Finsternisse* (Berlin 1899) • *142*

Glueck, N.: *The Other Side of the Jordan* (New Haven 1940) • *226*

Glueck, N. *et al.*: *Botanical Review, 7* • *247*

Glueck, N. *et al.*: *Botanical Review, 21* • *247*

Goell, Theresa: »Summary of Archaeological Work in Turkey in 1954«, *Anatolian Studies* (1955) • *175*

Gordon, Cyrus H.: »Abraham of Ur«, *Journal of Near Eastern Studies*, 17 (1958) • *169*

Götze, A.: »Das Hethiter-Reich«, in *Der Alte Orient*, XXVII,2 (Leipzig 1928) • *98*

Götze, A.: »Die Annalen des Mursilis«, *Mitteilungen, Vorderasiatisch-ägyptische Gesellschaft*, XXXVII (1932) • *100*

Götze, A.: *Mitteilungen, Vorderasiatisch-ägyptische Gesellschaft*, XXIX (1925) • *119, 129*

Götze, A.: *Mitteilungen, Vorderasiatisch-ägyptische Gesellschaft*, XXXVIII (1933) • *153*

Götze, A. and Pedersen, H.: »Mursilis Sprachlähmung, ein Hethitischer Text«, *Det Kongelike Danske Videnskabernes Selskab* (Copenhagen), *Historisk-Filogiske meddelelser*, XXI, I (1934) • *108*

Götze, A.: »Neue Bruchstücke zum grossen Texte des Hattusilis«, *Mitteilungen, Vorderasiatisch-ägyptische Gesellschaft*, XXXIV, Heft 2 (1930) • *119, 124f*

Götze, A.: »The Struggle for the Domination of Syria«, *Cambridge Ancient History* (3rd ed. 1975) • *217*

Grant, E.: *Ain Shems Excavations* (1298 : 31). Pt. III (Haverford 1934) • *236*

Güterbock, H. G.: »Die historische Tradition und ihre literarische Gestaltung bei Babyloniern und Hethitern bis 1200«, *Zeitschrift für Assyriologie*, XLIV (1938) • *98*

Güterbock, H. G.: »Carchemish«, *Journal of Near-Eastern Studies*, 1954 • *159*

Güterbock, H. G.: »The Deeds of Suppiluliuma as Told by His Son Mursili II«, *Journal of Cuneiform Studies*, Vol. X (1956) • *217f*

Guy, P. L. O.: *Megiddo Tombs* (Chicago 1938) • *229, 238*

Hall, H. R. H.: *The Ancient History of the Near East* (London 1913) • *86, 147, 180*

Hall, H. R. H.: »The Hittites and Egypt«, *Anatolian Studies*, presented to Sir W. M. Ramsey (London 1923) • *218*

Hall, H. R. H.: *The Oldest Civilization of Greece: Studies of the Mycenaean Age* (London and Philadelphia 1901) • *147, 197*

Hamilton, W. J.: *Researches in Asia Minor, Pontus and Armenia* (London 1842) • *142*

Hanfmann, G.: »Remarques stylistiques sur les Reliefs de Malatya; Ankara Universitesi Dil ve Tarih-Cografya, No. 53, Arkeoloji Entstitüsü, mo. 3, by Ekrem Akurgal«, *American Journal of Archaeology*, 51 (1947) • *166*

Haran, M. in *Israel Exploration Journal*, Vol. 8, Nr. 1 (1958) • *79*

Harris, James und Weeks, Kent: *X-raying the Pharaos* (New York 1973) • *200, 202, 214*

Hawkins, J. D.: »Assyrians and Hittites«, *Iraq* 36 (1974) • *216*

Hawkins, J. D.:»Building Inscriptions of Carchemish«, *Anatolian Studies*, 22 (1972) • *162*

Herzfeld: »Hettitica«, in *Archäologische Mitteilungen aus Iran*, 2 (1930) • *150*

Hill: *A History of Cyprus* • *221*

Hirschfeld, G.: »Die Felsenreliefs in Kleinasien und Das Volk der Hettiter«, *Philosophisch-historische Abhandlungen der Königlichen Preussischen Akademie der Wissenschaften*, 1886 (Berlin 1887) • *144*

Hitzig, F.: *De Cadyti urbe Herodotea* (Göttingen 1829) • *14*

Hogarth, D. G.: *Carchemish; report on the excavations at Djerabis in behalf of the British Museum conducted by C. Leonard Woolley and T. E. Lawrence*, Pt. 1, Introductory (London 1914) • *36, 38f, 46*

Homer: *Ilias* • *82, 221, 228*

Homer: *Odyssee* • *83, 228*

Houwink Ten Cate, Ph. H. J.: »The Early and Late Phases of Urhi-Teshub's Career«, in *Anatolian Studies Presented to Hans Gustav Güterbock* (Istanbul 1974) • *138*

Hrozny, B.: *Code Hittite* (Paris 1922) • *105*

Hrozny, F.: »The Hittites«, *Encyclopaedia Britannica*, (14th ed.) • *96*

Hume, W. F.: *Geology of Egypt* (1925-1937) • *221*

Hume, W. F.: *The Distribution of Iron Ores in Egypt* (Kairo 1909) • *221*

Jack, J. W.: *The Date of Exodus in the Light of External Evidence* (Edinburgh 1925) • *192*

278

Jack, J. W.: *Samaria in Ahab's Time* (Edinburgh 1929) • *240*

Jerusalem Talmud • *22, 60, 62*

Jidejian, Nina: *Byblos Through the Ages* (Beirut 1968) • *79, 87f*

Jirku, A.: *Zeitschrift der Deutschen Morgenländischen Gesellschaft* 86 (1933) • *41*

Josephus, Flavius: *Against Apion* (transl. H. Thackeray (Loeb Classical Library 1966)) • *86, 108f, 115, 121f, 125*

Josephus, Flavius: *Jewish Antiquities* • *12, 86*

Karo, G.: »Homer«, in Ebert's *Reallexikon der Vorgeschichte*, XV (1926) • *83*

Kêmi, *Revue de philologie et d'archéologie égyptiennes et coptes*, V (1935) • *18*

Kienitz, F. K.: *Die politische Geschichte Ägyptens vom 7. bis zum 4. Jahrhundert vor der Zeitwende* (Berlin, 1953) • *13f, 58*

Kiepert: »Vortrag über die geographische Stellung der nördlichen Länder in der phönikisch-hebräischen Erdkunde«, *Monatsberichte der Akademie der Wissenschaften zu Berlin*. 1859 (1860) • *177*

King, L. W.: *Bronze Reliefs from the Gates of Shalmaneser* (London 1915) • *38*

Kitchen, K. A.: *Ramesside Inscriptions* (1969) • *211*

Kittel, Rudolph: *Geschichte des Volkes Israel* (5th ed., Stuttgart 1923-25) • *23*

Koldewey, R.: *Das Ischtar-Tor in Babylon* (Leipzig 1918) • *119*

Koldewey, R.: *Das wiedererstehende Babylon* (1st ed.; Leipzig 1913) • *112ff, 116*

Koldewey, R.: *Die Architektur von Sendschirli* (Berlin 1898) • *36*

Koldewey, R.: *Die Hettitische Inschrift gefunden in der Königsburg von Babylon am 22. August 1899* (Leipzig 1900) • *148*

Koldewey, R.: *Die Königsburgen von Babylon* (Leipzig 1931) • *186f*

Körte, G. and A.: *Gordion* (Berlin 1904) • *148*

Kuentz, Ch. in *Annales du Service des Antiquités de l'Egypte*, XXV (1925) • *180*

Küthmann, C.: *Schweizer Münzblätter* I (1950) • *174*

Lamon, R. S. and Shipton, G. M.: *Megiddo I (Strata I-V)* (Chicago 1939) • *239*

Langdon, S.: *Building Inscriptions of the Neo-Babylonian Empire* (Paris 1905) • *59, 112, 120, 127, 129, 132, 179f, 184*

Langdon, S. H.: *Die Neubabylonischen Königsinschriften* (Leipzig 1912) • *104, 110ff, 119, 125, 179*

Langdon, S.: *The Venus Tablets of Ammizaduga* (London 1928) • *105, 177*

Larcher, P. H.: *Historical and Critical Comments on the History of Herodotus* (London 1844) • *14*

Leclant, J. and Yoyotte, J.: »Scarabée Commémoratif de la crue du Nil«, *Kêmi, Revue de philologie et d'archéologie égyptiennes et coptes*, 10 (1949) • *218*

Lefebvre, G.: *Romans et contes de l'époque pharaonique* (Paris 1949) • *131*

Lehmann, Johannes: Die Hethiter • *143, 165*

Leibovitch, J.: *Bulletin de l'Institut Français d'Archéologie Orientale*, XXXII (1932) • *80*

Lewy, Julius: »Forschungen zur alten Geschichte Vorderasiens«, Die Neubabylonische Chronik G, *Mitteilungen, Vorderasiatisch-ägyptische Gesellschaft*, XXIX (1925) • *102*

Libby, W. F.: *Radiocarbon Dating* (Chicago 1952) • *152, 247, 250*

Libby, W. F.: *Science, 140, 278* • *246*

Lidzbarski, M.: *Handbuch der nordsemitischen Epigraphik* (Weimar 1898) • *81*

Longwell: *American Journal of Science*, 1950 • *248*

Loon, M. N. van: *Urartian Art: Its Distinctive Traits in the Light of New Excavations* (Istanbul 1966) • *169*

Lucas, A.: *Ancient Egyptian Materials and Industries* (2nd ed., London 1934) • *219, 221f*

Luckenbill, D. D.: *Ancient Records of Assyria* (Chicago 1926-1927) • *20, 40, 85, 103*

Luckenbill, D. D.: »Hittite Treaties and Letters«, *American Journal of Semitic Languages and Literatures*, XXXVII (April 1921) • *122, 126, 137f, 177, 187*

Lucian: *The Syrian Goddess*, transl. H. A. Strong (London 1913) • *45f*

Lucretius: *De Rerum Natura* (transl. W. H. D. Rouse, London 1924) • *220*

Macalister: *The Excavation of Gezer* (1902-1909) • *225, 236*

Macdonald, J.: »The Na'ar in Israelite Society«, *Journal of Near Eastern Studies* 35 (1976) • *44*

Maçoudi: *Les Prairies d'or* (Paris 1861-1877) • *139*

Macqueen, J. G.: *The Hittites* (London 1975) • *98*

Mallowan, M. E. L.: »Carchemish«, *Anatolian Studies*, 22 (1972) • *162*

Manley: *Science News*, Penguin Publications, 1949 • *246*

Marcellinus, Ammianus • *46*

Maspero, G.: *The Struggle of the Nations* (New York 1897) • *21, 65, 218, 240*

May, H. G.: *Material Remains of the Megiddo Cult* (Chicago 1935) • *238*

Meissner, G. Bruno: »Die Beziehungen Ägyptens zum Hattireiche nach hattischen Quellen«, *Zeitschrift der Deutschen Morgenländischen Gesellschaft*, 72 (1918) • *136, 138, 230*

Menander of Ephesus: *Phoenician Record* • *86*

Ménant, Joachim: »Kar-Kemish«, *Mémoires, Académie des Inscriptions et Belles Lettres* XXXII (1891) • *44*

Mercer, S. A. B.: *Tutankhamen and Egyptology* (Milwaukee 1923) • *192*

Meriggi, P.: *Manuale di Eteo Geroglifico*, II/i (Rom 1967) • *148*

Messerschmidt, L.: »Die Stele Nabunaids«, *Mitteilungen, Vorderasiatisch-ägyptische Gesellschaft*, I (1896) • *104, 125*

Meulenaere, H. de: *Herodotos over de 26ste Dynastie* (Leyden 1951) • *14*

Meyer, Eduard: *Geschichte des Altertums* (2nd ed., Stuttgart 1931) • *76, 81, 177*

Midrash Rabba • *125*

Midrash Breshith Raba • *12*

Midrash Va'yikra Raba • *12*

Midrashim • *109, 124*

Montet, P.: *Byblos et l'Egypte, Quatre Campagnes de Fouilles à Gebel (1921-1924)*, (Paris 1928) • *71*

Montet, P.: *Isis* (Paris 1956) • *78*

Müller, Max: *Mitteilungen, Vorderasiatisch-ägyptische Gesellschaft*, VII • *216*

Muscarella, O. W.: »Hasanlu in the Ninth Century B. C., and Its Relations with Other Cultural Centers of the Near East«, *American Journal of Archaeology*, 75 (1971) • *167*

Naville, E.: »Did Mernephtah Invade Syria?«, *Journal of Egyptian Archaeology*, II (1915) • *194*

Newberry, P. E.: *Scarabs* (London 1906) • *233*

Olshausen: *Zeitschrift für Ethnologie*, 1907 • *223*

Origen: *Epist. ad Africanum* • *130*

Osten, H. H. von der: *Discoveries in Anatolia*, 1930-1931, Publications of the Oriental Institute of the University of Chicago (1933) • *151f*

Osten, H. H. von der: *Four Sculptures from Marash*, Metropolitan Museum Studies, II, 1929-1930 (New York 1930) • *152f, 172*

Osten, H. H. von der, Schmidt, E.: *The Alishar Huyuk*, 7. vols. (Chicago 1930-1937) • *149f*

Papyri, Elephantine • *67*

Papyrus Anastasi I, ed. and transl. by A. H. Gardiner: *Egyptian Hieratic Texts*, I (Leipzig 1911) • *69*

Papyrus Koller, ed. and transl. by A. H. Gardiner: *Egyptian Hieratic Texts*, I (Leipzig 1911) • *70*

Papyrus Raifet • *21*

Papyrus Sallier • *21, 23*

Papyrus Wenamon • *209*

Pensée IV, Spring-Summer 1973 • *206*

Pensée VI, Winter 1973-74 • *206*

Pensée: Immanuel Velikovsky Reconsidered I, May 1972 • *252*

Pensée: Immanuel Velikovsky Reconsidered IV, Spring-Summer 1973 • *252*

Pentaur: *Poem* • *21, 23, 25f, 33ff, 40, 43f, 61ff, 69*

Pesikta Rabba • *51*

Petrie, W. M. Flinders: *Abydos*, II (*Egyptian Exploration Fund, Memoirs*, Vol. 24; London 1903) • *223*

Petrie, W. M. Flinders: *A History of Egypt*, Vol III. (London 1905) • *14*

Petrie, W. M. Flinders: *A History of Egypt: During the Seventeenth and Eighteenth Dynasties* (7th ed., London 1924) • *193*

Petrie, W. M. Flinders: *Illahun, Kahun and Gurob* (London 1891) • *234*

Petrie, W. M. Flinders: *Six Temples at Thebes, 1896* (London 1897) • *229*

Petrie, W. M. Flinders, Murray, A. S. and Griffith, F. Ll.: *Tanis*, Pt. II, *Nebesheh (Am) and Defenneh (Tahpanhes)* (London 1888) • *185ff, 189*

Petrie, W. M. Flinders: »The Metals in Egypt«, *Ancient Egypt* (1915) • *222, 229f*

Pézard, M.: *Qadesh. Mission Archéologique à Tell Nebi-Mend, 1921 - 1922* (Paris 1931) • *22f 26, 39*

Philostratos: *History of India and Phoenicia* • *86*

Pinches, T. G.: »A New Fragment of the History of Nebuchadnezzar«, *Transactions of the Society of Biblical Archaeology*, Vol. 7, 188 D (1882) • *179*

Pliny: *Natural History* • *86, 221*

Plutarch: *De Iside* • *210*

Plutarch: *Lives* • *24, 170*

Prince, J. D.: »Chaldaea«, *Encyclopaedia Britannica* (14th ed.) • *172*

Pritchard, J. B. (ed.): *Ancient Near Eastern Texts Relating to the Old Testament* (Princeton University Press 1950) • *43, 47, 114f, 130f, 176, 180, 190, 240*

Pritchard, J. B. (ed.): *The Ancient Near East, Supplementary Texts and Pictures Relating to the Old Testament* (Princeton University Press 1969) • *114*

Procopius: *Histories* • *46*

Puchstein, O.: *Boghasköi, Die Bauwerke* (Leipzig 1912) • *147*

Puchstein, O.: *Pseudohethitische Kunst* (Berlin 1890) • *145*

Ramsey, W. M.: *Historical Geography of Asia Minor* (1890) • *202*

Reallexikon der Assyriologie • *216*

Reisner, Fisher and Lyon: *Harvard Excavations at Samaria* • *239f*

Renan, Ernest: *Mission de Phénicie* (Paris 1864) • *71*

Renan, Ernest: *Histoire générale et système comparé des langues sémitiques* (7th ed.) • *172*

Richardson, H. C.: »Iron, Prehistoric and Ancient«, *American Journal of Archaeology*, XXXVIII (1934) • *222*

Rickard, T. A.: *Man and Metals* (New York 1932) • *231*

Rogers, R. W.: *A History of Babylonia and Assyria* (6th ed.; New York and Cincinnati 1915) • *106, 111f*

Rowe, A.: *A Catalogue of Egyptian Scarabs ... Palestine Archaeological Museum* (Cairo 1936) • *237*

Sayce, Archibald H.: *Transactions of the Society of Biblical Archaeology*, 1876 • *91*

Sayce, Archibald H.: *The Hittites: The Story of a Forgotten Empire* (1888) • *173f*

Schaeffer, Claude F. A.: *Syria, Revue d'art oriental et d'archéologie*, 1929 • *226*

Schmidt, John D.: *Ramesses II: A Chronological Structure for His Reign* (Baltimore 1973) • *60, 138, 211*

Schorr, Eddi: *Pensée IV*, Spring-Summer 1973 p. 26: »Carbon 14 Dates and Velikovsky's Revision of Ancient History: Samples from Pylos and Gordion.« • *253*

Schumacher: *Tell el-Mutesellim* • *229*

Seder Olam • *12, 61*

Sellin and Watzinger: *Jericho*, (Leipzig 1913) • *235*

Sethe, K.: *Untersuchungen zur Geschichte und Altertumskunde Ägyptens*, Vol. II (1902) • *15*

Skinner, J.: *A Critical and Exegetical Commentary on Genesis* (New York 1910) • *94*

Smith, G. Elliot: »The Royal Mummies«, *Catalogue général des Antiquités Egyptiennes du Musée de Cairo* (Cairo 1912) • *200, 214*

Smith, R. A.: »Archaeology, Iron Age«, *Encyclopaedia Britannica* (14th ed.) • *222*

Smith, Sidney: *Alalakh and Chronology* (London 1940) • *77, 105*

Smith, W. Stevenson: »The Old Kingdom in Egypt«, *Cambridge Ancient History* (3rd ed.; 1975) • *217*

Spiegelberg, W.: »Zur Datierung der Ahiram-Inschrift von Byblos«, *Orientalistische Literaturzeitung*, XXIX (1926) • *76*

Texier, C.: *Description de l'Asie-Mineure* (Paris 1839) • *141*

The Cambridge Ancient History (3rd ed.; 1975) • *34, 47, 62, 100, 207, 217*

Thiele, E. R.: »The Chronology of the Kings of Judah and Israel«, *Journal of Near Eastern Studies* III (1944) • *65*

Toussoun, Omar: »Anciennes Branches du Nil«, *Mémoires de l'Institut d'Egypte*, IV (Cairo 1922-23) • *209*

Tractate Sanhedrin • *52, 60, 105, 130*

Tractate Shabbat • *52, 132f*

Tufnell, Olga: *Lachish (Tell ed Duweir)*, Vol. I, *The Lachish Letters* (1938) • *53*

Tufnell, Olga, Inge, C. H., and Harding, L.: *Lachish (Tell ed Duweir)*, Vol. II, *The Fosse Temple* (1940) • *53*

Tufnell, Olga: *Lachish (Tell ed Duweir)*, Vol. III, *The Iron Age* (1953) • *53*

Tufnell, Olga (ed.): *Lachish (Tell ed Duweir)*, Vol. IV, *The Bronze Age* (1958) • *53*

Ullman, B.: »How Old Is the Greek Alphabet?« *American Journal of Archaeology*, XXXVIII (1934) • *80ff*

Virolleaud, Charles: *Syria, Revue d'art oriental et d'archéologie*, IX (1928) • *227*

Velikovsky, I.: *Das dunkle Zeitalter Griechenlands* • *9, 253*

Velikovsky, I.: *The Assyrian Conquest* • *9, 14, 216f*

Velikovsky, I.: *The Dark Age of Greece* • *157, 253*

Velikovsky, I.: *Earth in Upheaval* • *247*

Velikovsky, I.: *Oedipus and Akhnaton* • *9, 84, 217*

Velikovsky, I.: *Worlds in Collision* • *107, 154, 247ff*

Velikovsky, I.: *Ages in Chaos, Vol I, From the Exodus to Kind Akhnaton* • *9, 21, 44, 70, 83f, 97, 176, 190, 216, 226, 239f, 247, 250, 253*

Velikovsky, I.: *Ages in Chaos, Vol. III, Peoples of the Sea* • *87*

Vyse, R. W. H.: *Operations Carried on at the Pyramids of Gizeh in 1837* (London 1840-1842) • *223*

Wainwright, G. A.: »The Coming of Iron«, *Antiquity*, X (1936) • *223, 225, 227, 229ff*

Walters, H. B.: *Catalogue of the Bronzes, Greek, Roman and Etruscan, in the British Museum* (London 1899) • *231*

Watzinger, C.: *Die Denkmäler Palästinas*, 2. vols. (Leipzig 1933-1935) • *149*

Watzinger, C. (ed.): *Tell el-Mutesellim* (Leipzig 1929) • *229, 237*

Weidner, E. (ed.): »Die Staatsverträge in akkadischer Sprache aus dem Archiv von Boghazköi«, *Boghazköi Studien*, VIII-IX (1923) • *177*

Weissbach, F. H.: »Die Inschriften Nebukhadnezars II im Wadi Brissa und am Nahr el-Kelb«, *Wissenschaftliche Veröffentlichungen der deutschen Orientgesellschaft* (Leipzig 1906) • *184*

Wheeler, J. T.: *The Geography of Herodotus* (London 1854) • *14*

Wilson, J. A.: »Egyptian Historical Texts« in Pritchard (ed.).: *Ancient Near Eastern Texts* • *176*

Wilson, J. A.: »The Legend of a Possessed Princess« in Pritchard (ed.).: *Ancient Near Eastern Texts* • *131*

Wilson, J. A. in Pritchard (ed.).: *Ancient Near Eastern Texts* • *43, 47, 130, 180, 190*

Winckler, Hugo: *Inschriften Nebukadnezar's*, Keilinschriftliche Bibliothek, III, 2 (1890) • *132*

Winckler, Hugo: *Mitteilungen der Deutschen Orientgesellschaft*, No. 35 (1907) • *95*

Winckler, Hugo: *Nach Boghaskoi* (1913) • *95*

Winckler, Hugo: *Orientalistische Literaturzeitung*, IX (1906) • *95*

Winckler, Hugo: *The History of Babylonia and Assyria* (New York 1907) • *179*

Winlock, H. E.: *Excavations at Deir el Bahari, 1911-1931* (New York 1942) • *17f*

Wiseman, D. J.: »Alalakh« in *Archaeology and Old Testament Study* (Oxford 1967) • *135*

Wiseman, D. J.: *Chronicles of Chaldean Kings (626-556 B. C.) in the British Museum* (London 1956) • *102, 110, 114, 117*

Wit, Constant de: »Het Land Bachtan in de Bentresjstele«, *Handeligen van het XVIIIe Vlaamse Filologencongres* (Gent 1949) • *130*

Woolley, C. Leonard: *Carchemish*, Vol. 2: *The Town Defences* (London 1921) • *36, 38, 41, 43, 67*

Woolley, C. Leonard: *Carchemish III* (London 1952) • *158, 161*

Woolley, C. Leonard: *Ur of the Chaldees* (London 1929) • *168*

Wreszinski, W.: *Atlas zur altägyptischen Kulturgeschichte*, Vol. II (Leipzig 1935) • *21, 25*

Wright, William: *The Empire of the Hittites* (London 1882) • *91, 96, 152*

Xenophon: *Anabasis* • *24, 170*

Xenophon: *Cyropaedia* • *170*

Young, R. S.: »Gordion: Preliminary Report, 1953«, *American Journal of Archaeology*, Vol. 59 (1955) • *155f*

Young, R. S.: »The Campaign of 1955 at Gordion: Preliminary Report«, *American Journal of Archaeology*, Vol. 60 (1956) • *155f*

Around the Subject

The Author

Immanuel Velikovsky was born in Vitebsk in White Russia in 1895. He studied medicine, science and other subjects, e.g. philosophy, ancient history and law at the Universities of Montpellier (France), Edinburgh (Great Britain), Moscow (Russia) and Kharkiv (Ukraine) in difficult circumstances caused by the discrimination and persecution of the Jews as well as the political and war-related chaos of the time. After getting his M.D. in Moscow in 1921 he emigrated to Germany, where he founded the scientific journal *Scripta Universitatis* in Berlin. In this project he came into contact with Albert Einstein, who was editor of the mathematical-physical section. This project, furthermore, laid the foundation for the Hebrew University of Jerusalem, the presidency of which was offered to Immanuel Velikovsky.

After getting married in 1923 Velikovsky settled in Palestine and started to practice as a physician. At the same time he studied psychoanalysis with Wilhelm Stekel, the first disciple of Freud, published several scientific papers about the subject and opened the first psychoanalytical practice in Palestine.

Doing research for a planned book project about Freud's dream interpretation and about a new view of Freud's heros Oedipus and Akhnaton, Velikovsky needed access to numerous literary sources. For this reason in 1939 he travelled to New York together with his family. Shortly afterwards World War II began and he had to extend his stay for an indefinite period, finally staying in the US for good due to his unexpected discoveries.

The next 10 years he spent with intensive research about the geological and historical facts he had discovered, and presented them to the public in 1949 in his book *Worlds in Collision*. By its contents, as well as by the scandalous reaction of the representatives of the scientific establishment, this book initiated such a far-reaching and revolutionary development in many areas of science and society that until today its actuality and importance have even increased.

Velikovsky himself, however, even after the publication of four more books, was confronted with a heavy up and down of overwhelming acceptance and devastating – unfortunately mostly very unserious – rejection, resulting in a grave psychological burden for him.

After moving to Princeton in the fifties he had a close and friendly relationship with Albert Einstein, discussing his theories with him. After Einstein's death Velikovsky's *Worlds in Collision* was found open on his desk.

Inspite of more and more recent research in geology and planetology supporting his theories, Velikovsky remained the victim of a discrediting campaign until his death, which is neither in proportion with his exact scientific methodology nor with the contents and importance of his works.

He died in Princeton in 1979.

Books by Immanuel Velikovsky:

- *Worlds in Collision* (1950)
- *Earth in Upheaval* (1955)
- *Ages in Chaos: From the Exodus to King Akhnaton* (1952)
- *Peoples of the Sea* (1977)
- *Ramses II and his Time* (1978)
- *Oedipus and Akhnaton: Myth and History* (1960)
- *Mankind in Amnesia* (1982)
- *Stargazers and Gravediggers: Memoirs to Worlds in Collision* (1984)
- *In the Beginning*

Further Reading:

- de Grazia, Alfred: *The Velikovsky Affair* (1966)
- Velikovsky Sharon, Ruth: *Aba – The Glory and the Torment* (1995)
- Velikovsky Sharon, Ruth: *Immanuel Velikovsky – The Truth behind the Torment* (2003)
- Internet: www.varchive.org
- Internet: www.velikovsky.info

Black Sea
Bosphorus
Macedonia
Thracia
Bithynia
Halys
Hattusa (Boghazkeu
Alisar
Lemnos
Aegaean Sea
Troy (Ilion)
Mysia
Gordium
Phrygia
Lesbos
Delphi
Thebes
Mycenae
Athens
Olympia
Argos
Heraea
Tiryns
Tegea
Sparta
Chios
Samos
Sardis
Lydia
Ephesus
Miletus
Caria
Halicarnassus
Cappa-
doci
Marash
Samal
Pamphylia
Cilicia
Lycia
Rhodes
Orontes
Knossos
Crete
Phaestus
Cyprus (Alasia)
Enkomi
Ugarit
(Ras Shamra)
Arvad
Hamat
Byblos
Beirut
Sidon
Damascu
Tyre
Acre
Mediterranean Sea
Sea of Galilee
Cyrenaica
Samaria
Jaffa
Jericho
Jerusalem
Askelon
Gaza
Lachish
Dead See
Rosetta
Alexandria
Tanis
Bubastis
Naucratis
el-Arish
(Rhinocolura)
Petra
Sinai Peninsula
Ezion-Geber
Elath
Libya
Memphis
Heliopolis
(On)
Heracleopolis
Nile
Mt. Sinai
Speos Artemidos
Hermopolis
Tell el-Amarna
Egypt
Panopolis
Abydos
Coptos
Deir el-Bahari
Medinet Habu
Thebes
(Karnak)
el-Qoseir
Red Sea
(Sinus Arabicus)
Syene (Aswan)
Elephantine

Caucasus Mts.

Mt. Ararat

Caspian Sea

ontus

Lake Van

Lake Urmia

Dur-Sharrukin

Arbela

Carchemish

Harran

Nineveh

Calah
(Nimrud)

Hierapolis

Assyria

Ashur

Tigris

Syria

Palmyra

Mari

Euphrates

Sippar

Babylon

Kish

Borsippa

Nippur

Susa

Babylonia

Erech

Larsa

Eridu

Ur

Persian Gulf

*Arabian
Desert*

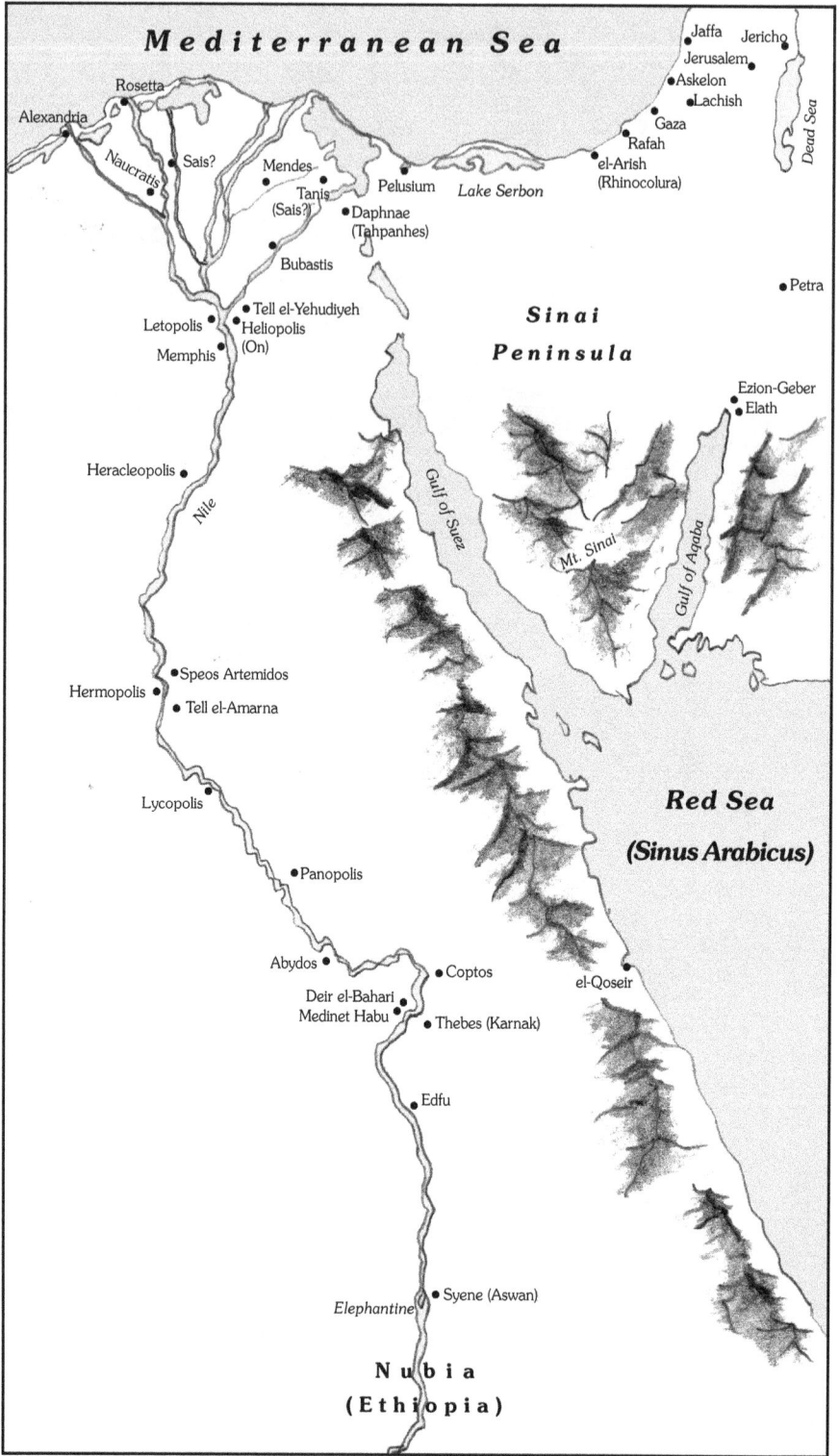

Mediterranean Sea

Jaffa
Jericho
Jerusalem
Askelon
Lachish
Dead Sea

Rosetta

Alexandria

Gaza
Rafah
el-Arish
(Rhinocolura)

Naucratis

Sais?

Mendes

Tanis
(Sais?)

Pelusium   Lake Serbon

Daphnae
(Tahpanhes)

Bubastis

Petra

Tell el-Yehudiyeh

Letopolis   Heliopolis
(On)

Memphis

Sinai

Peninsula

Ezion-Geber
Elath

Heracleopolis

Nile

Gulf of Suez

Mt. Sinai

Gulf of Aqaba

Speos Artemidos

Hermopolis

Tell el-Amarna

Lycopolis

Red Sea

(Sinus Arabicus)

Panopolis

Abydos

Coptos

el-Qoseir

Deir el-Bahari
Medinet Habu

Thebes (Karnak)

Edfu

Syene (Aswan)

Elephantine

Nubia

(Ethiopia)

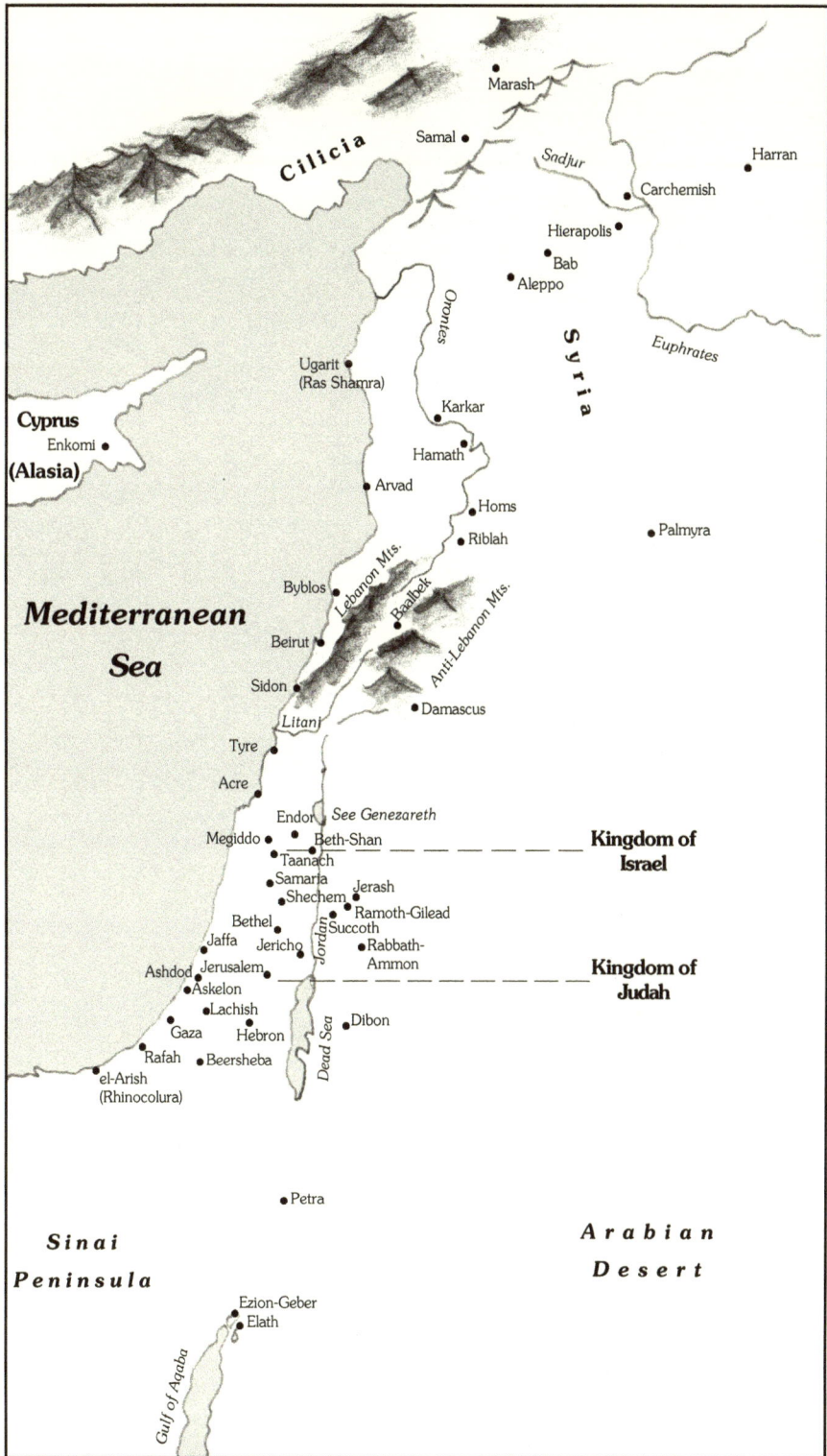

Cilicia

Marash

Samal

Sadjur

Harran

Carchemish

Hierapolis

Bab

Aleppo

Orontes

Syria

Euphrates

Ugarit
(Ras Shamra)

Karkar

Cyprus

Enkomi

(Alasia)

Hamath

Arvad

Homs

Riblah

Palmyra

Byblos

Lebanon Mts.

Baalbek

Mediterranean

Beirut

Anti-Lebanon Mts.

Sea

Sidon

Litani

Damascus

Tyre

Acre

Endor   See Genezareth

Megiddo   Beth-Shan   — — — — — — —   Kingdom of
                                          Israel
Taanach
Samaria   Jerash
Shechem
Bethel   Ramoth-Gilead
Jaffa   Jericho   Succoth
                    Rabbath-   — — — — — —   Kingdom of
Ashdod Jerusalem   Ammon   Judah
Askelon
Lachish
Gaza   Hebron   Dibon
Rafah   Beersheba
el-Arish
(Rhinocolura)

Dead Sea

Jordan

Petra

Sinai   Arabian

Peninsula   Desert

Ezion-Geber
Elath

Gulf of Aqaba

Peoples of the Sea

IMMANUEL
VELIKOVSKY

Vol. III of
Ages In Chaos

Immanuel Velikovsky

Paradigma Ltd.

ISBN 978-1-906833-15-2
(Softcover)
978-1-906833-55-8
(Hardcover)

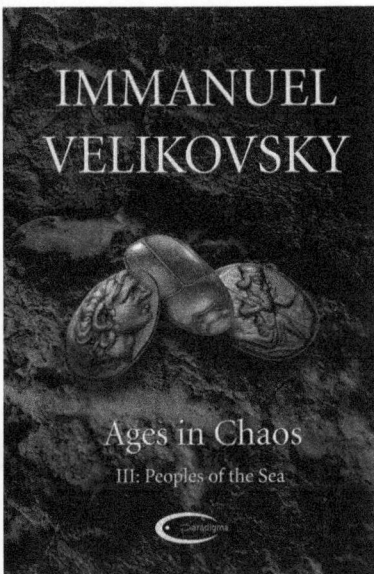

Peoples of the Sea is, in some sense, the culmination of the series *Ages in Chaos*. In this volume the erroneous time shift of classical history reaches its maximum span – 800 years!

With carefully documented evidence and indisputable arguments, Velikovsky places Ramses III firmly into the 4th century B.C. thereby solving, once and for all, numerous conundrums that historians had been confronted with in the past. He unveils the surprising identity of the so-called "Peoples of the Sea", clarifies the role of the Philistines and solves the enigma of the Dynasty of Priests.

This volume leads Velikovsky's revised chronology up to the time of Alexander where it links up with the records of classical chronology.

In an extensive supplement Velikovsky delves into the fundamental question of how such a dramatic shift in chronology could have come about. Analyzing the main pillars of Egyptian chronology, he points out where the most dramatic mistakes were made and addresses the misunderstanding underlying the "astronomical chronology".

In a further supplement he discusses the very interesting conclusions that can be drawn from radiocarbon testing on Egyptian archeological finds.

IMMANUEL VELIKOVSKY

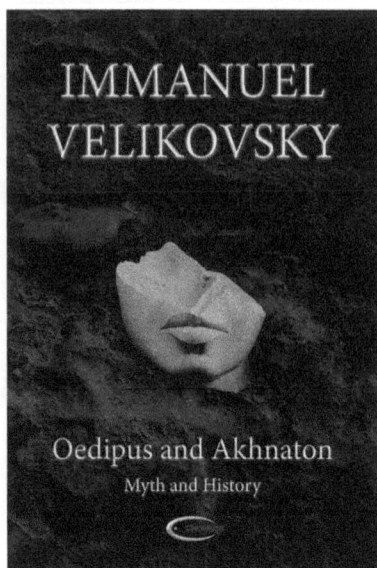

Oedipus and Akhnaton

Myth and History

Oedipus and Akhnaton

Immanuel Velikovsky

Paradigma Ltd.

ISBN 978-1-906833-18-3
(Softcover)
978-1-906833-58-9
(Hardcover)

Who hasn't heard of him – Oedipus, the tragic figure from Greek mythology whose shocking fate has moved so many generations, inspired so many writers and even found his way into modern psychology through Sigmund Freud?

Is it conceivable that this figure and his fate was not a creation of human fancy at all but the conversion of real historical happenings?

This question is posed by Immanuel Velikovsky in this book. Like a detective, he takes the reader on a unique investigation full of suspense, breathtaking surprises and insights while meticulously searching for traces of a finding that seems to be even more incredible than the original myth itself.

The most popular pharaonic family of all – Akhnaton along with his wife Nefertiti and his son Tutankhamen – are exposed as the real protagonists of the Oedipus saga.

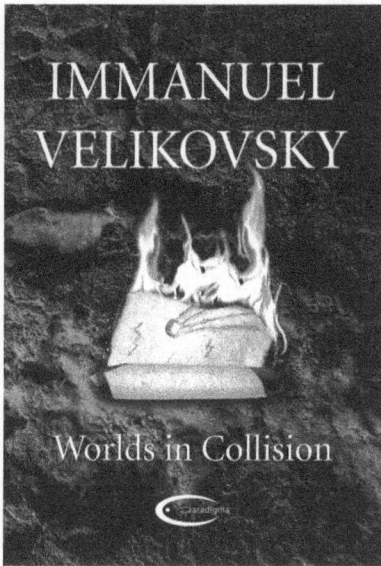

Worlds in Collision

Immanuel Velikovsky

436 pages
Paradigma Ltd.

ISBN 978-1-906833-11-4
(Softcover)
978-1-906833-51-0
(Hardcover)

With this book Immanuel Velikovsky first presented the revolutionary results of his 10-year-long interdisciplinary research to the public – and caused an uproar that is still going on today.

Worlds in Collision – written in a brilliant, easily understandable and entertaining style and full to the brim with precise information – can be considered one of the most important and most challenging books in the history of science. Not without reason was this book found open on Einstein's desk after his death.

For all those who have ever wondered about the evolution of the earth, the history of mankind, traditions, religions, mythology or just the world as it is today, *Worlds in Collision* is an absolute MUST-READ!

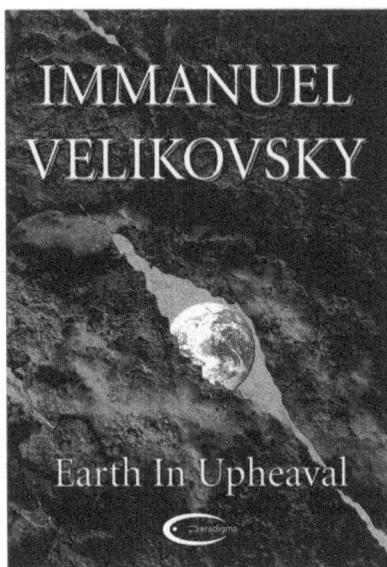

Earth in Upheaval

Immanuel Velikovsky

276 pages
Paradigma Ltd.

ISBN 978-1-906833-12-1
(Softcover)
978-1-906833-52-7
(Hardcover)

After the publication of *Worlds in Collision* Immanuel Velikovsky was confronted with the argument that in the shape of the earth and in the flora and fauna there are no traces of the natural catastrophes he had described.

Therefore a few years later he published *Earth in Upheaval* which not only supports the historical documents by very impressive geological and paleontological material, but even arrives at the same conclusions just based on the testimony of stones and bones.

Earth in Upheaval – a very exactly investigated and easily understandable book – contains material that completely revolutionizes our view of the history of the earth.

For all those who have ever wondered about the evolution of the earth, the formation of mountains and oceans, the origin of coal or fossils, the question of the ice ages and the history of animal and plant species, *Earth in Upheaval* is a MUST-READ!

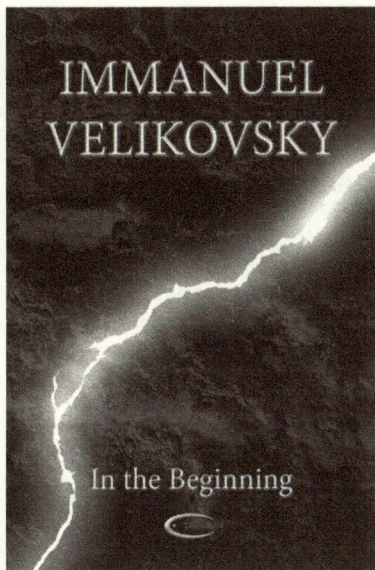

In the Beginning

Immanuel Velikovsky

Paradigma Ltd.

ISBN 978-1-906833-10-7
(Softcover)
978-1-906833-50-3
(Hardcover)

In his main work, the best-selling *Worlds in Collision*, Immanuel Velikovsky gave a detailed reconstruction of two global natural catastrophes based on information handed down by our ancestors.

He mentions there that, as part of his intensive research, he found numerous indications of even more catastrophes that took place earlier in the history of mankind.

In this book, the material collected by Velikovksy about this topic is presented to the public for the first time. His findings show just how turbulent the history of Earth and our planetary system was during the time of mankind and how little we actually know of all that today.

IMMANUEL VELIKOVSKY

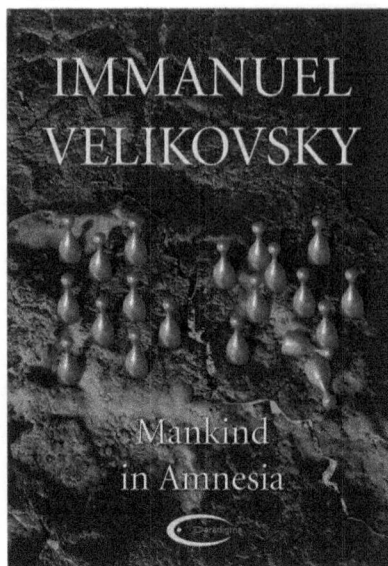

Mankind in Amnesia

Immanuel Velikovsky

196 pages
Paradigma Ltd.

ISBN 978-1-906833-16-9
(Softcover)
978-1-906833-56-5
(Hardcover)

Immanuel Velikovsky called this book the "fulfillment of his oath of Hippocrates – to serve humanity." In this book he returns to his roots as a psychologist and psychoanalytical therapist, yet not with a single person as his patient but with humanity as a whole.

After an extremely revealing overview of the foundations of the various psychoanalytical systems he makes the step into crowd psychology and reopens the case of *Worlds in Collision* from a totally different point of view: as a psychoanalytical case study. This way he shows that the blatant reactions to his theories (which are still going on today) have not been surprising but are actually inevitable from a psychological perspective – which equally holds for those who have defined our view of the world. At the same time he is able to reclassify the theories of Siegmund Freud and of C. G. Jung by finding a common basis for them.

A journey through history, religion, mythology and art shows the overall range of the collective trauma and gives us – the patients – a message of extraordinary urgency and importance for the future.

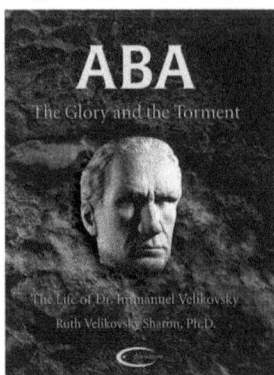

ABA – The Glory and the Torment

Ruth Velikovsky Sharon, Ph.D.

ISBN 978-1-906833-20-6

In this book you get to know Immanuel Velikovsky as a person. His daughter Ruth describes his childhood, his family environment and his eventful life.

Using plenty of background information, numerous anecdotes and many photographs she makes us familiar with her father, but also shows the personal dimension of the devastating campaign he encountered in the last decades of his life.

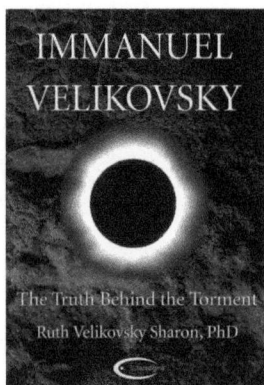

The Truth Behind the Torment

Ruth Velikovsky Sharon, Ph.D.

ISBN 978-1-906833-21-3
(Softcover)
978-1-906833-61-9
(Hardcover)

In this supplement to her father's biography, Ruth Velikovsky Sharon, PhD. depicts the true facts about the campaign against him.

She publishes informative letters in full length, that show the true nature of the undeserving. unscientific treatment of Velikovsky by the scientific establishment, a treatment that appears rather medieval than enlightened.

Ruth Velikovsky Sharon, PhD.

Immanuel Velikovsky's daughter is a psychotherapist herself, and has an extended professional consulting experience.
She has written some interesting books to present her insights to the public:

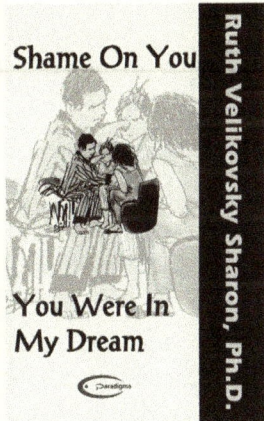

Shame on You – You Were in My Dream

Ruth Velikovsky Sharon, Ph.D.

ISBN 978-1-906833-01-5

Finally a new and easy guide to the understanding of dreams, which really makes sense! Ruth Velikovsky Sharon, PhD has developed a completely new understanding of the nature of dreams, which is fascinating because of its simplicity and its practical orientation.
This theory is presented in this book and makes it a valuable guide for parents.

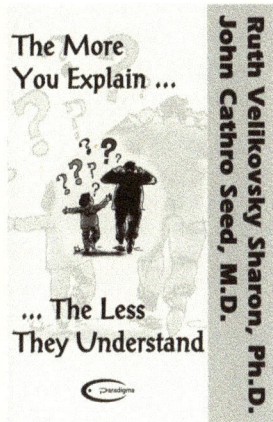

The More You Explain ... The Less They Understand

Ruth Velikovsky Sharon, Ph.D.

ISBN 978-1-906833-00-8

In this, perhaps the most encompassing of her works, Dr. Ruth Velikovsky Sharon brilliantly lifts the veil that shrouds the mystery of psychoanalysis, revealing intrinsic truths that can forever assist us in our journey to self-discovery and growth.
Harvard Medical School trained, Dr. John C. Seed's contribution of the Physical Health chapter will enlighten the medical community as well as the average reader, and if abided by, will help prolong life.

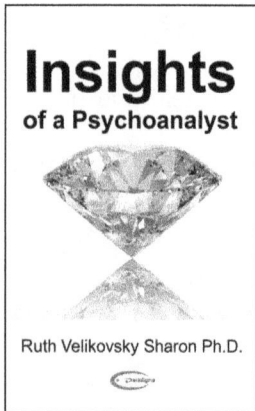

Insights
of a Psychoanalyst

Insights
of a Psychoanalyst

Ruth Velikovsky Sharon Ph.D.

Ruth Velikovsky Sharon, Ph.D.

ISBN 978-1-906833-04-6

In this booklet, Dr. Velikovsky Sharon, a renowned psychoanalyst, lets us partake in her rich professional experience.

Using short, clear statements she gives practical assistance for the questions of life every one of us is confronted with – even addressing points which many haven't been aware of so far in their busy everyday lives.

Imagine Art

Works of Art by
Ruth Velikovsky Sharon, Ph.D.
and Elisheva Velikovsky

ISBN 978-1-906833-02-2

The name of Velikovsky is mainly known from the scientific and historical discoveries of Immanuel Velikovsky.

Far less known is the artistic dimension in the Velikovsky family, mainly expressed by Elisheva (or "Elis") Velikovsky and Ruth Velikovsky Sharon, PhD., the wife and daughter of Immanuel Velikovsky. For everyone interested in and fond of visual and plastic arts this booklet will give an exhaustive overview of the remarkable range of the works of these two artists.